Praise for *Productive Failure*

"This book reveals the transformative power of Productive Failure through compelling narratives, insightful research, and practical strategies. Manu Kapur shows how embracing failure is a critical tool for progress, innovation, resilience, and triumph."

—John Hattie,
Melbourne Laureate Professor Emeritus,
Chief Academic Advisor, Corwin,
technical advisor to i-Ready Assessment, and
co-director of Hattie Family Foundation

"At a time when there is concern regarding the quality of outcomes in education, fresh approaches to learning and teaching are much needed. *Productive Failure* brings new and applicable thinking to values first espoused by Socrates, relating to the importance of failure in our learning journeys. Manu Kapur's timely research, detailed in this captivating book, encourages us to design for failure, to start with the problem rather than being fed the solution. It is affirming to all of us who have experienced failure and have thereby grown stronger."

—Sue Cunningham,
president and CEO, Council for Advancement
and Support of Education (CASE)

"An accessible mix of science and practice, Manu Kapur's carefully crafted argument about the value of Productive Failure is relevant in two important ways. First and foremost, it concretizes a fundamental human truth: deep learning and meaning making require engaged struggle with the issue at hand – a struggle that is immensely enriched by embracing failure. And beyond its universal educational implications, the book is also of special relevance today, when in all fields, the promise of generative AI could easily lure us into thinking that we now have tools to skip the struggling phase."

—Etienne Wenger-Trayner,
social learning theorist at Social Learning Lab,
Sesimbra, Portugal and author of Communities of Practice

"It's a truism these days that you have to fail to succeed. To learn from failure, we need a wise guide like Dr. Manu Kapur, who shows us that failure is the secret recipe of success. With his expert guidance, Dr. Kapur demonstrates how to fail productively in ways that move you forward instead of setting you back. Grounded in solid research and filled with practical advice, *Productive Failure* is a pleasure to read."

—Dr. Keith Sawyer,
professor at the University of North Carolina at
Chapel Hill and author of *Learning to See:
Inside the World's Leading Art and Design Schools*

Productive
Failure

Productive Failure

Unlocking Deeper Learning Through the Science of Failing

Manu Kapur

JB JOSSEY-BASS™

A Wiley Brand

Jossey-Bass, a Wiley imprint

Published by John Wiley & Sons, Inc., Hoboken, New Jersey.

Published simultaneously in Canada.

For general information on our other products and services, please contact our Customer Care Department within the United States at (800) 762-2974, outside the United States at (317) 572- 3993. For product technical support, you can find answers to frequently asked questions or reach us via live chat at https://support.wiley.com.

If you believe you've found a mistake in this book, please bring it to our attention by emailing our reader support team at wileysupport@wiley.com with the subject line "Possible Book Errata Submission."

Wiley also publishes its books in a variety of electronic formats. Some content that appears in print may not be available in electronic formats. For more information about Wiley products, visit our website at www.wiley.com.

Library of Congress Cataloging-in-Publication Data

Names: Kapur, Manu, author. | John Wiley & Sons, publisher.
Title: Productive failure : unlocking deeper learning through the science
   of failing / Manu Kapur.
Description: San Francisco : Jossey-Bass, a Wiley imprint, [2025] |
   Includes index.
Identifiers: LCCN 2024024149 (print) | LCCN 2024024150 (ebook) | ISBN
   9781394219995 (hardback) | ISBN 9781394220007 (adobe pdf) | ISBN
   9781394220014 (epub)
Subjects: LCSH: Learning strategies. | Learning, Psychology of.
Classification: LCC LB1066 .K36 2025 (print) | LCC LB1066 (ebook) | DDC
   370.15/23—dc23/eng/20240626
LC record available at https://lccn.loc.gov/2024024149
LC ebook record available at https://lccn.loc.gov/2024024150

Cover Design and Image: Wiley
Author Photo: Courtesy of Zakaria Zainal
SKY10081565_080924

For

Dev Kapur

and

Arvi Sudhir Kapur

Contents

Foreword

The year was 2005. My talk was over. The conference theater was almost empty. I wanted tea but a pesky PhD student stopped me. He was eager to show me some data, so I obliged, and we sat and looked at his data for a while. Education is rich in human values, but the sciences of learning are built on data.

I forgot his name but a few years later, I was setting up the program of a European conference when I read an intriguing paper. It was about learning in teams. The approach was exactly opposite to my own work. But the counterintuitive results were demonstrated with an unimpeachable rigor. I invited the author to give the keynote and he seduced the audience by the elegance of his proof. That was Manu Kapur, and it was his first keynote ever, on Productive Failure.

You will enjoy the same relentless logic while reading his book. The research findings interlock with each other, page after page, as the wheels of a Swiss watch. It is what it takes to demonstrate that a learning activity that has all the hallmarks of failure ends up producing better outcomes.

How people learn is a complex science. Learners and teachers are neither cells in a tube nor photons in a vacuum. Pupils for instance are not the same on a rainy day or when the first snow whitens the landscape, lighting up the pupils' eyes! Instead of tackling this complexity, some books depict learning and teaching in very general terms. Not this one. It clearly establishes evidence that trying to solve a problem before being told how to do so leads to better learning outcomes, despite the failure to solve this initial problem. Or more precisely, because of it. Some education experts try to sell a miracle method supposed to revolutionize education. Not this book. There is no miracle in education.

Instead, the magic of Productive Failure is demystified, chapter by chapter. At the core lies the intensity of cognitive engagement. No matter what the gurus of cognitive load claim, building knowledge is demanding. Learning is not a quiet river; some difficulty is desirable. The findings of this book are not only about cognition, but also about emotion. Manu integrates neuroscience findings to decompose the emotional rollercoaster along which we get the motivation to get mastery of difficult skills. The most important things we learn in our lives are not the easiest ones.

This book is about deep learning. Don't read it if you believe that all that matters is to store knowledge pieces in our brain as we put a book on a shelf and retrieve it later. Or rather, read it twice. Deep learning is about making meaning. Recently I came across the idea that if one travels at the speed of light, time stops. I understand every word of this sentence, I memorized it easily, but I am not able to do anything as I don't really get the meaning. Deep learning is about building actionable knowledge and it takes some failure to feel when and how some knowledge can be activated to tackle a real problem. Not simply to answer a quiz.

Twenty years later, Manu is giving keynotes around the world. At the end of his keynote, many pesky students will catch him with questions. Years later, one of them may write a book that Manu will preface. This is how the science of learning is moving forward.

But this book has not been written for a scientific audience. It speaks to all those who share our goal and our vision: to make learning and education more effective. This book is for them: learners, teachers, and policy makers, but also parents, sport coaches, and managers. All of us are learners.

Prof. Dr. Pierre Dillenbourg
Associate Vice-President for Education
EPFL - Swiss Federal Institute of Technology, Lausanne
Switzerland

Introduction: My Forays into Failure

All it took was a moment. I was 21. Till then, life was going exactly how I had dreamed of and trained hard for – becoming a professional soccer player. Then a snap, and I felt my knee give way. A bad tackle during a regular practice session had turned into my worst nightmare. It was a career-ending injury. My orthopedic surgeon assured me that I would walk again, but a professional career was not in the cards anymore. To this day, I am not completely over it. Like paper, once crumpled, it cannot be undone. Still functioning, but the scars remain for life.

People often ask me how I came up with the idea of Productive Failure, the notion that we could somehow *intentionally* design for failure and bootstrap it for deep learning. After all, many people have talked about the value of learning from failure. These accounts, however, are largely reactive; they talk about learning from failure *after* it happens. The idea of Productive Failure is to be proactive; that is, if failure is so powerful for learning, then we should not wait for it to happen. We should intentionally design for it for deep learning.

I like to believe that I came up with the idea in a moment of brilliance during my doctoral studies at Teachers College, Columbia University, in New York City. The truth, however, is that many things in my life led me to it. As Steve Jobs put it, "The dots connect looking back." My dots were my

1

failures, big and small, which slowly but surely nudged me toward it. But all of it only became clearer in hindsight. The lived experience was anything but.

Soccer Dreams

My journey started a long time ago, in my teenage years. I was in the sixth grade, doing stuff teenagers do. Falling in love was perhaps the most significant and consequential. However, unlike the first crush most people have in school, my first love was soccer.

As a teenager growing up in India, all I ever wanted to be was a professional soccer player. My father bought us our first color television just in time for the 1986 World Cup in Mexico. Diego Maradona was the man of the moment, and everyone I knew wanted to be like Maradona. I did too. Even though I was only in the sixth grade, I went for my high school team trials. In a country where everyone aspires to be the next cricket star, I took to soccer, and quite effortlessly so. And before the end of that academic year, I was the vice-captain and playmaker of my high school soccer team.

When I look back at my soccer years, a simple philosophy stands out. Training in the northern Indian city of Chandigarh in the foothills of the Himachal Mountains, my coach, Mr. Thomas, used to drill into us that matches are often won or lost in the last five to ten minutes of the game. Everyone can play well when they are fresh, he would say, but it is those who can push when extremely exhausted who make the difference in the last passage of play. Therefore, true to that philosophy, he designed our training to focus on preparing us for those game-changing moments.

How? By taking us to *the other side of failure.*

The idea was to train until you fail, and then you push just a little bit more. Do your push-ups and pull-ups till your arms buckle, and then push some more. Do your endurance training till your body cannot endure anymore, and then push some more. Of course, all this was done in a way that was safe to avoid injuries. Pushing just beyond the limit was sufficient. All the time to take the body to its limit, and then push a little bit more.

Why? Because good things happened on the other side of failure: this is where players maximized their physical and mental strength, and learned how to work the mind and the body together for optimal growth and performance. And our coach was right: when you look at tough games that go right to the end, quite often it is on the other side of failure where these games are won or lost. Lesson learned. In retrospect, this was the first of several dots I was to connect on understanding failure.

Unfortunately, just as I had made it to the national youth team, my soccer career ended with the injury. It was Spring of 1995. I remember it vividly. In one moment, everything that I had trained for in my life till then was gone. I was a case study in depression and failure. As effortless and enjoyable as soccer was, everything else after was quite the opposite, effortful and exhausting. Nothing seemed to work or make sense. So, the only thing I could do was to try to push through my backup option: finishing up my Engineering Bachelor's.

Struggling Through My Engineering Studies

It was not until my final year of engineering school that I started to take my studies seriously, for until then my life was all about soccer. In the final year of the engineering bachelor's degree, all students had to do a thesis. One could not graduate without completing a thesis. And I was certainly not in the mood for failing again. I was determined to succeed, but my professor and thesis advisor had other ideas.

First, I had to choose a project. Because other than soccer, the only other thing I was good at was math, I chose a project that involved a lot of mathematical analysis. My professor gave me a challenge to solve a special case of a differential equation in fluid dynamics. I was happy. It was mathematics and required neither an experimental setup nor building stuff. It was math and me, simple.

I tried several methods to solve the problem, without making any major inroads. After a couple of months, I saw my professor and showed him all I had done. He was quite pleased, even though I had not been "successful." He suggested I try a new approach, explaining the gist of it. I went back to the drawing table, working on it for a month, and still was not able to solve the problem. I could show that the professor's approach could not lead to a solution, but I wasn't able to actually improve upon it to solve the problem. When I saw the professor again, he was once again quite pleased, and gave me yet another approach. And again, the same result. This went on for three to four months; I'd follow through on all the approaches and suggestions, show that they couldn't solve the problem, but a full solution remained elusive.

By the end of the summer, I was panicking because I was nowhere near the end of this process, and I needed to graduate by the end of the year or else my scholarship would run out. I met the professor again at the start of the semester, sharing with him my predicament and concerns. He looked at me, and said, "Manu, all the strategies you have tried, including the ones I suggested, are known not to work." I was angry, but I tried not to show it. Why had he made me go through eight months of trying things that were known not to work? My professor explained, "Now that you have understood what does not work, you understand the problem way better than anyone else. Now I will tell you one last strategy. The problem cannot be solved mathematically. It has to be solved computationally."

It gives me goosebumps to this day when I think about that meeting. He was indeed right. Much as I hated admitting it at the time, I did understand the problem better and developing a computational solution and running simulations turned out to be straightforward. I did that quickly, and within a couple of months or so, I had completed the project and was even given the highest distinction for it. This was the second of several dots.

Looking back, both my soccer training and final year engineering thesis were the first two dots. In both, I was intentionally and repeatedly taken to the other side of failure. If I was paying attention, I would have connected the dots. I did not, or perhaps could not. Far from connecting the dots, I was merely happy just being able to graduate on time. I barely made it through with second-class honors, knowing very well that engineering was not what I wanted to do. My heart was simply not in it. I suppose, against the backdrop of a soccer career, it was hard for anything to come close.

It was time for trying out some other options. With some luck, I joined a management consulting firm, but within a few months even that did not work out, and I quit. Dot number three. Then, I ventured into the start-up world of the late Nineties during the Dot Com boom. This dream too fizzled out when the Dot Com boom turned into Dot Com doom. Dot number four.

By now, all my friends were already well into highly successful careers as doctors, lawyers, management consultants, and bankers; all I had to show was a string of failures – dots in a pattern that I had yet to realize – that I had in just about everything I had tried. I was running out of options.

And then, an opportunity to teach came along. Left with no other options at the time, and with bills to pay and make ends meet, I was forced into my fourth option: teaching.

Into the Classroom

Because I was reasonably good at math, I decided to become a math teacher, teaching the subject to high school kids for five years. It started as a one-year contract position, and I took it to give me some breathing space to figure out what I wanted to do with my life. As it turned out, this singular decision led directly to the discoveries that made my academic career a success and prompted me to write this book. However, these discoveries did not come from my prowess and skill as a teacher; instead, and as you will see, they are the direct result of my failure to teach mathematics to my students and my wondering why, exactly, this was so difficult.

I actually enjoyed teaching, and I still do. This did not mean I was good at it. I merely liked the idea of trying to help someone understand something new. And math, though a logical and well-structured domain, is known to be hard to learn, and consequently, hard to teach. I was up for the challenge.

My teaching philosophy was simple: I thought that if I could engage my students, explain the concepts as clearly as possible, then show them, step-by-step, exactly what to do and how to do it, I'd achieve transformational results. I spent a lot of effort and time preparing my notes and lectures, thinking about the best ways to explain difficult concepts. However, I quickly discovered that this method did not work well. Even after my preparation and my carefully planned lessons, at the end of the class, many of my students still did not fully understand the concepts we had covered.

How could these high school kids fail to see what I was trying to show them? How could it be that something I could so clearly explain, and draw their attention to, was still beyond their grasp? Well, if at first you don't succeed, try again, they say. And I did. I would repeat the lesson, going through the entire process of explaining the concept all over again, only to discover that the problem had persisted. Many students were still unable to see their way to the solution. Maybe some could to a certain extent, but, for most of them, a deep understanding of the concepts discussed and the ability to use them again in a different context, the holy grail of education, remained elusive.

Research on human learning by then had already developed a solid understanding about why we fail to understand when we are taught in this way. I unpack the major problems of learning in Chapter 1. Except at the time, I did not know about this research. I was at once frustrated and curious why my students could not see what I was trying to show them.

As you can imagine, teaching too didn't work out.

By now I was touching 30. Massively lost and confused and having spent my entire twenties trying and failing to figure out what I should do with my life, I decided to focus on my curiosity, and it was perhaps my curiosity stemming directly from my failure as a teacher that finally drove me to my fifth-choice career, in academia, searching for a scientific explanation for why teaching math was so hard and how it could be made easier. My close friends and colleagues often call me a reluctant academic. After all, academia was never in the cards, and when it happened, it was only after several tours and detours as a fifth-choice career.

Venturing into Academia

I enrolled in a doctoral program at Teachers College at Columbia University, majoring in the learning sciences – the science of human learning, how we learn, and how we can design better learning environments. I was immediately drawn to research into how best to teach new concepts. As I poured through scientific journals, I did not at first find the answer, but I started to notice a pattern across the research in my new academic field that echoed my experiences in the classroom. I had an epiphany, and I ended up writing a thesis on the science of learning from failure.

For a reluctant academic, I must say my years at Teachers College, Columbia University, were by far intellectually the most stimulating of my life. The formal training was of course rigorous and useful, but so was the informal experience beyond the confines of the formal courses, where encounters with diverse ideas challenged my thinking and broadened my perspectives in profound ways. Regardless of whether these interactions were planned or spontaneous, they formed the fertile ground from which new insights emerged and flourished. I claim these insights as my own, but in many ways they were the product of the collective experience.

A big part of this experience was reading and discussing what we read, and making sense of it. My focus was on how we learn new concepts, and how best to teach those concepts. Many of the studies I encountered described researchers who went into the classroom to observe how teachers taught their students. The teachers were almost always selected carefully: they were not just experts in their domains but also good at teaching. The researchers often found their lectures to be well-structured, engaging, and clear. Their students usually agreed and reported that they had learned a lot from the experience.

Yet, in study after study, when the researchers probed the extent to which students actually understood the concepts covered in the lectures, by giving them problem-solving tasks based on these concepts, they found that the understanding was largely superficial. Most students did not really understand the material, even though they felt like they did and reported that they had. I bet if you asked my high school math students, they would tell you I was a good teacher. Yet, as kind a judgment as that may be, I would bet doubly that chances are my well-structured and well-delivered lectures merely gave them the illusion of learning without actual deep understanding.

Almost everyone who has gone to school is familiar with this method of teaching. The teacher first teaches, then we practice, and, week in/week out, we learn new things and in a largely predictable manner. This is the "Direct Instruction" model, the standard approach for decades, and both the articles I had been reading and my own experience suggested that it was not effective, even if applied by excellent lecturers. The problem was not that we learn poorly from bad lectures, rather that we learn poorly from excellent ones.

Not learning well from bad lectures is understandable and explainable. Not learning well from good lectures is perplexing, even shocking. One can think of several reasons why. Maybe the material was not pitched at the right level. Maybe students needed to be supported better. Maybe students were only partially engaged with the material. Maybe more interactive learning was needed, and so on. And there are lots of studies in the literature that explore these explanations. No doubt these additional measures sometimes lead to incremental improvements, but they do not solve the problem of bad learning from good teaching.

To solve the problem, we need to know the cause.

Finding the Cause and Its Solution

Imagine you are watching a movie, a delightfully engaging and entertaining film. Now imagine that the person sitting next to you is an acclaimed director, an expert at making movies. Will you see the same movie as the director? In a sense, you will: the same sequence of images will appear before each of you. But what you will notice out of those images, the patterns you will see, the significance you will give to various elements of the movie, even the things you will see and will remember seeing – these are likely to be different unless you are an expert director yourself.

As we will see later in this book, decades of research on the difference between experts and novices has clearly demonstrated that experts see different things than novices. Novices tend to see superficial features, but experts see what is essential, the deep structure and critical features. It is seeing the deep structure that leads to understanding and powerful learning.

It turns out seeing is not simply a perceptual exercise but a cognitive one as well. We don't just see with our eyes, but with our minds: seeing is a function of what one knows. And herein lies the paradox (and challenge) of teaching a novice. A novice, by definition, does not have the knowledge to see what is critical. Yet, the novice needs to somehow be able to see the critical features to be able to develop expertise.

The solution to the paradox lies in realizing that the first job of teaching is actually not to teach. The first job of teaching is to prepare the novice to see with an expert's eyes. Indeed, my mistake as a math teacher was in assuming that my students could understand the principles I was trying to show them. Instead, I needed to activate my students' ability to see the critical features of the problem before I could expect them to fully grasp the solution.

How could I do that?

I realized that the best way to really teach something is to engage students in problem-solving activities specifically designed for them to productively struggle and even fail, and only then give them the correct explanation or lecture. Instead of waiting for failure to happen, I wanted to intentionally design for failure and then bootstrap it for learning from subsequent instruction, turning the initial failure into deep learning; that is, Productive Failure.

Since I made the realization, I have discovered by failing – and beginning to understand the reasons why they were failing – students could start to approach a problem in a way that enables them to see the critical features for success. They are then prepared to learn from subsequent explanation, instruction, or expert feedback.

In Chapter 2, I describe how I conceptualized Productive Failure, and designed the initial set of experiments to test its effectiveness, as well as the larger body of evidence that has accumulated over the years. As a teaser, let me just say that Productive Failure students have invariably demonstrated significantly deeper conceptual understanding as well as a greater ability to transfer what was learned to novel problems than students who had received Direct Instruction.

The bottom line: when learning something new, it is much too easy to find the path of least resistance. It is most natural to seek the easy way out. However, my research on Productive Failure shows that making learning easy does not always ease learning. If not intentionally designed to leverage failure in the initial stages, learning tends to be shallow and inflexible. But with it, learning is deep, flexible, and adaptive. Productive Failure suggests that making initial learning more difficult and challenging, where you may struggle and even fail to solve a problem or perform a task, can be beneficial for learning.

The Productive Failure model is in many ways simple yet paradoxical. Simple, because it turns the traditional mode of instruction on its head. Paradoxical, because it intentionally designs for and leverages failure in initial problem solving as the path to longer-term success; that is, deeper learning.

To be clear, the proposition of *Productive Failure* is not simply that failure, if and when it happens, should be seen and used as an opportunity to learn. Of course all of us make mistakes from time to time, we falter and fail. Everyone can relate to such experiences, and I do believe some of our deepest lessons can come from our failures.

In *Productive Failure*, the question I ask is: If failure is indeed such a good teacher, why do we wait for it to happen? Why not intentionally design for it? Take solar or wind energy as an analogy. We know these are natural sources of energy. Do we just wait for them to generate energy by chance? No. We intentionally design tools and technologies to tap the energy for our use.

The same goes for failure. The proposition being that instead of waiting for failure to happen, we should be more proactive, and intentionally and systematically design for it so that everyone can have the opportunity to learn from it. By designing so, we can accelerate the initial learning process, and achieve dramatic results.

Connecting the Dots

Some years ago, unfortunate circumstances forced me to embark on my fifth-choice career. Connecting the dots looking back, this book is the happy result. It is a story of my own forays on the other side of failure.

As I look back on my life, I realize now that many of my most important life lessons have come from Productive Failure. It was a misjudged tackle on the training field that derailed my career as a soccer player. In the period in which I reconciled myself to my new reality, the years I spent training and dedicating myself to skill at soccer have sometimes felt to me like wasted time. But I have come to understand that the lessons I learned during soccer were some of the most significant lessons of my life. It was only on the other side of failure, when I began to study how people learn, that I achieved success.

There are a number of stories of famous people who struggled with and overcame failures in their lives. Michael Jordan did not make his high school basketball team, Jack Ma failed his university entrance exam three times and was rejected by Harvard ten times, Steven Spielberg was rejected three times by a film school; the list is long. I do not know the full spectrum of learning experiences they had in their lives. Perhaps there was something in their schooling and upbringing that prepared them to be able to make the most out of the failures they faced. Perhaps they had something in them already, a clear vision and passion for what they wanted. Perhaps their experiences made them resilient and persistent. Most likely it was a bit of everything, with some luck thrown in for good measure.

Clearly, not everyone can be like them. Not everyone has the innate passion, ability, or preparation to cope with let alone learn from failure. What do we do about everyone else like the rest of us? Instead of waiting for failure to happen, what can we *proactively* do to prepare people to embrace failure, deal with it, and learn from it?

This naturally begs the question: How do we design such failure experiences in ways that promote more effective learning? Done wrong, failure can be detrimental. How do we maximize its benefits and avoid its pitfalls? After all, total, inexplicable failure can be intensely frustrating and can push students to drop a subject altogether. Repeated experiences of intriguing, constructive failure, however, when carefully curated to help develop resilience, creativity, and resourcefulness, can work miracles. What are the defining features of Productive Failure?

In Part III (Chapters 7 and 8) of this book, I describe evidence-based principles for how we can curate these experiences in a manner that is safe and affirming, so that failure is the norm, not the exception — a signal for learning, not the noise detracting from it. In Chapter 7, I describe these principles if you are designing learning for others, be it as a teacher, educator, parent, trainer, manager, coach, and so on.

However, these principles are not just for designing learning for others; they are just as powerful for taking charge of and designing your own learning. As an individual, maybe you want to learn new knowledge, language, sport, or a skill. In Chapter 8, I describe how Productive Failure can be so transformative for your own learning. From setting up goals that get you out of your comfort zone, to designing specific kinds of tasks that push the boundaries of your current abilities, to developing a mindset that supports your growth, I describe the full set of design principles to harness Productive Failure for your own deep learning.

Now, you may be tempted to jump straight to Part III to learn how to design for Productive Failure. I would suggest, however, that the design principles in Part III will make a whole lot more sense if you first read Part I, where I unpack the problems of learning (Chapter 1), followed by its solution —Productive Failure — and how it solves the problems (Chapter 2). An understanding of the problem and its solution would help you better understand the principles for designing the solution.

Part II (Chapters 3–6) focuses on the underlying science, and it is written especially for the science inclined reader who wants to dive deep into why the solution works, and why designing for failure instead of success results in deeper, more robust learning. Here I describe the four fundamental mechanisms – Activation, Awareness, Affect, and Assembly – of learning, dedicating a chapter to each one of them.

Note, however, that even though evidence for these mechanisms comes mainly from either lab-based or classroom-based experiments with students, the mechanisms themselves apply more universally, be it when you are learning by yourself or designing learning for others. Different ways of designing learning will invoke these mechanisms in different ways and to different degrees. And as you will see, Productive Failure is a powerful way of invoking these mechanisms to unlock deep learning.

I also hope that understanding the science of failure will encourage you to reconsider your own failures, place a greater value on them, and reflect on the learning and growth that resulted from them. And arming yourself with this understanding perhaps will empower you to intentionally design and use failure when learning something new.

That is what Productive Failure is all about. It is at once three things: a design, a science, and a mantra for life. As a *design*, Productive Failure shows us how to deliberately curate our learning experiences and those of others, so that we can harness the power of failure for deep learning. As a *science*, Productive Failure tells us how, when, and why that design works, so that you not only understand what it is but also why it is so powerful. And as a *mantra*, Productive Failure's true power is unleashed when we internalize it as a way of thinking, knowing, and being in this world, helping us seek, design, and harness the other side of failure, on a regular basis, until it becomes a part of us in everything we do, and perhaps it ultimately becomes us.

The Problem and Its Solution

The Fields Medal is widely considered to be the most prestigious prize in mathematics, often described as the Nobel Prize in mathematics. Unlike the annual Nobel Prize, however, the Fields Medal is awarded only once every four years, to up to four people. Since its inception in 1936, only 64 people have received the prize, making the winners of the Fields Medal a rare group of brilliant minds.

It does not take a brilliant mathematician to deduce that the chances that you actually know a Fields Medal winner are therefore exceedingly low. Unless of course you work at a university such as ETH Zurich in Switzerland, which has been home to many such brilliant minds over the years, one of them being my fellow colleague and friend, Alessio Figalli. He won the Fields Medal in 2018.

Over lunch one day, Alessio and I were talking about failure, and the role it plays in mathematics. I remember Alessio dropping a bombshell: "As a mathematician, I've come to realize that about 95% of my attempts are destined for failure."

Ninety-five! percent Now that is a high failure rate, making failure more of a core feature of mathematical practice than a bug. He went on to add, "This might sound disheartening, but failure is actually a vital part of the process. You see, every attempt, every struggle, every moment of puzzlement, is a necessary step toward understanding. When I confront a problem, I try, and often it doesn't work. So, I will try something else. It's a cycle of trying, failing, and persisting."

Failure was a necessary step toward understanding. Without failure, it would not be possible to understand the problem as well. According to Alessio, failure was instrumental in solving a key problem of understanding. Of course, I did not need much convincing but I wanted to hear his reasoning for why failure was so critical. He continued, "What many don't realize is that these failures are never in vain. Each one sheds light on the problem, helps me see a critical aspect or deep structure of the problem, and also clarifies what doesn't work. This process of elimination is crucial."

There it was. Failure seemed to help see what was critical, which led to understanding the problem better, and made it clear what did not work.

As a learning scientist, I was thinking that a failure to see and understand that which is critical is a key problem when we are learning something new, and that deep learning proceeds by tackling the problems of seeing and understanding and becoming aware of what does not work. And here I had a Fields Medal winner affirming exactly that, telling me that failure was the secret recipe of achieving mathematical success. Little did I expect that what was true for deep learning was also true in Alessio's work as a mathematician.

But there was more. For Alessio, these failures also served another purpose – they helped in "incubating" ideas. That sounded a lot like how transfer of learning might happen, so I urged him to elaborate. "You see, I've learned the importance of stepping back," he said. "When I'm stuck, sometimes the best approach is to let go of the problem. This break allows me to lose any fixedness in my thinking. When I return to the problem with fresh eyes, it's like meeting an old friend with new stories to tell. This fresh perspective often illuminates paths that were invisible to me before."

I could not believe what I was hearing. Failure was a core feature, not a bug. It helped see what was critical, and understand the problem better. And when multiple attempts of solving ended up in being stuck, it was good to step back, let ideas incubate, lose fixedness, and return to fight another day.

What was also striking to me was the contrast between how top mathematicians like Alessio Figalli approach mathematics and how mathematics is taught and learned in schools. For Alessio, mathematical problem solving does not proceed in a straight line. And he was quick to add: "Neither do mathematicians."

Yet, how we teach mathematics is often in a straight line – the Direct Instruction model – avoiding failure at all cost, and in the process undermining learning because it does not solve the problems of learning. And it is not just mathematics; the tentacles of Direct Instruction extend to much of schooling and instruction in most other domains and subjects too, all proceeding along the same suboptimal logic of Direct Instruction.

Therefore, I start your journey with this book by first articulating the key problems of learning: why we fail to remember, why we fail to understand, and why we fail to transfer (Chapter 1). And once armed with an understanding of the problems, only then do I describe how the solution – Productive Failure – solves these problems (Chapter 2).

1

The Problems
of Learning

I remember studying for my exams in school and university, and doing reasonably well on them, yet soon after, I would forget most of the material I had studied so hard to remember. I was and am not alone. This phenomenon plays out in schools around the world all the time.

Why do we remember so poorly?

One of the most well-documented curves in learning is the retention curve; that is, how well we can remember newly learned things over time. Unfortunately, these curves reveal a dismal picture. Retention is poor, and consistent with my experience, drops quickly and drastically. To understand the nature of this problem – why we fail to retain – we need to dive deep into how we store and retrieve things we learn. Retention, however, is not the only problem of learning. Even if we can retain information, it does not mean we understand it well.

Why do we understand so poorly?

When learning something new, one of the main reasons we do not understand it well is because we fail to see what is critical. Recall the movie thought experiment from the Introduction. The expert director would see different things from a novice while watching the same movie. Given the same stimulus, what makes experts see critical features easily, yet novices find it so difficult? Clearly, we cannot understand something deeply if we cannot

17

see that which is critical. However, seeing what is critical is necessary, but not sufficient. There is more to understanding than seeing, because understanding requires connecting and integrating new knowledge with prior knowledge.

And finally, if we cannot understand a concept deeply, then we cannot transfer it to novel contexts. Learning is effective when it allows us to do things in a new context, with new tasks, to adapt and apply our lessons to changing needs. This is called transfer. But why do we transfer so poorly?

In this chapter, I focus on the three problems as shown in Figure 1.1 – why we fail to remember, why we fail to understand, and why we fail to transfer – taking each in turn and unpacking the science behind it. Although I discuss them in turn, they are interconnected, each feeding off of one another. Only when we can understand the problems of learning, can we start to think of the possible solutions for learning.

Defining and understanding the problem is often the hardest part, which is why I have chosen to start with it. My hope is that by taking you through these deep dives into each problem you yourself will be able to remember, understand, and transfer why we fail to remember, understand, and transfer.

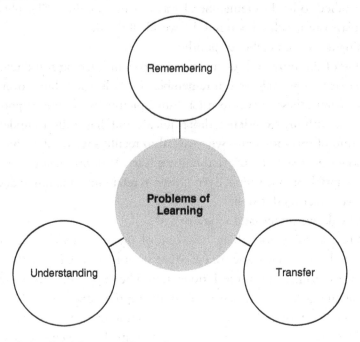

Figure 1.1   Problems of learning.

Failing to Remember

There are some things that are so deeply ingrained that we can never forget them. Think of your immediate family members, their names, their faces, what they do, and so on. Think of basic arithmetic you learned in school, or riding a bicycle, or how to swim. Think of key dates such as birthdays or anniversaries of people closest to us. Think of passwords you use all the time. Think of phone numbers you can still remember, if you are old enough to have lived in the pre-smartphone era, that is. Think of your go-to movie that you watch all the time. The list goes on. These are all examples of memories that are stored well and effortlessly remembered at any point in time. We say they have not only high storage strength but also high retrieval strength. When a piece of information has both high storage strength and high retrieval strength, it means that the information is deeply ingrained in memory and can be easily recalled in the present moment.

Then there are some things that you know you learned a while ago in school or outside, but you cannot remember them well. Think of those mathematical formulas and proofs that you had to learn repeatedly throughout schooling. Think of that foreign language course you did for a year or two. Think of a dance course you took for a bit. Think of the books you read, and so on. These are all examples of memories that were stored well because you learned them over a sufficiently long period of time but cannot easily be remembered right now. You would need to restudy or relearn them, and then perhaps you might be able to remember them better. At the time you learned them, however, they could be characterized by high storage and retrieval strengths. But as it stands now, these memories remain stored but not easily retrievable. When information has high storage strength but low retrieval strength, it means that the information is deeply embedded in long-term memory but is not easily retrievable at the present moment, often due to a lack of regular or recent exposure or use.

Now if you were to think of what you had for breakfast today, or the news headlines that caught your attention, or that pesky password change you had to make, your hotel room number during your vacation, the plot of the movie you watched recently, a recent event you attended, and so on, these are examples of memories that may not be stored deeply but in the short term, they can be remembered easily. Give them time, however, they are likely to fade away and become hard to recall. That is the reason my cramming strategy helped me pass my tests and exams at the time, but in the longer term, I would be hard pressed to remember the differential equations I learned in my engineering bachelor's. When information has low storage strength but high retrieval strength, it means that the information is not deeply ingrained in long-term memory but is easily retrievable at the moment, often due to recent exposure or relevance.

Finally, there are memories that are neither stored well nor recalled well. Think of the many introductions at a party or networking events; easy in, easy out as they say. Or random trivia facts that seem interesting in the moment but cannot be remembered soon after, casual chats, interesting jokes or memes that we come across – all get noticed in the moment only to be forgotten the next. There is low storage, and low recall. When information has both low storage strength and low retrieval strength, it typically relates to fleeting or superficial encounters with that information.

This dual-index model of our memory – storage strength and retrieval strength – was proposed by Robert Bjork and Elizabeth Bjork in 1992 (see Figure 1.2). They called their model the New Theory of Disuse.

What do storage strength and retrieval strength mean for learning? Four implications follow. The first three are intuitive, the fourth perhaps a little counterintuitive:

1. When we process new information, for example, when learning a new math or science concept or language, we increase storage and retrieval strengths.

		Retrieval	
		Low	**High**
Storage	**High**	Math learned in school, Foreign language learned years ago, ...	Parents' names, Key birthdays, Favorite password, ...
	Low	Names of people at a party, Random trivia, ...	Today's news, Hotel room number while on vacation, ...

Figure 1.2   Storage and retrieval strengths.

2. The deeper the processing of the new information, the higher the storage strength. For example, cramming does not work as well as persistent study and rehearsal over time, especially if we can connect the new information to what we already know.
3. The higher the storage strength, the slower the loss of retrieval strength. For example, you are unlikely to forget your parents' names no matter how long you do not see them.
4. The mere act of retrieving increases storage strength, the increase being greater when retrieval strength is lower than higher. That is, the lower the retrieval strength, the greater the opportunity for making learning gains, that is, increasing storage strength.

The fourth implication is the one that is somewhat counterintuitive. After all, shouldn't retrieving something we already know well make it even stronger? One way to think about it is that when retrieval strength is high, it means you can already easily access information that is stored. Yes, typing in your regular password one more time increases its storage strength, but this increase is not as great as when you are trying to retrieve something for which retrieval strength is low. Say, what is the capital of Greenland?

In the context of learning new things, this last point becomes crucial, for by definition, retrieval strength is low when we are learning something new. Many times, there is not much to retrieve in the first place because all of it is so new. Even if you did not know the capital of Greenland, just merely thinking about it or attempting it is useful, because if you were to Google the correct answer now, you will remember it better. As we shall see in this book, even when retrieval results in failure, it is still beneficial for learning the new information.

But here's an even more counterintuitive implication: having learned something new, it pays off to forget it a little. Why? When we learn something new, the first implication says both storage and retrieval strengths increase. If we have processed it deeply, the second implication says both storage and retrieval strengths will be high. At this point, we start to plateau. That is why after studying something for a while, you get to a point where the marginal gains start to drop. You reach a plateau.

To escape the plateau, we need to back off. Paradoxical, but true.

We have to let the retrieval strength drop off a little. We can do this by focusing on learning and doing other things for a period of time, could be hours, or days, or weeks, depending upon what you are learning. By this time if the retrieval strength has dropped off, and you try to recall that information, chances are you will find it a little challenging to do so, even fail to recall. But when you are then given that information again or have the opportunity to study the same thing again, the boost to your storage strength will be much greater than when you backed off.

My close friend and colleague, Ido Roll, likens this to how paths form when we walk on grass. Walk on a trail 100 times in one week, and a month later the weed returns. The path is forgotten. But walk on the same trail 100 times over 100 days – once a day – and the trail will be solid and deep.

This is perhaps the Disuse part of the New Theory of Disuse. After learning something new, we must allow for some disuse, that is, intentionally not using that information or allowing for some forgetting of that information, so that when we come back to it and try to retrieve it, we derive a strong boost in both storage and retrieval.

And that's the trick to remembering information. Learn, forget, retrieve, relearn, then repeat the cycle over time. The forgetting part is important, for it sets up the stage for retrieval. If retrieval is successful, it makes your storage stronger. If retrieval is unsuccessful, it creates an opportunity to re-study and re-learn, which will then enhance your storage and future retrieval.

We tend to think of forgetting as bad. It turns out forgetting can be good. We must remember to forget, so that we can use forgetting to remember. Productive forgetting.

Failing to Understand

How would you like to challenge a chess grandmaster to a memory game? Suppose I were to give you and the grandmaster a list of 20 random words or objects, nothing related to chess per se, to memorize in one minute. After a short break, I ask you both to recall as many words as possible. Who do you think would do better? If you are like most people I have put this question to, you would bat for the grandmaster. After all, chess is regarded as one of the toughest of mental sports, and it is not uncommon to have seen grandmasters play multiple games simultaneously, and win. Surely that is proof of their superior memory.

Except that is not the case.

What if instead of random words or objects, the task is to remember the positions of randomly placed chess pieces on a chess board? Surely this is a task that grandmasters would be better at. Except that too is not the case. As counterintuitive as it may be, it is true that, on average, grandmasters are no better than lesser skilled players or even you and me in remembering random things, allowing for the natural variation between people.

Only when the task is to remember positions of non-random chess pieces, authentic plays that may actually happen in a chess game, do grandmasters perform better at reproducing them from their memory.

In 1946, Adriaan de Groot was the first one to demonstrate this difference between grandmasters and lesser skilled chess players on reproducing authentic chess positions (his work was translated from Dutch to English in 1965). He found that after a brief exposure to authentic chess positions, grandmasters could reproduce the positions with almost perfect accuracy. The performance of lesser skilled players, even though these were not novices, was far inferior, demonstrating that it takes an exceedingly high level of expertise to be able to see chess positions and reproduce them almost perfectly.

The point was that it is not an overall better memory that helps the grandmasters. It is what they see in those non-random, authentic positions. It is their vast experience and expertise that allows them to see patterns of play that they recognize at once and as a whole. Instead of remembering individual pieces, their knowledge of the game allows them to see these deep structures, which a novice like you and me would not be able to do.

Following the seminal work of de Groot, in 1968, his student Riekent W. Jongman replicated de Groot's findings to show that even after a brief five-second look at authentic chess play positions, the performance of grandmasters was far superior. And in a twist, Jongman and his colleague W. Lemmens also compared grandmasters with lesser skilled players on reproducing random chess board positions. Although the study was not published, the result was striking: the superiority of grandmasters that was seen on authentic positions disappeared on random positions. Random positions after all do not have any deep structure to them, making grandmasters appear no different than lesser skilled players on reproducing random positions.

In 1973, William G. Chase and Herbert Simon reproduced de Groot's and Jongman's results by comparing chess masters and novices to find the same overall pattern of effects: given the same perceptual stimuli, experts see different things than novices when the stimuli is authentic, and not so much when it is random. Experts tend to use their prior knowledge to notice and see deep structure, whereas novices rely on surface features. In the absence of deep structure, as in the random positions, the differences between experts and novices tend to significantly reduce or vanish altogether.

This is true not just in chess, but in other domains as well. Chess is a well-defined, well-structured domain. How about something less structured, more subjective, like poetry, where structure is even harder to decipher?

You may have come across the excerpt shown in Figure 1.3 from Robert Frost's famous poem "Stopping by Woods on a Snowy Evening." If you are a novice reader of poetry like me, encountering this excerpt without prior knowledge of Robert Frost or his poetic style, you might interpret it more literally. For example, you might see the contemplation of the woods as a simple appreciation of nature's beauty. The repetition of the line "And miles to go before I sleep" might be understood as a statement of physical distance or a reference to a long journey ahead. Without the contextual understanding of Frost's thematic depth or his use of symbolism, a novice reader may not grasp the deeper layers within the poem.

However, for an expert in poetry, their prior knowledge of Robert Frost's style, historical context, thematic tendencies, and recurring motifs will play a significant role in the interpretation of a poem. They would approach this excerpt knowing Frost's use of nature, contemplation, and the juxtaposition of external landscapes with internal musings, to recognize the metaphoric quality of the woods, possibly interpreting them as a symbol of solitude, introspection, or even the journey of life itself. The repetition of the line "And miles to go before I sleep" could be seen as an emphasis on responsibilities, obligations, or the ongoing challenges one faces. These deeper layers of meaning (or deep structure) will likely be inaccessible to the novice.

> *"The woods are lovely, dark, and deep,*
> *But I have promises to keep,*
> *And miles to go before I sleep,*
> *And miles to go before I sleep."*
> _____
> Frost, Robert. *"Stopping by Woods on a Snowy Evening."* 1923.

Figure 1.3   Excerpt from Robert Frost's Poem.

Be it chess or poetry, experts tend to see different things from novices, because they can use their prior knowledge to see the deeper layers and make deeper meaning. Not only that; prior knowledge affects the very encoding of what they observe. It provides a different lens.

Experts not only see different things but also see things differently.

This is exactly what happens if, instead of playing chess or reading poetry, you are watching a football match alongside an expert coach or player. A novice is more likely to follow the ball, whereas a professional coach or player is more likely to also see what is happening off the ball, how the team is creating space, and configuring as a group, the strategies being deployed to exploit the weaknesses of the opponents and so on. Same match, same perceptual stimulus, but experts see critical features and structures, novices less likely so.

The pattern extends to mathematics or science or art as well, whether you are looking at an elegant math proof alongside a mathematician, or the equations of motions alongside a physicist, or examining a painting alongside an artist, and so on. Novices tend to see superficial features, but experts see what is essential, the deep structure and critical features.

Seeing depends upon what we know. We use our knowledge to see things. The exercise is not merely perceptual; it is also a cognitive one. And it is seeing the deep structure that leads to understanding and powerful learning. In the context of learning something new, we quickly run into a paradox. If you are learning something new, you are a novice with respect to that target knowledge. Therefore, by definition, you do not have the knowledge to see what is critical. Yet, somehow you need to be able to see the critical features to be able to develop expertise. When learning something new, novices therefore get caught in this conundrum, between a rock and a hard place.

Prior knowledge is key. It not only helps us see critical features, it also helps us connect with and integrate new knowledge. Both seeing and connecting are key to making meaning and developing deep understanding.

To see why connecting is important, consider what happens when we learn a new language. For example, I do not know Greek, or many other languages such as Mandarin, Russian, Japanese, Tamil, just to name a few. If you were to talk to me or ask me to read something in any of these languages, I would turn up a blank. These languages have an entirely different script. But if I were to try to make sense of something in French or German or Spanish, I would fare a little better. Why? Because I know English, and there is some overlap between the letters and words in English and languages like French, German, and Spanish, but not with Greek and the others listed above. I could use my prior knowledge of English, and leverage the overlap to connect with the French and German words, to make some sense of the new language. And that gives me an entry, a way in, to learn a new language.

Learning math, science, history, art, or any other domain is not that different. Each domain has a formal language, with its own words, symbols, meanings, grammar, structure, and ways of using and thinking with it. A domain expert is akin to a native speaker of the language. To a novice, however, it is altogether a new language, a new way of thinking and being, and an entirely new culture even.

From the perspective of the student, it is not unlike finding yourself in a foreign country where you do not speak the language, and are trying to find the train station. Someone notices you are lost and starts giving directions in their language. Seeing your puzzled look, they slow down and repeat the directions more slowly and clearly. Much as you appreciate their effort, it does not help much because you do not have any prior knowledge to understand the language to begin with.

A similar thing unfolds in classrooms around the world. For a student new to a topic, the concepts and terms are like a foreign language. Even if a teacher explains these "foreign" concepts slowly and clearly, the student may still find it hard to understand. The situation may not be as stark as trying to understand a completely foreign language, but it is not that different either. It is a matter of degree, not kind. This is exactly what I used to do as a teacher. As you already know, I was not successful with it.

Just because the teacher, as an expert, can see the critical features and deep structure and explain it clearly, it does not mean the student, as the novice, can also see it and connect with it. Because they simply do not have the necessary prior knowledge to see the critical features and connect with it; they are learning a new "language" made up of symbols, terms, and ways of thinking. The language analogy is telling because it is not uncommon for students to come out of a lecture and say: "That was all Greek to me!"

Teachers, and experts in general, often assume that if they just explain what they know clearly and engagingly, that that should work. As in my experience, but also more widely, it does not work well. In fact, this is something researchers have known for a long time.

In an influential 1988 paper, Alan Schoenfeld reported on his study of what most would intuitively consider good teaching. He observed the classrooms of good mathematics teachers, teachers who manage the class well, explain the concepts in a clear and well-structured manner, engage the students, where even students themselves report to have understood the concept as explained by the teacher – by all accounts these were well-taught mathematics classes. Yet, when he probed students' understanding of the concepts, he found it to be shallow. Change a small thing, or a superficial feature, and they were completely thrown off.

What Alan Schoenfeld was suggesting was that the problem was not that we learn poorly from bad lectures, rather that we learn poorly from excellent ones. He titled his paper "When Good Teaching Leads to Bad Results: The Disasters of Well-Taught Mathematics Courses." I wish I had read his paper before I started teaching.

Seeing and connecting are key. And prior knowledge holds the key to both. But the prior knowledge key is precisely the key novices do not have. And without that key the door to understanding cannot be opened.

In 1998, a decade after Alan Schoenfeld's paper, Daniel Schwartz and John Bransford wrote another equally influential paper arguing for, as the title of the paper suggested, "A Time for Telling." That is, the first job of teaching is not to tell, but to prepare the novice to see. And the first job of learning is not to be told, but to prepare for the telling. There is a time for telling, but only after the learner has been prepared for it.

How does one do that?

As you may have guessed, one powerful way of preparing novices to see is through failure, and we will see that in the chapters to come. For now, it is more important to understand the problem of why we fail to understand when learning something new. We fail because we do not have the prior knowledge key, the very key we need to see the critical features in and connect with new knowledge.

Failing to Transfer

Suppose you are asked to remember two lists of words, each comprising 36 randomly chosen two- or three-syllable words from a word bank. The first list is to be learned sitting 20 feet underwater in full diving gear, with the words being narrated one by one through a recorded tape. This is the Wet learning condition. The second list is to be learned sitting on dry land, also via a recorded tape. This is the Dry learning condition. After a break, you are then asked to recall as many words as possible from each list, except that the recall takes place both underwater (Wet recall) and on land (Dry recall).

Therefore, as Figure 1.4 shows, there were some words that were learned and recalled underwater – the WW words. Others were learned and recalled on dry land – the DD words. And then there were words that were learned underwater and recalled on land – the WD words, or learned on land and recalled underwater – the DW words.

What would the pattern of recall look like? To answer this question, in 1975, D. R. Godden and A. D. Baddeley reported on an experiment similar to the scenario described above.

They found that people had the best recall for words learned on land and recalled on land. This might seem intuitive, no surprises here. What was intriguing was people had just as good a recall for words learned and recalled underwater. Statistically speaking, there was no difference between these two sets of words; that is, people performed equally well in recalling WW and DD words. But for words learned underwater and recalled on land or vice-versa, people had the worst recall.

It seemed that when the learning and testing contexts were the same, recall was better. When they were different, recall suffered. A simple, yet delightfully creative, demonstration that context matters. We seem to encode not just the words but also the context in which they are learned. Given that recall in the same context was better, it means that context also provides cues for us to remember the words.

Learned \ Recalled	Wet	Dry
Wet	WW words	WD words
Dry	DW words	DD words

Figure 1.4 Learning by recall matrix of words.

Context therefore gets encoded together with whatever we are trying to learn, and then serves as a cue for retrieving that information. Which is why if learning and testing are in different contexts, we perform worse than if they are in the same or similar contexts. This pattern of effects is not just from one study. In 2001, Steven Smith and Edward Vela examined 75 different studies on the effect of context on memory, and they found a reliable effect that our memories are indeed context dependent.

Context matters.

And if context matters, then it must influence transfer. Transfer, by definition, is the idea of using what we learned in one context and applying it in another context, which may be similar or different than the one we learned in. Here, context is to be interpreted broadly. Where you learn and how you learn are both part of the context.

The experiment above demonstrated that where you learn matters. The place itself gets learned and coupled with what you are learning. For example, dancers learn routines in a studio, associating moves with familiar cues in the learning environment. On a new stage, absent these cues, performance can falter, which is why rehearsing on stage becomes critical for enhancing memory and live performance. Similarly, a basketball player who practices free throws in a certain gym might find that they perform better in that same gym because they have associated the visual cues of the space with the muscle movements of shooting.

Where we learn, the place, matters.

Context also means practices, that is, how we learn what we learn. We can learn new content, say math or science, from a lecture by listening and taking notes individually, or we can learn it by engaging in problem solving, working both individually and collaboratively. The two sets of practices are different. Likewise, the practices within which we learn a new language, say formal classroom versus cultural immersion, are different, and will therefore influence how well we learn and transfer the new language.

How we learn, the practice we engage in, matters.

However, the kinds of practices we engage in while learning need not be and are often not the same as the practices we need to use that knowledge in. And when this happens, we find it difficult to transfer what we have learned to new places and practices. Hence, the frequent lament amongst employers that even though students learn a lot of knowledge and skills throughout their schooling years, they find it difficult to apply them in the authentic complexities of work and life.

The late neurosurgeon, Paul Kalanithi, beautifully illustrated this problem of transfer as he reflected upon his experience of transitioning from being a medical student to a practicing doctor.

> *"It was becoming clear that learning to be a doctor in practice was going to be a very different education from being a medical student in the classroom. Reading books and answering multiple choice questions bore little resemblance to taking action, with its concomitant responsibility. . .I stood still, unsure when to act or what to do."*
>
> —*Paul Kalanithi,* When Breath Becomes Air *(pg. 63)*

Not surprisingly, a similar dynamic plays out for other domains as well. Although students learn substantial amounts of formal knowledge in their subject area, they find it difficult or are often unable to apply this knowledge. Or, as Paul Kalanithi describes, they are *"unsure when to act or what to do."*

Why does this happen?

In a landmark article in 1989, John Seely Brown, Allan Collins, and Paul Duguid put forth what is perhaps the most compelling case for how our cognitions and learnings – memory, knowledge, skills – get tied to the context – place and practices – in which they are learned.

They called it *Situated Cognition*, the simple idea that what you are learning, where you are learning, and how you are learning become inextricably linked. When you learn something new, it is not just the facts or skills themselves that stick in your brain. It is also the whole experience – where you are, what is around you, and what you are doing at the time. So later on, when you are in a similar situation, it can trigger those memories and make it easier to recall what you learned. Your brain links what you are learning with the environment and practices.

This linking between learning and context is more generally true as well. If you learn to cook a new dish while listening to a specific type of music, say Italian opera, you might find that hearing opera again makes you think of the recipe steps and even the tastes and smells of the dish you prepared. Or if you wore a specific perfume or cologne during a memorable summer vacation where you learned to surf, smelling that fragrance again might bring back memories of surfing, even if you are nowhere near the beach. This is why pilots train in simulators that mimic the cockpit of an airplane. The context of being in an actual cockpit can enhance the recall of the procedures and checks learned during simulation. This is also why sometimes studying in the same place where you take a test can help you remember better, but also make it harder if the learning and testing places are different.

One can also think of situated cognition as the home advantage effect, borrowed from the sporting world, where teams tend to perform better at home than when they are away. When a team practices and plays regularly in their home stadium, they become deeply familiar with many aspects of the environment: the feel of the playing surface, the way the ball bounces, the sounds of their specific crowd, the layout of the facilities, and even the routine they follow in their own locker room. Their bodies and minds form a connection between these contextual elements and their playing strategies and skills. During home games, all these familiar cues can help trigger the athletes' memories and instincts, improving their performance. Conversely, when teams play away games, they are in an unfamiliar environment with different sights, sounds, and routines, and the unfamiliarity can disrupt their concentration and increase stress levels, potentially leading to poorer performance compared to when they are at home surrounded by familiar contexts.

In all of these scenarios, the environmental and situational factors during the learning process are not just background details – they are integral parts of the learning experience that can significantly influence memory recall and skill execution.

If our cognition and learning are indeed situated, we can derive an important hypothesis for transfer: when there is an overlap or alignment between the context of learning and the context of use or application of that learning, then transfer is easier. If not, transfer is harder. The overlap or alignment creates a home advantage, so to speak.

One of the clearest and most intuitive examples supporting the hypothesis comes from how we learn words and language in schools. Miller and Gildea's 1987 study cast doubt on traditional vocabulary teaching methods that treat knowing words and using them as two separate processes, that meanings of words could be learned independently of the context of their use. They pointed out that in schools, students often learn new words through dictionary definitions and a handful of example sentences. This practice is clearly quite different from how people typically learn language outside the classroom, which is through regular conversation and exposure to language in context.

According to situated learning hypothesis, one would expect formal language learning to be situated in schooling practices of learning through dictionaries and examples and therefore not transfer well to authentic contexts of use, whereas language learning outside of school would be situated in authentic practices of daily life and transfer well to such contexts, which are the real contexts of use.

True enough, as Miller and Gildea argued, this real-world practice of language learning is incredibly efficient, as evidenced by the fact that by the time someone is 17 years old, they usually know on average about 80,000 words, having acquired them at a remarkable rate of about 13 words per day over the years. In stark contrast, school-based vocabulary lessons that rely on abstract definitions and decontextualized sentences are slow and ineffective. There is simply not enough time in school to teach more than a few hundred words a year.

Worse, many of these words do not end up being useful to students, as they do not use them meaningfully. For example, students tend to make errors like "Me and my parents *correlate*, because without them I wouldn't be here," when what they mean to say is that they are related to their parents, or "I was *meticulous* about falling off the cliff," when what they really mean to say is that they were very careful, or "the *redress* for getting well when you're sick is to stay in bed," when what they really mean to say is not *redress* but *remedy*, and so on.

Miller and Gildea's study always reminds me of my Physics teacher in high school, who exhibited exactly such patterns. To be fair, he was a good Physics teacher, but English was neither his native language nor his strongest suit. For example, it would not be unusual for him to come to class and say "Open the windows so that the atmosphere can come in," or when he found us loitering in the corridor he would admonish us by saying "Stop rotating about the corridor and go to class," and many other hilarious uses of the English vocabulary. Perhaps he too had relied heavily on dictionary learning and not as much on meaningful contextual practices.

Indeed, a 2023 meta-analysis by Stuart Webb, Takumi Uchihara, and Akifumi Yanagisawa examined 24 studies in second language vocabulary learning and showed that when vocabulary learning was situated in meaningful contexts, it had strong effects on learning and transfer, precisely as predicted by the theory of situated cognition.

All of this calls into question how we design learning environments. Let us consider an easy and intuitive example first. How would you teach someone how to ride a bicycle? Much like children learning formal definitions of words first, would you first give them all the theory about why the bicycle is constructed the way it is, the forces and the dynamics behind it, before getting them to cycle? Or much like learning words in an authentic context, would you get them onto the bicycle, and have them try to cycle, get a feel of it, fall and get up and try again, and as they are engaged in this, give them tips and explanations at the right moments? You would always choose the latter.

Now consider the same, but this time replace riding a bicycle with learning math or science, or for that matter most subjects we learn in school. Is learning something more abstract such as math or science really that different from learning how to ride a bicycle? The situated nature of our cognition and learning would suggest that the underlying dynamics of both kinds of learning are not that different.

And yet, how do we teach? We decouple knowledge about mathematics from the practice of mathematics, knowledge about science from the practice of science, and so on. In so doing, the practices within which students learn mathematics or science or language are not aligned with practices within which they might be expected to use that very knowledge. And because of that, students find it difficult to apply or transfer what they have learned.

Situating learning in decontextualized practices of schooling is a big reason why we fail to transfer.

Any solution for learning should address the three problems of learning. In the remainder of this book, we will see how Productive Failure does that, and more.

Key Takeaways

1. We **fail to remember** because of low retrieval strength. However, forgetting can be good because retrieval practice is an effective way to increase both storage and retrieval strengths.

2. We **fail to understand** because, as novices, we do not have the prior knowledge to see and connect with new knowledge. Therefore, when learning something new, we should first prepare or be prepared to see, and not go straight into teaching or telling.

3. We **fail to transfer** because learning is situated in the context in which we learn, which means that if the context of learning and context of use or transfer differ a lot, then transfer becomes hard.

2

The Solution: Productive Failure

Let us start with a little thought experiment. Imagine you are a child, and you love playing with toys. Suppose you were part of an experiment, and I randomly assign you to play in one of two groups: Group 1 or Group 2.

To both the groups, I say: "Hey kids, here is a *new* toy" (and I show you the toy). You have not seen this toy before. Do you want to play with it? Both groups enthusiastically show they want to play with the new toy.

To Group 1, I say: "Wait, this is a new toy, so let me first show you how to play with it. Watch and learn, and then I will let you play with the toy as you like." Once I am done showing, I give them the toy and I observe how they play.

To Group 2, I say: "Okay, here's the toy, play as you like." I give them the toy and I observe how they play.

Both groups are allowed to play freely with the toy as they like, except only Group 1 is first shown how to play with the toy. The question is: Which group do you think would be more inventive in playing with the new toy? I have done this thought experiment with thousands of people who have attended my talks and workshops over the years. Invariably, most people intuit in favor of Group 2. And then I ask another question: Which group will better learn how the toy works? This time, most people intuit in favor of Group 1.

What if this was not just a thought experiment, and there was actual scientific evidence to test the two intuitions? Luckily, there are precisely such studies, for example, by developmental psychologists Zi Lin Sim and Fei Xu (2017), that help us answer the two questions empirically. In a nutshell, studies have shown that when children are allowed to play freely with the toy (like Group 2), they are more than three times as inventive as when they are first shown how the toy works and then allowed to play (like Group 1). This supports our first intuition.

However, when it comes to learning how the toy works, both groups learn equally well. This does not support our second intuition. It turns out that Group 2 children play in a way that helps them generate evidence not only about how the toy works but also how it does not work, that is, failure evidence, which was crucial for them learning on their own how the toy works. And if one knows both how something works and does not work, then it is reasonable to assume that the learning is deeper. In other words, Group 2 children not only learned how the toy worked but also how it did not, and together it helped them learn more deeply without any explicit instruction whatsoever.

What is additionally intriguing about these findings is the lower inventiveness of Group 1 children compared with Group 2 children. Group 2 children went into free play without knowing how the toy worked. Group 1 children went into free play knowing how the toy worked. Even armed with more knowledge, in fact correct knowledge, Group 1 children still did not exhibit more inventiveness during free play. Shouldn't knowledge aid invention? Or could it be that more knowledge somehow constrained them in their inventiveness? Something to ponder, for we shall return to it later on.

If a child's free play with toys is so powerful, perhaps we can start to think of new knowledge, concepts, ideas also as toys. Not as physical toys, but conceptual toys. We could then argue that deep learning and inventiveness come from playing with new toys, new concepts, new ideas, exploring them, tinkering with them, connecting them, and of course failing as well. What implications might this have for how formal learning in the schools is organized? For the most part, and evidence backs it up, formal schooling, or training in general, largely follows Group 1. Mine was definitely so, and chances are you were mostly in Group 1, too.

If the bulk of our learning experiences are in Group 1, that is, when we are shown how to play with new conceptual toys first, before any opportunity to play and explore, are we not being robbed of the opportunity to develop the very basis for deep learning and inventiveness?

The answer depends upon the extent to which formal concepts and ideas in the various domains (math, science, language, humanities, and so on) can be treated as toys. It is one thing to figure out how a toy works, akin to figuring out how to put together an IKEA item with minimal or no instruction. It is quite another to learn formal, and often abstract, concepts such as algebra, gravity, grammar rules and so on. It is highly improbable that a student in high school would be able to self-generate principles of algebra or calculus on their own without any explicit help or instruction. Therefore, one could expect a similar pattern of effects in formal learning environments in schooling and beyond. If, however, there is something decidedly different about formal concepts, then we obviously cannot expect the pattern to hold.

Once again, we can ask science to either confirm or refute our intuitions. It turns out there is a whole body of scientific research that compares Group 1 versus Group 2 in formal learning contexts. In this body of research, Group 1 is typically called Direct Instruction, whereas Group 2 is called Discovery Learning (or pure Problem Solving).

Direct Instruction vs. Discovery Learning

Imagine you're learning to cook. Direct Instruction would be like following a step-by-step recipe, with exact measures and detailed instructions. Discovery Learning, on the other hand, would be more like experimenting in the kitchen with different ingredients and techniques, tasting as you go, and figuring out what works best without any guidance from a recipe.

Or imagine a math class on how to solve quadratic equations. The teacher presents the problem, and explains the solution step-by-step on the blackboard. Students then practice solving similar equations on their own. The process is straightforward: the teacher imparts knowledge, and students absorb and apply it. This is Direct Instruction, or Group 1. However, if the teacher presents the problem and asks students to figure out how to apply their existing knowledge and discover the solution themselves without any guidance or instruction, that would be Discovery Learning, or Group 2.

The underlying logic of Direct Instruction is that if you do not know the concept, the best way to learn is to tell you exactly what to do and how to do it, much like children in Group 1 who were first shown how the toy worked and then asked to play with it. Whereas Direct Instruction is heavily structured and explicit, Discovery Learning emphasizes active engagement and self-exploration as the primary drivers of acquiring new knowledge.

The underlying logic of Discovery Learning is that learners should be given opportunities to learn through problem solving with minimal or no guidance, so that they can explore and discover new knowledge themselves, much like the children in Group 2 allowed free play to discover how the toy works.

Direct Instruction and Discovery Learning therefore represent two ends of a spectrum in teaching methodologies.

We can now return to the question: Which is better in formal learning contexts: Direct Instruction or Discovery Learning? When pitted against each other, science is clear and robust on this question. Direct Instruction beats Discovery Learning hands down. In experiment after experiment, regardless of age, gender, domain, and so on, students who learned through Direct Instruction outperformed those in Discovery Learning on a range of learning outcomes.

It seems the pattern of effects we saw in free play with toys does not extend to formal learning contexts. Playing with physical toys to figure out how they work is different from learning domain-based formal concepts. The learning method that optimizes the former seems to fail spectacularly for the latter.

By the time I started my doctoral studies in the Fall of 2003, this was largely the state of this debate. All done and dusted. Direct Instruction had won. Direct Instruction was King. Discovery Learning had lost.

Searching for a Problem

The hardest part of doctoral studies is finding a problem. This intellectual odyssey, while daunting, is a rite of passage in a doctoral student's academic growth. To quote Albert Einstein: The formulation of a problem is often more essential than its solution. In my experience, it is not unusual for a doctoral student to take years to find and formulate a problem well. Solving the well-formulated problem is usually relatively fast by comparison. But it has to be a problem that is worthy of solving.

One of the frequent arguments that junior doctoral students make when proposing a problem is that no one has yet solved that problem. I confess I too have made this argument as a doctoral student, and my doctoral students have also made this argument. Although logical, this argument is weak. Maybe no one has solved the problem because it is not a significant problem to solve. Best leave it alone. Instead, find a problem, which if solved, will advance the field in a significant way, and in doing so, contribute to our understanding of human learning.

How does one find a problem like that? As a doctoral student, I remember spending weeks and months thinking about this. This quest, like an intellectual treasure hunt, demands patience and grit. It can be quite a frustrating journey. One has to wrestle with vast amounts of literature, each study a potential clue. Ideas emerge, flicker, then fade under scrutiny. Rigor battles creativity, while the specter of "insignificance" looms large. It's a cerebral marathon that not only shapes the thesis but also one's academic identity. And one never knows how long it would take or when we might stumble upon an insight.

And then one day, I was discussing Thomas Kuhn's book *The Structure of Scientific Revolutions* (1962) with my close friend and fellow doctoral student, John Voiklis. We were discussing Kuhn's description of the paradigm shift from Ptolemy's geocentric model of the solar system to Copernicus' heliocentric model. It was fascinating in and of itself how the entire shift happened; insightful for anyone wanting to understand how scientific revolutions come about. But it was also particularly insightful for me as a doctoral student.

The geocentric model (that the Earth is at the center of our solar system), proposed by Ptolemy, was the prevailing paradigm for centuries. It had complex explanations for why the planets moved as they did, including epicycles (little circles the planets made while orbiting Earth). But over time, astronomers began noticing anomalies. The planetary movements didn't always align with the geocentric model's predictions. Copernicus proposed a radical new paradigm: the heliocentric model (that the Sun is at the center of our solar system), where Earth and the other planets orbit the Sun. His model explained the observations more simply and accurately.

As classic and beautiful the story of this paradigm shift is, it didn't happen quickly. What struck me was how a string of anomalies with the geocentric model led to the questioning of its most fundamental assumption (that the Earth is at the center), which allowed Copernicus to entirely revise centuries of established science. By questioning just one fundamental assumption, he had changed our understanding of the solar system. Much like a Jenga tower, you remove one critical foundational block, and the whole thing falls apart.

I went back to thinking about the debate between Direct Instruction and Discovery Learning, and how Direct Instruction had basically won. But there was a problem.

Actually, not one but at least three. First, even though Direct Instruction was the prevailing model, there were still lots of anomalies or problems with the Direct Instruction model. As noted in the previous chapter, especially Alan Shoenfeld's seminal paper on when good teaching leads to bad results, reports of Direct Instruction resulting in shallow understanding were coming in thick and fast. Retention problems, understanding problems, transfer problems.

Evidence on the problematic aspects of Direct Instruction had started to gather momentum, much like the accumulation of anomalies in the geocentric model.

Second, even though Direct Instruction had won, and it was the prevailing model, it did not mean a new model couldn't be better. Just like the heliocentric model was better than the geocentric model, there could be models that were even better than Direct Instruction.

Third, just because Discovery Learning lost, it did not mean all was lost. No doubt students do not succeed in solving problems without any guidance or support. But that does not necessarily mean the problem solving experience has no value. Maybe there was some value in the problem solving efforts, in the struggle, in the frustration, in the exploration that ultimately results in failure. Maybe this value needed to be extracted somehow. There had to be a way.

This was my *Aha!* Moment. I remember it vividly. It was neither grand nor explosive, just a quiet triumph. Everything else seemed distant in that moment, muted against what felt to me at the time a striking insight. I could zone in on the fundamental assumption, and go after it.

I now understood why the Direct Instruction model assumed that the best way to teach a new concept was to explain clearly and exactly what the concept is. There was no point in learners struggling with problems when you could tell them exactly how to solve them. Tell them what to do and how to do it. There it was, nestled in the complex workings of the model – a subtle yet fundamental assumption that could very well turn out to be its fundamental flaw: *making learning easy eases learning*. This was to me the foundational block in the Direct Instruction Jenga tower. With this singular insight, which in hindsight seems so obvious, my intellectual landscape shifted, a gentle earthquake that vigorously shaped what was to come next.

What if I were to question this fundamental assumption? What if exactly the opposite could be true? Instead of making it easy, could the best way to teach be to make initial learning hard? Counterintuitive as it sounded, I decided pursuing this line of argument would be the focus of my doctoral research.

Quickly I ran into two questions: How does one make initial learning hard? And how hard is hard enough?

The first question was relatively easier to figure out. One simple way was to get students to solve problems that required knowledge of concepts they did not know yet. Problems that were beyond their knowledge base. Clearly such problem solving will be hard.

The second question was not so easy because operationalizing hard is itself hard. Where does one draw the line? Luckily, I could resort to an old trick in the science playbook: look at the extreme-case scenario. The extreme opposite of making things easy is not to make them hard but make them so hard that it results in failure. My logic was that if I could demonstrate the hypothesis in the extreme case, then the middle ground would be easier to sort out later. I needed to engage students in problem solving that was not just hard but one that led to failure. Speaking of extreme, if I could demonstrate the hypothesis in a domain that was known to be hard to learn, for example, mathematics, even better.

What would such math problem solving look like?

Designing for Failure

Imagine the following scenario. You are a high school student, and today's math lesson is on the concept of standard deviation – a basic math concept that measures how much variation there is in a distribution. For example, if everyone in your class is of the same height, then there is no variation in height, the standard deviation of heights is zero. If, however, there are lots of different heights, with tall and short students, then the standard deviation is large. How large exactly? Well, that's the mathematical formulation that is captured by standard deviation.

As a student, you do not know this concept, probably never even heard of it until the lesson. You are a novice. So, you come into the class, sit down at your desk, and get ready for the lesson. Your teacher comes in and starts the lesson. You expect her to teach you in the good old Direct Instruction way, except she adopts a different approach. Instead of teaching you the concept of standard deviation first, she gives you the challenging problem shown in Figure 2.1.

She explains the problem to you and gives you about half an hour to attempt it. She asks you to try your best to solve the problem, and emphasizes that your goal is to invent as many solutions as possible without worrying about getting them right or wrong.

Take a moment to think about how you might approach this problem as a high school student who has not yet learned the concept required to solve this problem correctly. If you have time as you are reading this, take a few minutes to even have a go at it. List three to five ideas you might generate.

When I ask people to estimate the kinds of solutions students might be able to generate, two things typically happen. First, they find it quite hard to think like a novice, especially if they already know the concept of standard deviation. This happens a lot with math teachers. Second, they tend to underestimate what students can generate, typically limiting them

Amy and Ben are two basketball players in a league. The table shows the number of points they scored in the 9 games they played. Invent as many ways as possible to determine who the more consistent player is. Just be creative; without worrying about getting it right or wrong.	Amy	Ben
	11	12
	12	14
	13	17
	14	15
	14	11
	14	16
	15	12
	16	16
	17	16

Figure 2.1 An example of a productive failure problem.

to a few standard ideas such as means and graphs. Ideas that you can find in textbooks. But when I actually show what students are typically able to produce, they are invariably and pleasantly surprised. And mighty impressed too. Teachers like it particularly because they can see the creativity and play of imagination that students can engage in.

Likewise, there is also a big surprise for students, for they are themselves surprised that they could generate as much as they actually do. There is a big gap between what they think they could do at the outset, and what they are actually able to do. When faced with a challenging problem, a problem that is beyond our current knowledge and skills, we tend to underestimate our capabilities, and those of others, too. Data, however, shows that we have far greater resources for creative production if only we are given well-curated opportunities to do so.

So, let's look at this data to see what novices are capable of producing when they try the basketball problem in Figure 2.1. Remember, they have not been taught the concept (of standard deviation) required to solve this problem.

The Ideas of a Novice

When faced with the basketball problem in Figure 2.1, students typically start by trying to figure out what consistency really means. Are we looking for the better player or the more consistent player? Is there a difference even? One of the common things students, and even adults actually, do is to confuse the two. Being better is not the same as being more consistent. A straight Fs student is more consistent than a student who gets As and Bs. At least statistically speaking. Just eyeballing the data also suggests that Amy gets better over the games, but not Ben. Does this mean Amy is more consistent? These kinds of questions and discussions spontaneously emerge as students go about solving the problem.

Other students may jump directly into computing something. After all, given a bunch of numbers, that seems the path of least resistance. The lowest hanging fruit is to calculate totals; that is, the total number of points scored by each player and compare the two. Averages are also intuitive, so they calculate the means, and if they have learned the concepts of median and mode, they might find those out too. It turns out the problem is designed in a way that the totals are the same. Both Amy and Ben have scored a total of

126 points over nine games, which also means that their averages are also the same; that is, 14.

Amy's Total = 11 + 12 + 13 + 14 + 14 + 14 + 15 + 16 + 17 = 126

Therefore, Amy's Average = 126/9 = 14

Ben's Total = 12 + 14 + 17 + 15 + 11 + 16 + 12 + 13 + 16 = 126

Therefore, Ben's Average = 126/9 = 14

This is deliberately designed into the problem. I will discuss the design principles in greater detail in Chapter 3, but the idea is that the problem invites students to use their intuitive as well as formal knowledge learned in school, yet the problem is designed in a way that those solutions do not work. Because totals and averages are the same, they cannot distinguish between Amy and Ben. This way, it becomes clear to the students that they have to think of something else.

Another common solution is to draw graphs, most frequently by plotting the number of goals on the y-axis against the game on the x-axis, as shown in Figure 2.2.

This way they can see how the graph changes from game to game. If it goes up and down a lot, has a lot of changes or fluctuations, then the player is inconsistent. If, however, the graph does not change much or has only small fluctuations, then the player is more consistent. One can clearly see from the graph that Amy's graph either stays the same or goes up, but never down. Ben's graph never stays the same, and goes either up or down. Hence, Amy is perhaps more consistent, they would argue.

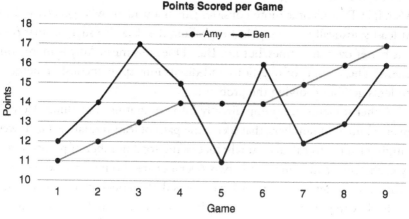

Figure 2.2   Graph of the scores per game over the nine games.

Other visual representations that frequently emerge are tally tables, frequency polygons, or histograms. These visual representations are indeed a great way to get a feel of the problem, but they do not constitute the solution in and of themselves. In that sense they are necessary but suboptimal. We praise students for generating visual representations to understand the problem and look for patterns, but then we push them to use these representations to generate solutions that are quantifiable and more precise, just like mathematicians would.

The cycle of invention needs to carry on. Having looked at the totals and averages, students start to look at the ends. What were the maximum and minimum numbers of points scored by each player? In other words, what is the range of scores for Amy and Ben? As you might have guessed, the problem is designed in a way that the minimum (11), maximum (17), and the range (maximum − minimum = 6) are the same for the two players. Once again, the problem invites their prior knowledge, but it is not solvable by that knowledge. They need to think of something else.

Here is where things start to get really interesting. One intuitive solution that turns up frequently is to calculate the difference between the points scored from one game to the next; that is, the second game minus the first, the third minus the second, and so on until the ninth minus the eighth game – a total of eight game-to-game changes. Adding all these eight differences gives the sum total of all the changes from one game to the next. If you calculate this, then Amy's total game-to-game change turns out to be:

$$12-11 + 13-12 + 14-13 + 14-14 + 14-14 + 15-14 + 16-15 + 17-16$$
$$= 1 + 1 + 1 + 0 + 0 + 1 + 1 + 1 = 6$$

Similarly, Ben's total game-to-game change turns out to be:

$$14-12+17-14+15-17+11-15+16-11+12-16+13-12+16-13$$
$$= 2 + 3-2-4 + 5-4 + 1 + 3 = 4$$

Since Ben's total is smaller than Amy's, perhaps Ben is more consistent. Or so they would argue. Some students notice that Amy never has any negative changes, but Ben has both positive and negative changes, which cancel each other out. This is of course not fair, they would argue, and hence propose that only the magnitude of the change ought to be considered, and not the sign. Upon recalculation, Amy's total game-to-game magnitude of change is still 6 (because she has no negative changes) but Ben's is now 24. What a jump from 4 to 24! Clearly Ben is now more inconsistent by this measure. Finally, some students go on to calculate the average magnitude of the change. For nine games, there are eight changes, therefore the average magnitude of change from Amy equals 6/8 or 3/4, whereas for Ben it equals 24/8 or 3. By this measure, Amy is again the more consistent player.

There are now several such studies with thousands of students around the world. Not just on the topic of standard deviation but many topics from elementary to middle to high school and universities. In math but in other domains too. I use the basketball problem here as an illustrative example.

Altogether, the idea is to design problems so that students are able to generate about four to six solutions. In the case of the basketball problem, it is often a mix of totals, averages, range, graphs, and varied calculations of game-to-game changes. This typically takes 30–45 minutes of problem solving. While all the solutions are highly intuitive, they are either incorrect (e.g. totals, averages), or at best suboptimal (graphs, range, game-to-game changes). None of these solutions are correct from a canonical standpoint, which is calculated using the formula for standard deviation – the targeted concept for the lesson. Therefore, one may ask: What is the point of engaging in such an exercise when it results in either incorrect or suboptimal solutions?

This is precisely the reaction of the proponents of Direct Instruction. When they look at this, their immediate reaction is: See? We told you students will not be able to generate the correct solution on their own. You have just wasted time. What could possibly be gained from engaging in such an exercise? If students don't know the concept first, what is the value of getting them to solve problems that require knowledge of that very concept? You should have taught them first!

Yet, when I share this data with people, most of them, particularly teachers, educators, parents, and even students themselves, find it intuitively obvious that there is something there even if students are not able to generate the correct solution. It is like Group 2 children playing with the toy without knowing how to play with it. But to others, especially the proponents of Direct Instruction, such an exercise carries no value whatsoever.

It was clear. Even though it is intuitively obvious to many, including myself, that such an exercise has intrinsic value, intuitions cannot be admitted as scientific evidence. It was not sufficient to merely illustrate students' capabilities when they engage in problem solving deliberately designed to lead to failure. I also needed to find a way to extract or bootstrap that failure for deep learning.

How does one do that?

Turning Direct Instruction on Its Head

The answer lay in the Direct Instruction model itself. If one is going to turn the fundamental assumption on its head, then why not turn the model on its head too? When Copernicus questioned the fundamental assumption of Ptolemy's geocentric model, he generated the alternative model by turning the model on its head; that is, instead of Earth being the center of the solar system, he made the Sun the center. Likewise, if making learning easy does not necessarily ease learning, then maybe the alternative model is to turn the Direct Instruction model on its head.

As we saw earlier, Direct Instruction involves explicit instruction followed by solving problems. Learn first, solve later. It is a two-phase model: an Instruction Phase followed by a Problem Solving Phase (Figure 2.3). The Instruction Phase provides clear, explicit instructions and demonstrations, immediate feedback, and correction. The Problem Solving Phase provides opportunities for learners to apply what they have learned by solving problems. And this sequence of Instruction followed by Problem Solving (or I-PS) can repeat as often as desired or necessary.

Turning the model on its head would mean starting with Problem Solving followed by Instruction (or PS-I), as in Figure 2.4. Solve first, learn later. That was it. Quite simple. The way to extract the value of failure in problem solving was to follow it up with explicit instruction. After all, it is conceivable that the process of generating suboptimal or incorrect solutions to the problem can be productive in preparing students to learn better from the subsequent instruction that follows. Thus, Productive Failure is not the same as Discovery Learning, for it combines the benefits of constrained discovery learning through problem solving, followed by instruction.

However, like intuition, being conceivable is not enough. Just because something is intuitive or conceivable does not mean it is true. I needed to turn the conceivable into demonstrable. I needed an experiment. A clean way to compare Productive Failure and Direct Instruction; an experiment that would demonstrate that engaging students in problem

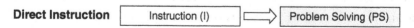

Figure 2.3   Direct Instruction: Instruction followed by Problem Solving.

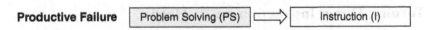

Figure 2.4   Productive Failure: Problem Solving followed by Instruction.

solving activities deliberately designed for them to fail could in fact help them learn better from subsequent instruction, than engaging them in Direct Instruction.

Setting Up the Experiment

The experimental logic itself is fairly simple, but designing a good experiment requires thorough planning and attention to detail. And as hard as it is to design a good experiment, it is sometimes even harder to recruit people to participate in the experiment, especially when the experiment is on something called Productive Failure. Nobody wants to be a guinea pig, especially if it involves failing, a lesson I learned after I approached several schools and explained the experimental study I was planning to do, its underlying logic and hypothesis.

Nobody bought it. Everyone wanted some evidence first, which was fair enough. But how was I supposed to get such evidence if no one gave me a chance in the first place? Besides, the mere presence of the word *failure* seemed to throw them off. And they would throw me out. Even with the qualification *Productive*, they would focus their attention on Failure. It was undesirable to position failure so overtly and explicitly in the foreground. Perhaps it was fair that I had to go through the process of failure trying to prove the point that failure can be productive.

But good things can happen on the other side of failure. I finally got the nod from one school whose principal decided to take a chance on me. It was pure luck amidst all the trying to stumble upon a school whose principal happened to be my high school math teacher. In the years since, she had gone on to become a school principal. I don't quite know why she took a chance on me, but I will always be grateful that she did. She assigned one of her math teachers to work with me. One school, one teacher, and her math students. The study was on. We could now begin designing the experiment proper. And there were a number of things to consider and design for.

Giving Chance a Chance

Once I had a sample of students who agreed to participate in the experiment, I would randomly assign students into one of the two conditions: Productive Failure or Direct Instruction. Randomization is key. Imagine picking teams for a game. If you handpick the best players for one team, that would not be fair. The same goes for scientific experiments. If we do not randomly assign participants to different conditions (like different teaching methods), we risk bias – pre-existing differences in abilities or knowledge or skills might affect the results, not the variable we are studying. By giving chance a chance, random assignment ensures each participant has an equal chance of being in any condition, making the groups comparable. It's like shuffling cards before dealing them, ensuring a fair game, where differences in outcomes can be attributed to the strategies used, not the initial deal. This way, randomization ensures that any differences in learning outcomes can be attributed to the teaching methods, not to students' prior abilities or characteristics.

All Else Being Equal

Next, one has to control all variables except for the teaching method. Imagine you are trying to find out if a particular spice enhances the flavor of a dish. You would want to keep all other ingredients, cooking time, and techniques the same, changing only the amount of the spice. If you simultaneously alter other factors, like adding a different ingredient or changing the cooking time, you cannot be sure if the change in taste is due to the spice or these other changes. Similarly, in scientific research, controlling variables means keeping all factors constant except the one we are studying. All else being equal, you change the one thing that you want to study the effect of. In my case, the teaching method. Therefore, I ensured that all students were from the same school, learning the same curriculum, the same concept, with the same teacher, for the same duration, at a similar time of day, and in a similar environment, and so on. In a lab experiment, these variables are easier to control. In an actual school or a formal learning environment, it becomes hard. But one must try as best as possible.

Tuning It Up

Equally important is for the two learning methods to be designed well. Imagine a Formula 1 race where two teams have developed innovative but vastly different designs for their cars. One team has focused on creating a more aerodynamic shape to reduce drag, while the other has put their energy into developing a more powerful engine for greater speed. Before they compete, however, it is essential that each team ensures their car works well with its respective design. Both designs need to be well-tuned before comparing. If the aerodynamic car has not been properly wind tunnel tested, or the powerful engine has not been finely tuned, it would be premature to compare them. The race would not accurately reflect the potential benefits of the different design strategies, but rather the effectiveness of the implementation and preparation. Similarly, when comparing two learning methods, both should be thoroughly developed and optimized within their respective design frameworks. Both should be conducive to learning. If one method has not been adequately prepared or tested, it is disadvantaged from the start. A number of iterations and piloting goes on in the lead-up to an experiment just to make sure both methods are working well before we subject them to a comparison. Only then can we truly determine which method is better, as the differences in outcomes can be attributed to the effectiveness of the methods, and not poor design.

Capturing the Signal

One can design a nice experiment, but if the measurement is not good, the whole thing falls apart. Measurement is like the heartbeat of any experiment, the compass that guides our exploration. Good measurement ensures we are not just collecting any data, but the right data – precise, accurate, and relevant. We need to capture the signal if there is one; that is, if there is an effect in favor of one condition or the other – the signal – our measurement should be able to detect it. For example, a test that is either too easy or too hard would fail to detect any difference because both conditions will end up performing either well or poorly respectively. The trick is to design tests and surveys that are good at picking a signal when there is one. There is a whole body of science behind the development of measurement systems. Suffice it to say, a whole lot of work goes into designing instruments that provide valid and reliable assessments of students' knowledge and skills, before, during, and after the experiment. It is like taking snapshots at different stages of a journey. You can observe where the students started, how they progressed, and where they ended up, providing a comprehensive picture of their learning journey.

Before the experiment, we assess the students' pre-existing knowledge and incoming characteristics (e.g. gender, age, grades, and so on) to establish a baseline. During the experiment, we keep track of how students interact, what they produce, and survey their experience on a number of variables like engagement, interest, motivation, anxiety, and so on. After the experiment, we evaluate what they have learned using a variety of instruments designed to pick up the signal. When comparing Productive Failure with Direct Instruction, we are interested in three types of signals: procedural knowledge, conceptual understanding, and transfer. These three signals largely map onto the three problems of learning – remembering, understanding, and transfer – described in Chapter 1.

The Three Signals: How, Why, and Apply

Procedural knowledge is like knowing the recipe of a dish. It's about knowing the steps to solve a math problem – the "how." For example, if you're taught a specific method to solve a quadratic equation, and you can apply that method correctly to solve such equations, that's good procedural knowledge. In science, it might be the method to conduct titration in a chemistry lab. In language, procedural knowledge might be understanding how to structure a five-paragraph essay.

Conceptual understanding, on the other hand, is about understanding the "why." Recall from the previous chapter that understanding requires seeing and encoding the critical features and the deep structure of the concept. It is the stuff that novices really struggle with. It is like understanding why certain ingredients in a recipe work well together. In math, it is about understanding why a certain method or formula works. Why do we "carry the one" in addition? Why does the Pythagorean theorem hold true? In science, it could be explaining why increasing the temperature can accelerate a chemical reaction. In language, it might involve comprehending why certain literary devices, such as metaphor or foreshadowing, are effective in conveying a story's theme. If you can demonstrate these abilities, you have good conceptual understanding.

Finally, transfer is about taking something you have learned in one context and applying it to another context, often a new context – it is like using a recipe you know to come up with a new dish. In math, if you can use your knowledge of addition to understand and solve multiplication problems, or apply your understanding of geometry to solve real-world problems like calculating distances or areas, that is a successful transfer. In science, it could mean using the principles of physics to understand why a curveball in baseball behaves the way it does. In language, it could be about employing critical thinking skills learned in literature class to analyze and interpret current events or historical situations.

As you can imagine, the "how" can be hard but most people can learn that. Any learning method worth its salt should at least develop the "how," or procedural knowledge, robustly. The "why," or conceptual understanding, is much harder. A good learning method ought to be able to develop not just the "how" but also the "why." In doing so, it would address the problem of why we fail to understand. But the hardest of them all is transfer, the ability to apply your "how" and "why" in novel contexts, contexts that you have not encountered before, thereby requiring you to flexibly adapt and apply. I will call it the "apply" signal.

On the one hand, what is the point of learning anything if you cannot transfer it to new contexts and problems? On the other hand, and as you can guess, research suggests that transfer is indeed the hardest, and consequently rare, and therefore, is often called the holy grail of learning. A learning method that can develop robust procedural knowledge, deep conceptual understanding, and demonstrate transfer is worth its metaphoric weight in gold.

With the experiment well-designed, the teaching methods finely tuned, the measurement set up to capture the key signals, it was time for the battle of the methods.

The Battle: Productive Failure vs. Direct Instruction

At the operational level, comparing Productive Failure with Direct Instruction, be it in a lab or in the classroom, essentially boils down to Figure 2.5: When learning a new math concept, should learners be first taught the concept and then solve problems (Direct Instruction), or solve problems

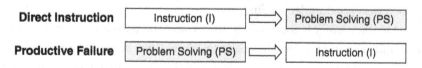

Figure 2.5   Comparing Productive Failure versus Direct Instruction.

that lead to failure first and then be taught the concept (Productive Failure)? After running several such studies, for a range of topics (e.g. ratios, statistics, and many others), in a number of schools, what did we find?

Figure 2.6 shows that both methods led to high levels of procedural knowledge about the targeted concepts. This is the "how" signal, the kind of knowledge that gets tested on standardized tests: facts, procedures, and some basic problem solving. However, if you look at the second set of bars in Figure 2.6, you can clearly see that Productive Failure students demonstrated significantly (denoted by ★★★) deeper conceptual understanding than Direct Instruction students. This is the "why" signal, which if you recall, had remained elusive from my teaching days. The same was also true for transfer, the "apply" signal. The third set of bars in Figure 2.6 show that Productive Failure students demonstrated significantly (denoted by ★★★) better transfer to novel problems. Although not salient in Figure 2.6, statistically speaking, the effect on transfer was much stronger than on conceptual understanding. Engendering both deep understanding and transfer was therefore a stellar achievement. I call it the *Productive Failure Effect*.

A quick note about what we mean when we say that something is statistically significant: Statistical significance is simply a way to determine how probable it is to get the difference between the two methods purely by chance. If the chance of getting a difference between two methods purely

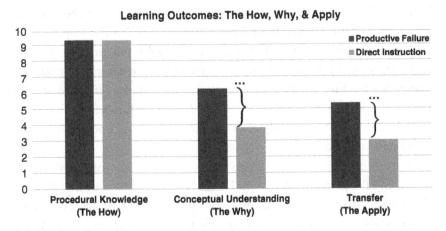

Figure 2.6   Learning outcomes of Productive Failure versus Direct Instruction.

by chance is high, then we cannot deem it significant, because there is a high probability of getting the effect just by chance. It is what we might call a random effect. However, if the chance of getting the difference is small, then we can be more confident that it is not a random effect, that one method is indeed better than the other. How small is small enough depends on the domain. In my domain – the learning sciences – anything less than 5% is deemed significant. That is, if there is less than 5% (or one in twenty) chance that the effect could be random, it is considered significant. We give it one star (★). If there is less than 1% (or one in a hundred) chance that the effect could be random, then we give it two stars (★★). And if there is less than 0.1% (or one in a thousand), we give it three stars (★★★). The effects on conceptual understanding and transfer were both three-star effects. In other words, there is less than one in a thousand chance that the Productive Failure Effect is merely a random effect.

I then investigated how much better was learning from Productive Failure over Direct Instruction? Once again, statistics give us a way of benchmarking how strong the size of the effect is. Think of effect size as the "oomph" of our experiment. It tells us not just if Productive Failure was more effective (that is what the statistical test does), but precisely how much more.

It is one thing to say Amy was faster than Ben in a race, it is another to say she was a full minute faster. Now if the race lasted on average 10 minutes, then it is a 10% effect, but if the race lasted on average 100 minutes, it is only a 1% effect. Quantifying the effect gives us a sense of the practical significance of the finding. If a new diet improves health outcomes by 1%, you are not likely to switch. But if it changes health outcomes by 10% or more, you would at least think about it. Likewise, a teacher may not want to change her teaching method if the new method makes a difference of only 1%, but if a new method makes a 10% or a 20% or perhaps a 50% difference, then the teacher is more likely to pay attention to it and potentially switch to the new method.

Furthermore, it is important to not rely on just one or a few studies comparing Productive Failure with Direct Instruction, because a small sample of studies may not be able to produce a stable and robust signal of effects. One may also be accused of bias if one relies only on their work alone. What one needs is to look at a large number of studies from other labs, in other contexts and domains, carried out independently. After all, science thrives on independent replications and extensions. And the gold standard technique for extracting the pattern of effects across a large number of studies is called a meta-analysis.

So, we carried out a meta-analysis of more than 50 studies (Sinha and Kapur 2021), reporting more than 160 experimental comparisons of students in four different continents (and counting). Our meta-analysis showed that the relative effect of learning from Productive Failure was up to three times (that's 300%) that of learning from a good teacher for one year. Another way to benchmark the relative effect is in terms of schooling years. It seemed as if Productive Failure students were performing up to two academic years ahead of Direct Instruction students. What we have here is not an incremental effect, but a breakthrough that is practically highly significant.

And because more than 80% of the studies in the above meta-analysis were independent replications, that is, I or my students were not involved in them, it lends even more credence to the breakthrough findings.

Let's go one step further. What would be even more credible is if there was an independent analysis in which I was not involved at all. Luckily, there are several but most notably, in 2023, an even more comprehensive review of the literature (de Jong et al. 2023) by 13 eminent scholars from leading universities in the world led by Ton de Jong largely demolished the case for Direct Instruction, and concluded that the most effective method for deep learning is something that combines inquiry and direct instruction. Productive Failure does precisely that.

The Basic Knowledge Fallacy

Another way to interpret these findings is this. We have two groups of students who appear strikingly similar and highly proficient on procedural knowledge – the "how," the basic or foundational knowledge – but appear different on conceptual understanding – the "why" – and transfer to adapt and apply in novel contexts. Oftentimes people argue that the foundation is extremely important, and that everyone should have a strong foundation. So far so good. But then they argue that higher order things like deep understanding and transfer could be developed after we have built a strong foundation. So let us build the basics as efficiently as we can, which is usually through Direct Instruction, and we can worry about the deep understanding and transfer later on. This is a fallacy.

I call it the basic knowledge fallacy. What my results show is how one learns the foundational knowledge influences how well they understand it and can transfer it. The learning path matters. Two different ways of learning the same basics can result in significantly different understandings and transfer. Learning is path dependent. If we do not pay attention to how we are learning the basics, then we might be shooting ourselves in the foot. The damage to developing deep understanding and transfer capabilities might already be done. And a lot more work is needed downstream if we do not fix the upstream problem of learning the basics in a way that builds understanding and transfer, like in Productive Failure.

The Creativity Fallacy

Remember Group 1? They were the group of children who were first shown how to play with a new toy and then asked to play as they liked. Intriguingly, even though they had the correct knowledge of how to play with the toy as well as the freedom to play as they liked, they still weren't as inventive as Group 2 children in their free play. Group 2 was more than three times as inventive as Group 1 if you would recall.

Well, a similar pattern unfolded with Direct Instruction students. They were given the correct knowledge of the concept, and then asked to solve the problem targeting that concept. In my experiments (see Figure 2.5), the same problem that was given to Productive Failure students to start with was given to Direct Instruction students after they had learned the correct knowledge. And with the same instruction to invent as many ways of solving the problem (e.g. see Figure 2.1). So I could compare the creativity with which they invented solutions to the problem. To be clear: we are comparing the creativity with which Productive Failure students solved the problem *before* learning the required concept with that of Direct Instruction students who solved the same problem, but *after* learning the required concept.

Whereas all Direct Instruction students were typically able to solve the problem correctly because they had just learned the concept, none of the Productive Failure students ever produced the correct solution. Understandable of course, as they had not learned the required concept yet. However, the diversity and creativity of ideas, solutions, and representations produced by Productive Failure students was far greater than that of Direct Instruction students, who largely stuck to the correct (taught) ways of solving the problem. When we noticed that they were sticking to the correct solutions mostly, we prompted them again to think outside the box, and invent other ways. In spite of the prompting, they found it hard to go outside the box, so to speak. What was striking to me here is that correct knowledge, when given too early, seemed to constrain the development of inventiveness and creativity. Much like it did for Group 1 students.

We are used to thinking of knowledge as a file on a computer. It does not matter how you get that file; if you have it, you can use it as you like. The reality is that knowledge can be a double-edged sword when it comes to creativity. While knowledge in a domain facilitates action and work in the domain, it can also constrain from thinking outside the domain. Whether you are playing with new toys or learning a new concept, more and more research is suggesting that how you learn the new toy or concept – the learning path, or the teaching method – actually influences how creative and inventive you can be with it. Creativity is path dependent too. In this way, the creativity fallacy is a corollary of the basic knowledge fallacy.

The challenge for us is not to shun knowledge, but to marry it with experiences that harness and develop curiosity and open-mindedness. And one way to do it is to design such experiences when learning new things, to situate and support the learning of the new things in creative and inventive and explorative problem-solving practices. After all, the goal is not just to know more, but to also think differently. And sometimes, thinking differently requires delaying knowing a little. And that is precisely what Productive Failure does in a nutshell.

Instead of starting with Direct Instruction on the targeted concepts, Productive Failure engages students to generate multiple ideas, solutions, and strategies for solving novel problems that target concepts they have *not* learned yet. It is important to understand that these are not just any hard problems. These problems (e.g. Figure 2.1) are carefully designed in a principled way (more on this in Part III of the book) to admit multiple solutions, activate students' formal as well as intuitive knowledge and ways of thinking, induce failure in problem solving to make students aware of the limits of their own knowledge, and increase the motivation for and situational interest in learning the correct solutions. In a curated and safe way,

Productive Failure engages students in the creative and design processes of divergent exploration and invention, reinvention, and refinement, while persisting through struggles and failure in problem solving. And it is precisely this failure that prepares them for learning from subsequent consolidation and knowledge assembly orchestrated by the teacher or an expert source.

In a nutshell: Fail First, Learn Later.

Key Takeaways

1. **Direct Instruction trumps pure discovery learning.** But that does not make Direct Instruction the most optimal model for learning.

2. **Productive Failure designs for and bootstraps failure for learning.** Even though students fail at solving problems targeting concepts they have not learned yet, the failure is designed to prepare them to learn from subsequent instruction.

3. **Productive Failure trumps Direct Instruction.** Robust evidence shows Productive Failure produces significantly better understanding and transfer outcomes than Direct Instruction.

4. **Making learning easy does not necessarily ease learning.** There is a time for failing and a time for telling.

PART II

The Science of Failure

A 15-year-old high school student passionate about basketball tried to get selected onto the high school team. When the results came out, his name was not on the list. He was told he was not tall enough. Devastated and feeling like a complete failure, he was almost ready to give up. His mother convinced him otherwise. From then on, he used his disappointment and failure as motivation. Far from letting failure demoralize or destroy him, he harnessed it to spur him to train harder. As he said, "Whenever I was working out and got tired and figured I ought to stop, I'd close my eyes and see that list in the locker room without my name on it, and that usually got me going again." The rest is history: Michael Jordan went on to become one of the greatest basketball players of all time.

Even as a professional basketball player playing at the top of his game, Jordan was no stranger to failure, honestly admitting, "I've missed more than 9,000 shots in my career. I've lost almost 300 games. Twenty-six times, I've been trusted to take the game-winning shot and missed. I've failed over and over and over again in my life. And that is why I succeed."

Jordan is just one example of many who have experienced the trials and tribulations of failure in their lives and come out successful. Such stories are not only inspiring but also demonstrate that it was failure that led to learning, and learning that led to growth and success. In doing so, they reveal the underlying mechanisms of Productive Failure, which will form the focus of Chapters 3–6. It is easy to see that failure *activated* something in them, and helped them see what is critical and essential, stripping away all else. Failure made them *aware* of who they were and what they really wanted. Helped them focus. Failure created the *affect*, the motivation to push harder toward that focus. And with the right help at the right time, whether from friends, family, coaches, or mentors, they managed to put it all together, *assemble* it, and made their failure productive. Activation, Awareness, Affect, and Assembly – the 4As at the heart of Productive Failure.

In the problem-solving phase of Productive Failure, students generate multiple solutions to the problem, but as expected, they fail to solve the problem correctly. This, however, results in a strong activation of the cognitive system because it activates relevant prior knowledge needed for learning. Failure is crucial here, as it also builds awareness of a gap between what we know and what we need to know. This awareness in turn drives affect – needs, interest, curiosity, motivation, and emotions – to learn from subsequent instruction.

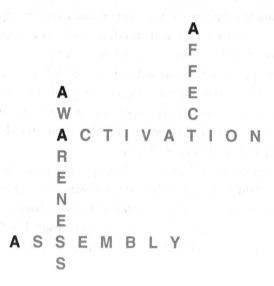

Figure P.1   The 4As mechanisms driving Productive Failure.

With activation, awareness, and affect all set up and aligned in the problem-solving phase, we are now ready for the instruction phase of Productive Failure, for this is when an expert or a teacher can help assemble our knowledge into the correct concepts and ideas. What seemed to be failure in the problem-solving phase can thus be bootstrapped for deep learning, making it not just any kind of failure, but Productive Failure.

In Part II, I will describe the science behind the 4As mechanisms and explain the string of experiments that discovered how and why these mechanisms form the scientific basis of Productive Failure. That said, the mechanisms are fundamental in nature; that is, they apply in all learning situations. Whether you are learning by yourself, working in teams, or designing learning for others, different ways of learning invoke these mechanisms in different ways and to different degrees. The point being that not all ways of learning are equal; certain ways, like Productive Failure, are particularly good at optimizing the synergistic effect of the 4As. And that's what makes Productive Failure powerful.

3 | Activation

What if there was a simple trick or a hack to help us all remember things better? Indeed there is, but to illustrate and appreciate it better, here is a memory challenge comprising nine statements. Each statement is about someone doing something. Your challenge is to commit all of them to memory in about 20 seconds. Ready? Go.

1. Shourav wrote a play
2. Jean made a discovery
3. Lara ate an apple
4. Carol pressed the light switch
5. Ken set for sail
6. Vivek made a movie
7. Petra sang a song
8. Clarence played football
9. Karen performed a dance

Now, without looking at the list, try to recall who did what. Write down your answers, and then compare how many you could successfully recall.

1. Who wrote a play?
2. Who made a discovery?
3. Who ate an apple?
4. Who pressed the light switch?
5. Who set for sail?

6. Who made a movie?
7. Who sang a song?
8. Who played football?
9. Who performed a dance?

For most people, this is a tough task. There are 81 combinations if you cross "who" with "what" they did. When I have done this quick-and-dirty experiment with people, on average, they can recall about five such combinations correctly. Because the order in which I ask the questions is the same as the original order of the sentences, people recall the first few and the last few sentences better than the ones in the middle. However, if they are particularly into some of the domains, for example, movies or sports, they might recall them better. Still overall, average performance is typically around five items.

What if I told you that on another list of nine such items, similar to the original one, I could make you remember all of them effortlessly? Not only that; this time I would make the challenge much harder by jumbling up the order in which I asked the recall questions.

So, here are nine more statements similar to the original list. As before, your challenge is to commit all of them to memory in about 20 seconds. Ready? Go.

1. Shakespeare wrote a play
2. Einstein made a discovery
3. Adam ate an apple
4. Edison pressed the light switch
5. Columbus set for sail
6. Spielberg made a movie
7. Madonna sang a song
8. Messi played football
9. Michael Jackson performed a dance

Now, without looking at the list, try to recall who did what by responding to the questions below. Write down your answers, and then compare how many you could successfully recall.

1. Who set for sail?
2. Who sang a song?

3. Who played football?
4. Who wrote a play?
5. Who ate an apple?
6. Who performed a dance?
7. Who pressed the light switch?
8. Who made a movie?
9. Who made a discovery?

Note that the order in which I ask the questions is not the same as the original list. It is much harder now because I have jumbled it up. But even so, you are probably able to remember all of the sentences, and quite easily too. As an external stimulus, it has similar demands on your memory as the first one. Yet, now most people can recall all the items perfectly.

What changed? Clearly, the names of the people doing the various things. I changed the names based on certain assumptions I made about where in the world you are reading this book. If you are in the West or western-educated contexts, the second challenge would have been easy because of the prior knowledge you are likely to have about the various well-known people and their domains of expertise, from Michael Jackson to Albert Einstein. These priors are also likely to have high storage strength and high retrieval strength, making it effortless for you to remember them. But if you do not have these priors, then the second challenge would be equally difficult as the first one if I had kept the order of the questions the same, and even more difficult because of the jumbled-up order of the questions. Of course, given all of this is in the English language, the base assumption is that you have a good grasp of the language itself.

What is instructive is that simply by changing the task at hand, by designing it in a way that activates your prior knowledge, the task becomes easier. And it does not matter if it is a simple memory task or a complex interpretation of a poem, if it is learning abstract mathematics or analyzing historical text, if it is learning a new language or to write an essay; activating relevant prior knowledge is key to processing new information and learning.

That begs the questions: What are the ways in which one can activate prior knowledge? Are some ways better than others, and why? We are ready for the multiple ways that can be placed on an *activation spectrum*.

The Activation Spectrum

Suppose you are learning a new language by yourself, say French, and you encounter the word "bibliothèque."Your mind starts scouring its vast storage of information, seeking connections. If you have knowledge of other languages, it might latch onto similar words like the German "Bibliothek" or the Spanish "biblioteca." But what happens if you're completely new to these languages? In that case, you may have to cast an even wider net, perhaps to English (which I presume you know if you are reading this book), and connect with the English word "bibliography," a list usually found at the end of books, thereby helping you infer that "bibliothèque" might have something to do with books, leading you to understand that it means "library."

This is the basic mechanism by which the mind processes new information. It always tries to find and connect to relevant prior knowledge that we have. Recall that prior knowledge holds the key to both seeing and connecting, and that is the way to deep understanding. If we are unable to find any relevant prior knowledge to connect to, processing and understanding new information becomes extremely hard. For example, learning Mandarin when you only know English would be hard because there is little to connect to. Still doable, and people do learn, but this is the kind of learning that would be hard for a non-native Mandarin speaker. On the other hand, if we can find a lot of relevant prior knowledge, we would find it relatively easier to process new information and learn. The more relevant knowledge we can activate, the easier the processing, the better the learning.

This is why, in formal education settings, a teacher may use a range of strategies to activate learners' prior knowledge when teaching them something new. On one end is a teacher, like I used to be, who might believe in giving a clear, engaging, and structured lecture on the new concept. The lecture may include examples designed to activate students' prior knowledge, with explanations to help them process new knowledge, the absolute minimum a teacher ought to do.

Another teacher, say in teaching reading, might start the lesson by asking students to share their personal experiences related to the book's topic. If the students are about to read a story about a trip to the beach, the teacher might encourage them to recall and share their own beach experiences. This strategy not only makes the upcoming text relatable but also activates their prior knowledge about the beach, setting the stage for a deeper understanding of the text.

Or in a literature class, a teacher might use the metaphor of a journey to explain the narrative arc of a story. They might describe the protagonist's conflicts as mountains to climb and their periods of growth as smooth stretches of road. This metaphor not only activates the students' experiences and understandings of journeys but also illuminates the dynamic nature of narratives.

Like metaphors, analogies can also be powerful activation devices. For example, a physics teacher introducing the concept of electricity might use the analogy of water flowing through a pipe. They could compare voltage to water pressure, current to the flow rate, and resistance to pipe size. This may help students understand electrical circuits by linking the concept to their experiences with water systems, making the abstract notion of electrical flow tangible.

Employing real experiences, analogies, or metaphors works by linking the new concept to something familiar to students. Of course, analogies and metaphors can backfire too if they are applied literally, but they can be used judiciously to bridge the gap between the known and the unknown, enabling students to transfer their prior knowledge to the new context.

Some teachers may go one step further. Instead of merely presenting information or using relatable experiences, analogies, and metaphors, they get students to engage in problem solving. For example, consider a math teacher introducing fractions to elementary school children. Instead of going straight into direct instruction, the teacher presents a problem: "If you and three friends share two pizzas equally, how much does each person get?"

To solve this problem, students tap into their prior knowledge of equal distribution, an experience common from sharing food or toys. They intuitively understand that each person gets half a pizza, thus leading them to the concept of fractions. Following this, the teacher formalizes the understanding by introducing the notation "1/2" representing "half." The teacher could extend this with further pizza-related problems involving adding or subtracting fractions. Through such a problem-solving approach, the teacher activates the students' prior knowledge, linking everyday experiences to formal academic concepts, fostering meaningful and lasting understanding. This method not only makes learning more engaging but also showcases the practical relevance of new knowledge.

In all the examples above, prior knowledge is activated in diverse ways to help process new information. Whether you are learning a language yourself, listening to a lecture, learning by analogies and metaphors, or problem solving, in all cases, relevant prior knowledge is activated. But what is different is the degree of activation.

In 2009, Michelene Chi, winner of the 2019 Rumelhart Prize, which is widely regarded as the Nobel Prize in Cognitive Science, proposed a framework for placing the different degrees of activation on a spectrum. She called it the Interactive, Constructive, Active, Passive (ICAP) framework, arguing that interactive activities will lead to better activation than constructive activities, which in turn would be better than active, and finally passive will be the lowest on the spectrum. Therefore, the higher one is on the spectrum, the better the learning outcomes.

Figure 3.1 shows a simple way to imagine the *activation spectrum*: On the lower end, simpler activities like listening to lectures or watching instructional videos elicit narrower activations, and lower cognitive effort on the part of the learner. On the higher end, complex tasks like problem solving, when designed well, typically engender a broader activation of relevant prior knowledge, but they also require more effort and engagement on the part of the learner. Because the more relevant knowledge we can activate, the easier the processing, the better the learning, we can expect

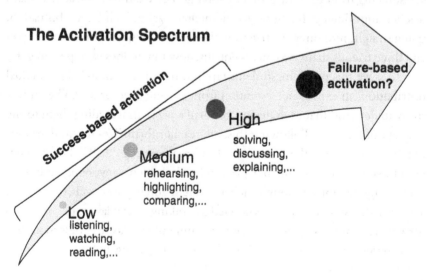

Figure 3.1   The activation spectrum.

methods on the higher end of the activation spectrum help us learn better than those at the lower end.

Note, however, that all the methods thus far largely focus on activation that does not deviate too much, if at all, from the narrow path that leads a novice to learn the correct concepts and ideas. The degree of activation differs, they are different points on the activation spectrum, and hence the efficacy for processing and learning varies, but all the methods focus on activation of correct ideas and concepts. We can call these activation methods success-based activation methods. In these methods, failure is neither designed for nor desirable.

What if we could extend the activation spectrum? Indeed, one way to think about my research on Productive Failure is that my goal was to extend the activation spectrum, to design even more powerful ways of activating relevant prior knowledge, and in doing so, achieve transformative effects on learning. A direct consequence of the epiphany I had, that engaging learning in problem solving that leads to failure prepares them to learn from subsequent instruction, was to explore whether such failure resulted in better activation of relevant prior knowledge. Productive Failure thus created a paradigm shift by moving from success-based activation methods to explore failure-based activation.

Failure-based Activation

Why does failure-based activation work? It all comes down to the benefits of generating knowledge prior to learning the target concept.

The Generation Effect

Imagine that you are participating in a psychological study. Your first task, labeled the Generation task, involves a bit of mental effort. You are presented with a word, for example, *rapid*, and it's your job to generate a second word. Let's say it has to be a synonym, starting with the letter *f*, the correct answer being *fast*. Together, they form the complete word pair. You're actively engaged as you are presented with several such word-pair generation tasks, thinking about relationships between words to generate the pair.

Now, let's shift to the second task, the Read task. Here, you are simply given pairs of related words such as *bread-butter* or *cat-mouse*. There's no requirement for you to puzzle out any connections this time. You just read several such word pairs, committing them to your memory as best you can.

You might think, okay, that was interesting, but what's the point? Here comes the twist. After a while, and without any forewarning, you are tested on your recall of the second word in each pair; that is, given the first word, recall the pair.

Would you recall the Generate or Read pairs better?

A series of such studies were conducted by Norman Slamecka and Peter Graf in 1978. Their experiments showed that participants in the Generate group remembered significantly more words than those in the Read group, hence the term "generation effect." Generating the words requires more cognitive effort and a deeper processing of the information, and a deeper, more semantic processing of information leads to better retention. Several experiments and independent replications followed.

Almost 30 years later in 2007, Sharon Bertsch and colleagues published a meta-analysis, examining the pattern of effects in 86 studies since the 1978 seminal paper, and reaffirmed the robustness of the generation effect across a variety of tasks and experimental conditions. In other words, the generation effect is not a random effect found in one obscure study, but an independently replicated and robust effect across a number of studies.

And if you recall, that is the same philosophy of failure-based activation: students are asked to generate multiple representations and solutions to challenging problems before learning the required concept. The act of generation itself therefore is one of the reasons why failure-based activation works. But it cannot be the only reason.

Why? Perhaps not immediately obvious, but it is easy to argue that generation effect works as long as you generate the correct response. As noted earlier, the generation task was supported in two ways to increase the likelihood of correct pairs being generated. First, participants were told the relationship between the pairs, for example, that they are synonyms (*rapid-fast*), or antonyms (*long-short*), or associative (*bread-butter*), and so on. So, given the first word *rapid*, you could easily think of synonyms *fast* or *quick* as the second word. Additionally, they were given the first letter of the second word as well. Therefore, if the first letter of the second word was *f*, then you are more likely to generate *fast*, or if it was *q*, then *quick*. This was a clever way of keeping errorful generation to a minimum, reportedly only 6% in the seminal study.

However, that makes one wonder if generation alone is sufficient or must it be generation of correct responses. Maybe it should have been called the "Correct Generation Effect," for it raises the possibility that maybe generation that involves generating incorrect or failed response(s) may not be good for learning. We need to test the effects of generating incorrect or failed responses as well. We turn to this next.

The Failed Generation Effect

Ever had that awkward moment at a party or conference, when someone tells you their name, and in an instant, it's gone? *Poof!* Vanished, like a ninja in the night. It is a weirdly universal experience, as if our minds have a secret trapdoor where names fall into the abyss as soon as we hear them, trying to recall if the person who we were just introduced to was a Sarah, a Sam, or a. . . um, what was it again? It's like trying to catch fish with your bare hands; you think you've got a good grip, and the next moment, it's gone. And the worst part? It happens to everyone. We all forget names. We may not remember a person's name, but we all remember what it's like to not remember.

So here's the big question: Can we do anything about this name amnesia? Maybe it's about paying more attention, or repeating the name a few times in conversation, or many other memory techniques advocated by a number of gurus. Perhaps there is a simple one.

Imagine a party with new rules, where introductions are turned on their heads. The name of the game is no longer introducing yourself but guessing the name of the other. You can introduce yourself to someone only after they have tried to guess your name. So, if I am at such a party, the following might ensue:

Me: Hi, are you Julia?
Stranger: No, I'm Samantha.
Me: Ah, hello Samantha.
Samantha: And are you Mark?
Me: No, I'm Manu.
Samantha: Ah, hello Manu.

I have never been to such a party or organized anything quite like this, but it would be fun to try. Because the idea behind it is that when people are given a chance to guess and fail, they are more likely to remember the correct name when they are subsequently told so than if they were told immediately. I would predict, in such a party, people would be more likely to remember names of people they met than in a regular party.

The basis of my prediction is what, in the literature, is called the unsuccessful retrieval effect, or simply the failed generation effect: attempting to answer questions about some topic before learning improves learning even if the initial answers were incorrect. Simply designing opportunities for people to guess and fail helps them learn the correct information later, an idea demonstrated beautifully by Nate Kornell and colleagues in 2009.

Imagine the same word pair study by Slamecka and Graf, but with a twist. Instead of designing word pairs to make it easy for participants to generate the correct answer, Kornell and colleagues designed to make it hard for participants, so much so that most people would generate the incorrect answer. Whereas Slamecka and Graf used strongly associated word pairs (e.g. *rapid-fast, long-short*) governed by a rule (e.g. synonyms, antonyms) and supported with the starting letters (rapid-*f__*, long-*s__*), Kornell and colleagues use weakly associated word pairs (such as *mouse-hole, whale-mammal*) without giving any rule or starting letters. This clever trick ensured that most people would fail to generate the second word most of the time.

And the trick worked. In their experiments, they used a total of 60 word pairs, and people could generate the correct answer on only 1 or 2 of those pairs, or an average 1.5 times out of 60. Said another way, on average, participants got 58–59 answers out of 60 wrong. That is a high failure rate indeed. Perhaps one might have a better success rate at guessing the names of 60 strangers at a party, but for an experimental demonstration, having such a high failure rate was perfect.

As shown in Figure 3.2, they randomly assigned participants to one of two conditions: the Read condition or the Test condition. In the Read condition, participants were shown a word pair (e.g. *mouse-hole*) and given 13 seconds to study it. In the Test condition, participants were shown the first word of the pair for eight seconds (e.g. *mouse - ____*), during which they were asked to generate the second word. If they could generate the second word in the eight seconds, great. If they could not, it was captured as a blank. Then, the correct answer was shown for five seconds. So, everyone got 13 seconds for each of the 60 word pairs. Participants in the Read

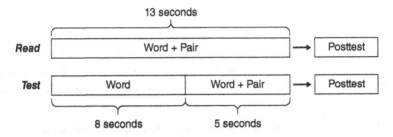

Figure 3.2 Adapted from Kornell et al. 2009 experimental design.

condition studied it for 13 seconds, and those in the Test condition tried to generate an answer in the first eight seconds and only then were shown the correct answer for five seconds.

After the 60 trials were completed, participants were given a distractor task, unrelated to the word pairs. They were asked to list the names of as many countries as possible in five minutes. Distractor tasks are often used in psychological experiments, with the goal of keeping the participant's mind busy so that they do not rehearse or think about the material that was just presented to them. To capture the experimental effect, one needs to ensure that people do not have the opportunity to think about or rehearse what they have just learned, for if they did, one would not be able to tell apart the effect of the experimental manipulation from that of the rehearsal. A quick distractor task is therefore often deployed between the learning and testing phase.

Finally, in the testing phase, participants took a cued-recall test of all the 60 items. The first word of each pair formed the cue, and participants had to recall the second word. As you might have guessed, participants in the Test condition performed significantly better than the Read condition on the cued-recall test. Failed generation followed by immediate feedback was much better than studying the same material for the same amount of time.

But if failure was indeed driving the learning, a final nail in the coffin would be to check if people did better on the items on which they had failed than those they left blank. Being unable to generate is not the same as generating an incorrect answer. It turned out that about three quarters of the time, people generated incorrectly. One quarter of the time, they left it blank. And indeed the final nail in the coffin was that people recalled incorrectly answered items better than the ones they left blank.

It was not simply generation but failed generation that resulted in better recall and learning. Like in that party, I would remember Samantha as Samantha better if I first guessed her name incorrectly as Sarah (or any other name really), and then be immediately corrected. So, if you were in doubt about organizing the party with the new rules, these findings should be encouraging.

The failed generation effect has since been replicated in other learning contexts as well. For example, in 2014, Rosalind Potts and David Shanks from University College London wanted students to learn the definition of 60 unfamiliar English words such as *valinch, frampold*, and so on (see Figure 3.3). The definitions were essentially in the form of synonyms of the unfamiliar words. They designed three types of learning trials – Study, Choice, Generate – each with 20 words.

1. In the Study trial, students were given 17 seconds to read the word and its correct synonym, similar to how one might consult a dictionary. The word and its synonym were presented together for students to read and remember.

2. In the Choice trial, students were given 10 seconds to read the word and select the synonym from two choices (one correct, another a lure). True enough, given the unfamiliarity with the words, their performance on selecting the correct definitions was at chance levels, that is, about 50%. After that, they were then shown the correct synonym for seven seconds, so that the total time remained the same as in the Study trial.

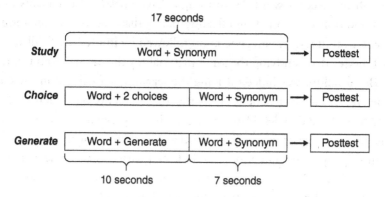

Figure 3.3 Adapted from Potts and Shanks 2014 experimental design.

3. In the Generate trial, students were given 10 seconds to read the word and generate a synonym by themselves. So, what do you think the words *valinch* and *frampold* mean? If you do not know, just make a guess and jot it down. At first, I too did not know either of the words. The same for the students. Because the words were highly unfamiliar, students made a lot of errors in generating the definition, with a spectacular failure rate of about 94%. After that, they were shown the correct synonym for seven seconds, so that the total time remained the same as in the Study and Choice trials.

After the learning phase, all students were tested on all the 60 words to see if and to what extent they could remember the definitions. Students remembered the definitions of the words in the Generate trials significantly more than the words in the Read or Choice trials, and there was no difference between the Read and Choice trials. Even though generating almost always produced the wrong definition, and this failure was deliberately designed for by choosing highly unfamiliar words, it still produced much better learning than reading the correct definition or choosing between two definitions.

It turns out *valinch* means tube, and *frampold* means quarrelsome. If you had genuinely guessed and failed, your retrieval and storage strengths should have been boosted, and chances are you will now remember the meanings.

Beyond vocabulary learning, the failed generation effect has been demonstrated in learning from texts and videos as well. In 2009, Richland and colleagues asked students to read an essay about human color blindness caused by brain damage. By design, they chose a topic that students would be unfamiliar with, and checked with the students that this was indeed the case. Therefore, students were in a situation where they were learning something new.

Figure 3.4 shows the experimental design. In one condition, students were given 10 minutes to read the essay, reflecting a commonplace situation where one might read an article or webpage or passage in a textbook to learn something new. In the other condition, for the first two minutes, they pretested students on the concepts in the essay before they read the essay. In the remaining eight minutes, students read the essay, making sure that the

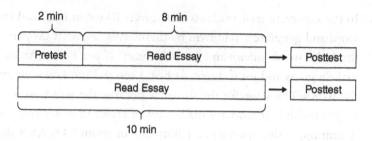

Figure 3.4   Adapted from Richland et al. 2009 experimental design.

total time (10 minutes) was the same for both groups of students. In the end, all students answered a posttest on the concepts covered in the essay.

Students who were pretested largely failed on the pretest, answering about 95% of the questions incorrectly. This was expected given that the pretest, by design, occurred before reading the essay. Yet, these very students performed significantly better than those who only read the essay. Remarkably, failed generation prior to reading an essay was more effective for learning than an extended time to read.

Given how much of our learning happens from reading text, be it on paper or on the computer or our mobile devices, these findings are highly relevant to our own learning. That said, we do not just rely on text-based sources, but also videos and online lectures. Wouldn't it be nice if these effects also extended to learning from instructional videos?

That is precisely what Toftness and colleagues demonstrated in 2018. Using a similar design as the essay study earlier, they pretested one group of students before watching a 20-minute educational video on an unfamiliar scientific topic (signal detection theory). The other group was not pretested but watched the same video. In the end, all students answered a posttest on the concepts covered in the video.

As expected, the pretested students failed on the pretest, answering only about 30% of the questions correctly. Yet on the posttest, they outperformed those who were not pretested, demonstrating that answering questions incorrectly when one does not know the targeted knowledge helps us learn from subsequent instruction on that knowledge. Toftness and colleagues then replicated the findings for another unfamiliar scientific topic (autobiographical memory), further bolstering evidence for the failed generation effect (Pan and Sana 2021).

In short, the failed generation effect shows that attempting to answer questions about an unfamiliar topic before learning improves learning of that topic even if the initial answers were incorrect, and the effect holds whether you are learning words, reading texts, or learning from videos.

All of this begs the question: Why does failed generation work?

Why Does Failed Generation Work?

There are broadly three main and mutually reinforcing mechanisms – Processing, Preparation, and Priming – that are responsible for the effect. Although we now turn to them sequentially, note that the three work as a system.

Processing

I have always had a special place for art, but I am admittedly challenged both in knowledge and capability. Still, with its kaleidoscope of colors, brush-strokes, and untold stories, for me it holds a mystical allure that captivates our senses and speaks to the depths of our souls. Behind every stroke of the brush lies the heart and mind of an artist, weaving their unique tales on canvases that transcend time and space. Luckily, we have museums that bring these tales to life.

Picture yourself standing at the entrance of two excellent museums, each offering a different curation approach to showcasing their treasures. In Museum A, the curatorial concept is "Clustered Artists." It could just as well have been themes or chronology, but let's say it is organized by artists. That is, you encounter a series of rooms, each dedicated to the paintings of a renowned artist, like Monet, Renoir, Degas, and so on. Each room being a microcosm of an artist's brilliance, inviting you to immerse yourself in the unique styles and genres of that artist's creations.

In Museum B, a different adventure unfolds. Here, the concept of "Mixed Artists" reigns. You encounter the same paintings by the same artists in the same number of rooms, except each room carries paintings from multiple artists. So, instead of a Monet room, Renoir room, and Degas room, imagine witnessing a juxtaposition of artistic creations in each room. The collision of styles and genres sparks a kaleidoscope of inspiration, as you explore the interplay between contrasting visions and discover unexpected connections.

Now, given a choice, which museum would you choose? And if you were in there to actually learn about artists and their art, which curatorial concept would lead to better learning of an artist's style and genre? In Museum A, the clustered artists offer a focused exploration, making it easier for you to engage with the paintings of one artist at a time. On the other hand, contrasting styles and paintings in Museum B allows you to constantly compare and contrast, switching from one artist to another, making it harder to detect patterns and styles and voices.

On average, most people prefer Museum A, which is organized by a pre-selected category. Above I chose artists as the organizing principle or category, but it could just as well have been themes or chronology. People not only prefer this, and museums typically curate according to these preferences, but people also think that it is Museum A that will lead to a better learning of each artist's style and genre. If there was a test at the end of each museum, where you were shown unknown paintings by the various artists, you would be able to attribute them to their creators.

However, as shown by Kornell and Bjork's 2008 lab study version of the above thought experiment, it is Museum B that is more likely to lead to better learning, because making the learning experience a little harder pushes your brain to put in more effort to process the information. Provided you do not give up, initially you may find it difficult to make connections, detect patterns, even have several unsuccessful retrievals or miscategorizations, but this deeper processing leads to better learning in the long run.

In other words, deliberately making the initial learning phase difficult can be beneficial for retention and transfer, a phenomenon coined as *Desirable Difficulties* by psychologist Robert Bjork in 1994. He is the same guy who co-developed the New Theory of Disuse, using the constructs of storage and retrieval strengths.

Generation involves retrieval from long-term memory, and the act of retrieval increases the storage and retrieval strength, and helps you remember better. Recall, however, that the greatest boost to our memory comes when retrieval strength is low, and failed generation basically means that retrieval strength is zero or close to. That is as low as it can get. But that is precisely where we stand to derive the strongest boosts in both storage and retrieval strengths.

Desirable Difficulties refers to the idea that introducing certain well-designed challenges or difficulties during the learning process can actually enhance long-term retention and transfer of knowledge. Difficulties here refers to items with low retrieval strength, which make them difficult to remember if at all. Although these difficulties may slow down the initial learning phase, they may ultimately lead to better retention and understanding in the long run. And that is what makes them Desirable. This is why techniques like pretesting yourself can be more effective than simply reading material. This is why the party with the new introduction rules is likely to be more effective in remembering names.

Desirable Difficulties can be applied to various educational settings and learning domains, and research has shown that these techniques can lead to improved learning outcomes.

Language Learning

For example, in 2013, Sean Kang and colleagues demonstrated the effectiveness of Desirable Difficulty in second language vocabulary learning. They randomly assigned fluent speakers of English to learn words in Hebrew by either imitation or retrieval. In the imitation condition, participants first heard a Hebrew word with the corresponding picture of the object that it referred to, and then were asked to repeat the Hebrew word aloud. In the retrieval practice condition, participants were shown the picture of the object, and were asked to produce the Hebrew word aloud, followed by hearing the Hebrew word.

After 40 such words, they were tested on comprehension (given the Hebrew word, select the picture that the word referred to) and production (given the picture, produce the Hebrew word). These tests were given immediately after the learning phase in the first experiment, and with a two-day delay in the second experiment. In both experiments, the performance of retrieval practice students suffered during the learning phase, yet they outperformed imitation students on both comprehension and production. In fact, the effects were stronger on production, which is the harder of the two to learn.

Motor Skill Learning

Similar patterns of effects extend to motor skill learning as well. Imagine a simple motor skill such as throwing bean bags into a target placed at a distance, much like throwing a basketball into the net. In a classic experiment in 1978, Kerr and Booth had elementary school children learn this motor skill: throwing bean bags into a target. Some students were asked to practice throwing from four feet away, and others from either three feet or five feet but never from four feet. After several weeks, they were all tested from four feet away.

If you were in the first group, you got to practice throwing from four feet away, and weeks later, tested from four feet away, precisely the distance at which you practiced. This is called blocked or massed practice. You practice the same thing again and again in a block. If you were in the second group, you got to practice throwing from either three or five feet and never from four, but were tested from four feet away. This is called varied practice, where you are constantly switching from one distance to another.

Which group – blocked practice or varied practice – would perform better? If practice makes perfect, then we would expect blocked practice students to perform better. After all, they practiced at four feet and were tested exactly at the same distance. If, however, there was some benefit to the increased difficulty that varied practice students faced, then we might expect them to perform better. The increased difficulty came from having to switch, which meant they were switching what they were retrieving. After all, even though they did not practice at four feet, they spent more time coordinating across multiple variables and strategies (controlling strength, angle, direction, etc.), and perhaps learned how to modulate and encode these variations better, which in turn made them more flexible and adaptive.

And that is precisely what the findings also revealed. Varied practice students outperformed blocked practice students, a finding which is both counterintuitive and hard to believe. Practicing a motor skill under varying conditions, even though it is harder, can lead to better performance when the skill needs to be adapted to new situations. Since then, these findings have been replicated in several experiments, in different ways, for different tasks, making it fairly robust evidence for Desirable Difficulty while learning simple motor skills.

By now, we have seen how Desirable Difficulties trick the brain into deeper processing in a number of areas, from memory tasks to vocabulary learning, to learning about art and artists, to motor skills. The list goes on. I have deliberately chosen a diverse set of domains just to illustrate the point. I end with yet another domain: Music.

Music Learning

Why music? Because music is another area where my ambition far exceeded my talent. I love listening to music but I'm hopelessly challenged at it. Still, if I were to learn how to make music, say play a piano, how might I use Desirable Difficulties for deeper processing?

Imagine you are learning to play a short melody on the piano, but like me, you've never played piano before. You get three chances to practice a nine-note sequence, but the time between each practice session is different. You can choose to have only five minutes between each practice session; or six hours between your practice sessions; or a full day between the sessions.

Massing our practice with five-minute breaks seems the most intuitive. Leaving six hours or a whole day seems like a bad decision, for you may not even remember the nine-note sequence, making the second and third practice sessions that much harder. Yet, a 2012 study by Amy Simmons demonstrated that if you waited a full day between practice sessions, your accuracy improved a lot more by the second session than if you only waited five minutes or six hours. But by the third session, the groups who waited six hours or a full day showed even more speed improvements, while the five-minute group didn't improve as much. This did not mean the five-minute or six-hour spacing was bad, for everyone was able to play faster with practice, no matter how long they waited. Just that one derived a much better boost if you made it harder by spacing out the practice sessions.

This suggests that while we might feel like practicing over and over without long breaks will make us better faster, what really helps us improve is spacing out our practice sessions. When we wait between sessions, we allow for some forgetting to take place, and our brains have to work a little harder to recall and reinforce the learned skill. This "struggle" actually aids in embedding the learning deeper, leading to better accuracy and speed. More precisely, retrieval becomes harder because the passage of time allows for some forgetting; disuse is good for reducing retrieval strength. So, rather than cramming in a learning session, we should embrace the Desirable Difficulty of spaced practice for better mastery.

Failed generation results in deeper processing, but it is not just deeper processing that matters; the nature of that processing also matters. What we do during deeper processing prepares us for learning.

Preparation

Let's imagine you are a high school student assigned a physics project. The task is straightforward: figure out how and why something floats or sinks. You're simply given two different materials – two wooden balls of different sizes and two clay balls also in the same two sizes as the wooden balls, and two liquids – water and honey – in a jar. Your job is to design as many experiments as needed to figure out how and why something floats or sinks.

You have not formally been taught the physics of floating, or buoyancy to be specific. Therefore, for a start, you might rely on your daily experiences of what you already know about floating and sinking. You may have observed that heavy rocks sink in water, while lighter objects, like twigs or leaves, tend to float. But you also remember seeing a huge ship, much heavier than a small rock, floating effortlessly. You realize that the question of floating or sinking is a bit more complex, and interesting.

Maybe you decide to drop the smaller wooden and clay balls in the water jar. Both are of the same size, but you see that the clay ball sinks while the wooden one floats. From this, you may infer that there must be something about "what" the object is made of that matters. Maybe it's the size, so you repeat the same setup but with the bigger balls. Again, the same result, suggesting that in this context, the size of the object does not affect whether it floats or sinks as long as the material remains the same. But this seems to be at odds with your initial conception that bigger means heavier, hence sinkable.

Then, you may repeat the process up till now with the honey jar. This time, both the clay and the wood float, for both the sizes. This suggests that there must be something about the liquid that also matters. Intuitively, honey is thicker than water as one might say, and you conjecture that it may have something to do with that.

Throughout these experiments, you're not just following a set procedure; instead, you're actively manipulating variables, observing results, and generating and testing intuitions and understandings based on those observations. You may not even design clean experiments where only one thing is manipulated at a time. You may well be able to use your experiments to conclude that there is something about the material and also about the fluid that determines whether things float or sink, yet most likely you will not be able to formalize your ideas into the correct explanation; that is, relative density is what determines whether an object floats or sinks.

What is the point of engaging in such an exercise? This is the same question the proponents of Direct Instruction always ask. After all, much like the basketball problem in Chapter 2 (Figure 2.1), you generated different ideas and experiments and explanations, but you were not able to get to the formally correct answer by yourself.

It turns out that such generation, when designed well, serves a key preparatory function, in that it prepares you to learn from instruction. Much like a gardener wishing to plant a variety of seeds in their garden, before they can plant anything, they'd like to prepare the soil. If they just scatter seeds on unprepared ground, something will surely grow but it may not be the most optimal. The soil may be too hard for the seeds to penetrate, too acidic or alkaline for certain plants, or lacking in the nutrients that seeds need to germinate and grow. To avoid this, the gardener spends time tilling the soil, testing its pH, and adding necessary nutrients or compost to create an environment conducive to growth.

The same preparatory process applies to learning. Before learners can successfully grasp and apply new knowledge or skills, their minds – like the garden soil – must be adequately prepared. Preparation could come in many forms: activating relevant prior knowledge, helping learners develop appropriate learning strategies, or engaging them in tasks designed to help them notice key features or concepts.

For example, in our previous scenario, the student designed and performed various experiments on buoyancy. These experiments served as the "tilling" process, helping the student "soften" their existing understanding of buoyancy, "test the pH" by identifying gaps or misconceptions in their knowledge, and "add nutrients" by creating a variety of experiences with floating and sinking objects.

When the teacher later introduces formal instruction about buoyancy and relative density, the student is ready. They have a rich set of experiences and observations to connect with the new information, much like a seed planted in well-prepared soil has all the resources it needs to grow. The teacher's instruction, then, is like the sunlight and water that help the seed sprout and flourish.

This gardening analogy underscores the concept of *preparation for future learning* developed by learning scientists Daniel Schwartz and John Bransford in 1998. It emphasizes that initial preparation, although it may not immediately result in visible learning outcomes (or plant growth), is crucial for successful learning in the long run. By preparing the "soil" of the learner's mind, we can better ensure that future "seeds" of knowledge will take root and grow.

How is such preparation crucial for future learning? It does four things that get us ready to learn: activate relevant prior knowledge, differentiate prior knowledge, encode variability, and build cognitive flexibility.

Activate Priors

First, it activates relevant prior knowledge, both formal knowledge that you may have learned in school, but also your informal and intuitive knowledge from lived experiences. By invoking everyday experiences and existing knowledge of floating and sinking, these experiments make the new information more accessible and meaningful. As we have seen earlier, we need to activate prior knowledge to make sense of new information. The more relevant knowledge we can activate, the more we can connect new information with our priors, the better we are prepared to process the new information, and such failure-based generation is high on the activation spectrum. It gets the soil ready.

Differentiate Priors

Second, by generating multiple solutions – experiments, observations, and inferences – we have a created activation that is also diverse, varied, or as I call it, differentiated. Differentiation simply refers to activation that tries to get to the targeted concept in not one but many different ways. It's like trying to get to a destination but trying multiple paths to get to it, even if the paths do not get you there, or lead to dead ends. Not the correct path that Google suggests, but a set of differentiated navigation paths. Whether you are generating solutions to the basketball problem or experiments to explain floating and sinking, or learning how to use a word in different contexts, or cooking a dish in different ways, the idea behind differentiation is that it creates: a) a set of contrasts between the multiple solutions, b) a network of multiple paths to get to the targeted knowledge, and c) conditions for the development of cognitive flexibility.

Contrasts hold the key to the problem of seeing. By contrasting what is similar and different between several things, we can see features that are critical and those that are not. The wooden ball floats but the clay ball sinks in water, regardless of size. But they both float in honey, regardless of size. It is contrasts that help us notice critical features that matter, in this case something about the object and the fluid. And also notice features that do not matter, in this case the size of the balls. Recall that without being able to see the critical features, we cannot possibly understand anything deeply.

Consider another example. If you are trying to learn the difference between two types of trees – say, a spruce and a fir. Just reading about them or seeing them separately might not help you distinguish one from the other effectively. But when you examine them side by side, noting the differences in needle shape, cone structure, and bark texture, you are more likely to notice and remember the distinct features of each tree. From a perceptual standpoint, our brains are wired to notice differences. And the same is true from a cognitive standpoint as well. Armed with features that matter and do not matter, you are now ready to learn the formal concepts.

Encode Variability

In addition to contrasts, differentiated activation helps us leverage the power of *encoding variability*. The principle behind encoding variability is straightforward: when we encounter and process information in different ways, we create multiple pathways or "traces" in our memory. Each of these traces provides a unique route for information retrieval.

Suppose you run into a new person – let's say, "John." If you only hear the name once, your memory of the name will depend on a singular auditory encoding. Now, if John introduces himself to you and shakes your hand, you have additional sensory information to encode – the sound of his voice, his face, the feel of his handshake, etc. If you later see John perform at a local theater, your memory encoding now includes this performance context. All these experiences provide different angles or contexts from which to recall John's name, increasing the likelihood of successful recall.

Let's look at a more complex example, like studying for an exam. If you only read your notes, you are relying on a single method of encoding – the visual processing of written text. However, if you also discuss the material with classmates, create mind maps, write summaries, or teach the material to someone else, you are encoding the information in multiple ways. Each method engages different cognitive processes and contexts, creating a richer and more interconnected memory trace. Consequently, you increase your chances of recalling the information during the exam because you've set up multiple retrieval paths.

In everyday life, encoding variability happens all the time. Consider learning to cook a new dish. You might read a recipe (visual), watch a video tutorial (audio-visual), physically prepare the dish (kinesthetic), and smell and taste the ingredients (olfactory and gustatory). These varied experiences create a robust memory trace of the cooking process, aiding future recall and performance. Similarly, if you're learning a foreign language, and you only memorize vocabulary lists, your recall might be limited. But, if you also listen to music, watch movies, converse with native speakers, and practice writing in that language, you're diversifying your encoding strategies. This encoding variability not only improves your recall of the language but also helps you understand the language in different contexts and nuances.

In a nutshell, encoding variability is like building a web of interconnected memory traces. Each interaction or encoding of information serves as a node in this web, and the connections between these nodes are the pathways for recall. The more diverse the encodings, the more robust and interconnected the web becomes, thereby enhancing the ability to retrieve the information when needed. The power of encoding variability lies in its ability to create a resilient, multifaceted memory that can be accessed from different angles and contexts, enhancing our learning and memory recall capabilities.

Cognitive Flexibility

It is easy to see how generating multiple solutions and solution paths to solve a problem, even if those solutions and solution paths do not lead us to the correct solutions, creates this web of interconnected memory traces that are not only useful for processing new information but also for retrieving it later. There is also an added benefit of setting the learner on the path of developing *cognitive flexibility*.

In the context of learning from Productive Failure, cognitive flexibility is the ability of a learner to adaptively navigate and experiment with various problem-solving approaches, drawing from a range of prior experiences and knowledge, even when facing initial failure. It is the capacity to pivot in one's thinking, reorganize information, and consider multiple solutions or perspectives before arriving at a deep understanding or solution. In other words, it is the mental agility displayed when someone encounters challenges or mistakes in the learning process but can still shift, adapt, and use different strategies or perspectives to ultimately grasp and master the concept or skill.

Just as a city with many roads has more routes to a specific location, and therefore more flexibility in getting from one point to another, a brain with varied encodings has more ways to access a particular piece of knowledge in flexible ways. This improves the robustness of memory recall because even if one path (cue or association) is forgotten, other cues or associations can still guide you to the desired information. The network is by definition more flexible because it affords multiple ways of connecting, routing, and assembling knowledge.

The network is properly activated, differentiated, and interconnected. It is prepared for learning. Not just prepared, but also primed for learning; for priming, as we shall see, is an added benefit over and above deeper processing and preparation.

Priming

Back in high school, I had an English teacher who had a counterintuitive strategy for tackling reading comprehension questions in exams. For those unfamiliar, reading comprehension sections typically present a passage followed by a set of questions to assess your understanding of the passage. The conventional approach, which I used to follow, was to read the passage first, then answer the questions. My teacher, however, advised us exactly the opposite: read the questions first, then the passage.

She believed this method would direct our focus, making the reading more goal-oriented. Although I was initially skeptical, I decided to give it a try. I skimmed the questions, creating mental markers of what to look for, then delved into the passage. It felt less like wandering in a textual maze and more like having a map to find treasures of answers. The questions provided context, even without attempting to answer them, making the passage more accessible and easier to navigate.

This shift in approach, as simple as it was, changed my interaction with the text, making the daunting exam a more manageable task. It was a practical, straightforward strategy that has stuck with me, and the beauty is that it does not require any generation in the sense we have been discussing in the previous sections whatsoever, and therefore no failure as such. Just thinking about a few questions before navigating through dense material did me wonders.

Two decades later, when I was in doctoral school, I realized that my teacher's approach was supported by science. And that is the power of priming.

Improving Attention

Recall the 2009 study by Richland and colleagues from earlier, where students were asked to learn something new by reading an essay on an unfamiliar topic (human color blindness caused by brain damage). In that study, students either read the essay first, just like my conventional approach, and then took a posttest to test their knowledge of the essay. Or they took a pretest first, read the essay, and then took the posttest. In support of the failed generation effect, recall that the study found that the pretested students performed better on the posttest in spite of failing on the pretest.

In a twist to the pretest group, Richland and colleagues (2009) inserted a third group to their fifth experiment (see Figure 3.5): they gave some students just the questions on the pretest, without asking them to answer them, and then had them read the essay. I call this the prequestions group, because unlike the pretested students who actually attempted the pretest questions and failed to generate the correct answers, students in the prequestions group merely studied the questions without attempting to answer them, much like my teacher's approach to reading comprehension.

If pretested students outperformed the prequestioned students, it would show that just giving the questions is not sufficient. It pays off to actually answer the questions on a new and unfamiliar topic even if you get them wrong. And they found exactly that. The pretested group outperformed the prequestions group on learning from the essay. Failed generation is more effective even than studying the questions before learning something new from an essay, giving support for the deeper processing and preparing mechanisms.

But remember there was the conventional group too, who were neither pretested nor prequestioned, who directly read the essay and then took the posttest, much like my approach to answering reading comprehension questions.

To test my English teacher's strategy, one would have to compare the performance of the prequestions group with the conventional group. If the prequestions group did the same as the conventional group, then

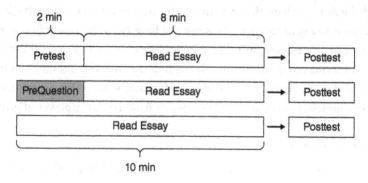

Figure 3.5   Adapted from Richland et al. 2009 experiment five design.

perhaps there was no value to reading the questions before reading an essay. But if the prequestions group outperformed the conventional group, not only would that support my English teacher's strategy from two decades earlier, but it would also show that merely knowing the questions beforehand primes us into how we go about reading the essay and learning from it.

And that is exactly what they found. The prequestions group outperformed the conventional group on the posttest, showing that even without any generation, let alone failed generation, just questions alone can prime us for subsequent learning. Such priming is key, as it shapes our subsequent learning behaviors by at once improving attention and reducing mind wandering, as well as focusing our search for answers to the questions.

Reducing Mind Wandering

Intriguingly, a 2020 study by Steven Pan and colleagues added some empirical weight to the notion that pretesting can increase attention and reduce mind wandering during subsequent learning. Using mind-wandering probes, they uncovered that participants who underwent pretesting reported lower levels of mind wandering and therefore greater attention while learning from subsequent video lectures compared to those who did not pretest. It was as if the pretest questions focused their attention to look out for the answers, and made them wander less. In the absence of a pretest, such focus may not be as strong or well structured, and people tended to wander more.

Better attention and reduced mind wandering are great, but not sufficient. What one does with that during the learning also matters.

Focusing Search

In a related 2020 study that came out around the same time as above, Kyle J. St. Hilaire and colleagues found that the pretesting effect worked only if the people could actually remember the pretest questions. In a series of experiments, students were either given a pretest or not before watching a lecture video. Of course, they expected greater attention and reduced mind wandering from their pretested students, but they wanted to more closely examine what students did during the watching of the video.

To understand what students did while watching the video, they asked some of the students to jot down what they thought was important information in the video lectures with no reference to the pretest questions, while instructing others to specifically try to find answers to the questions on the pretest. By analyzing participants' notes, they found that the benefits of this pretest were only seen when students could notice and select answers to the pretest questions during the video, suggesting that the success of pretesting hinges on the students' ability to remember and focus on the questions asked earlier.

Given that the pretested students performed better than those who were not pretested, it means that the pretesting also serves a priming function of helping students spot and grasp the answers during the video lecture.

In sum, the mechanisms of processing, preparation, and priming work together to bring out the effects of failure-based activation, and set us up to understand the boundaries – an awareness – of what we know and what we do not.

Key Takeaways

1. **Activating relevant prior knowledge is key.** Activated priors not only work like hooks for the new knowledge to latch onto, they also help integrate new knowledge.

2. **Not all ways of activating are equal.** Activities such as watching and listening fall on the lower end of the activation spectrum, whereas activities such as problem solving, explaining, and discussing fall on the higher end of the spectrum, especially failure-based activation through problem solving as designed in Productive Failure.

3. **Failed generation is effective.** Attempting to answer questions about an unfamiliar topic before learning improves learning of that topic even if the initial answers were incorrect.

4. **Processing, preparation, and priming.** Failure-based activation:
   a) induces deeper *processing* even if generating solutions to challenging problems is difficult, for some difficulties are desirable.
   b) *prepares* us for subsequent instruction or learning by activating our priors, differentiating them, encoding variability and cognitive flexibility.
   c) *primes* us for subsequent learning as well by enhancing attention, reducing mind wandering, and focusing our search for answers.

4

Awareness

The great philosopher Socrates is well known to have said "awareness of ignorance is the beginning of wisdom."

Philosophically, Socrates' dictum can be understood as an articulation of intellectual humility, a recognition that the scope of what one does not know far exceeds what one does. This acknowledgment of ignorance is not a defeatist perspective but rather a starting point for genuine inquiry. Socrates famously claimed that he was wise not because he knew much, but because he understood the extent of his own ignorance.

The Socratic method, derived from this approach, involves asking a series of probing questions to challenge assumptions and reveal contradictions in one's thought. This method is not aimed at finding a correct answer but to lead to aporia, a state of puzzlement, impasse, or doubt, which is the fertile ground for philosophical investigation. It is in this state of aporia where one becomes open to acquiring wisdom because one has admitted to not having it.

Consider the following hypothetical dialogue (see next page) between Socrates and one of his students.

This hypothetical dialogue is designed to show how Socrates guides the student to the realization that failure, and the recognition of one's own ignorance, is not only unavoidable but also beneficial in the pursuit of knowledge and skill. Through his questions, Socrates helps the student become aware of a gap in their understanding – the role of failure in learning – leading to a deeper insight into the nature of acquiring wisdom.

> **Socrates:** Tell me, do you believe that one can be good at something without ever having failed at it?
>
> **Student:** Yes, I believe so. If someone is naturally talented, they can be good without failing.
>
> **Socrates:** A reasonable belief. Now, have you ever observed someone learning to play a musical instrument?
>
> **Student:** Of course.
>
> **Socrates:** And did they play flawlessly from the beginning?
>
> **Student:** Not exactly. They often made mistakes in the beginning.
>
> **Socrates:** So, they failed in playing the correct notes at first?
>
> **Student:** Yes, that's true.
>
> **Socrates:** If they had not been aware of their mistakes, could they have corrected them?
>
> **Student:** No, they needed to recognize their errors to improve.
>
> **Socrates:** Then, would you say awareness of their failures was necessary for them to become good musicians?
>
> **Student:** I suppose so.
>
> **Socrates:** Does it not then follow that one's awareness of their lack of skill or knowledge – in other words, their ignorance – is a step toward their improvement?
>
> **Student:** I see your point. One must be aware of their ignorance to improve.
>
> **Socrates:** So, would you then agree that to be truly good at something, one must first become aware of their failures or gaps in knowledge?
>
> **Student:** I agree, Socrates.
>
> **Socrates:** And so, would you still hold that one can be truly good at something without ever having failed at it?
>
> **Student:** No, Socrates. I now understand that failure and the awareness of one's own ignorance are necessary to achieve true skill and wisdom.

This pursuit of wisdom is therefore intrinsically linked to the concept of learning from failure. In recognizing our ignorance, we also recognize our fallibility – we are prone to mistakes and misjudgments. Each failure is a manifestation of our ignorance, and in reflecting on these failures, we learn not only about the subject at hand but also about the limitations of our reasoning and understanding.

By embracing our failures as learning opportunities, we embody the Socratic principle that wisdom begins with the awareness of our ignorance.

From Socratic Dialogue to Tutoring

Imagine you are trying to learn physics, working through a few problems with the help of a tutor. How the dialogue between you and the tutor unfolds will influence what and how much you learn. A good tutor, perhaps like Socrates, might be able to help you learn more than others who are not as skilled, which is why examining such tutorial dialogues is of keen interest to researchers.

What makes some tutoring sessions more successful than others?

In 2003, a group of researchers led by Kurt VanLehn looked into this by carefully analyzing conversations between students and their physics tutors. They wanted to figure out what happens in those dialogues that leads to actual learning. Precisely what features of dialogue result in learning. They searched approximately 125 hours of tutorial dialogue between 42 university students and 2 experienced adult physics tutors for events that resulted in learning. And what they found was intriguing.

They found that sometimes students were able to solve the problem without getting stuck, but at other times they would get stuck and not be able to move forward. They called these getting stuck moments impasses. They found that not only were such impasses strongly associated with learning gains, but when students did not encounter such impasses, they hardly learned anything no matter what the tutor said or explained.

Successful learning, it seems, almost requires that you reach an impasse. Why would it be so critical to reach an impasse?

Figure 4.1 shows the basic process of what happens after an impasse. When a student gets stuck, they immediately become aware that there is

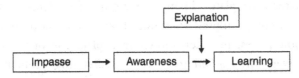

Figure 4.1 How impasses lead to awareness of knowledge gaps and learning.

something wrong. They become aware that there is a gap in their current knowledge, and this awareness is key to them seeking a resolution. The impasse then becomes a strong learning opportunity, forcing the student to think harder, ask questions, and understand the concept deeply to move forward. What VanLehn and colleagues found out was that only when students were at an impasse, were the tutor's explanations helpful and resulted in learning. When students were not at an impasse, the tutor's explanations did not result in learning.

Struggling a bit with the problem helps you learn better than if someone just explains the answers. Before we can repair or resolve our misconceptions or failures, we need to become aware of them in the first place. Even in tutoring situations, there seems to be a time for failing, a time for an impasse followed by a time for telling.

If you find yourself in a tutoring situation, then make sure you give your tutee a chance to work through problems on their own and encourage them to think deeply about where they are getting stuck. And only when they get stuck and become aware of it, explain how they might proceed, and help them get unstuck. Equally, if you are the tutee, remind your tutor to withhold explanations until you are stuck, because explanations are more likely to be useful in those moments than others.

If impasses are so critical for building awareness of a knowledge gap, and learning, then, as the logic of Productive Failure goes, we should not wait for them to happen, and instead intentionally design for them to engineer awareness and learning.

Intentionally Designing Impasses

Emilio Sánchez and colleagues tried to engineer impasses in their 2009 study with undergraduate students learning about geology, specifically about tectonic plates.

Figure 4.2 presents the experimental design. First, all students first saw a video on tectonic plates. Then, one group of students – the impasse condition – were prompted to think about a common misconception about tectonic plates, and then shown an explanation of the misconception. They were then asked to solve a challenging problem regarding tectonic plates that students were unlikely to be able to solve. They were then given the explanation for the solution to the problem.

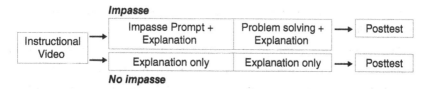

Figure 4.2 Experimental design for comparing the effect of intentionally designed vs no impasse conditions on learning.

The other group – no impasses condition – did not have to think about the misconception or solve the challenging problem, but did receive explanations for both. Therefore, the only difference between the two groups was the misconception prompt and the challenging problem, both of which worked like triggers of impasse because they made students think about something they could not resolve on their own.

After learning, all students took a posttest where they were tested on how much they remembered the material and how well they could apply their knowledge to solve problems. On both measures, students who received impasse triggers significantly outperformed those who did not, demonstrating one way in which impasses can be designed to increase awareness of knowledge gaps while learning something new.

The same group of authors, this time led by Santiago Acuña, replicated the above findings in 2010 by showing that merely providing a prompt of possible misconceptions before presenting an instructional explanation can foster learning, especially for students with lower prior knowledge, as the warning helps students to become aware of their own knowledge gaps.

Being warned of possible misconception is quite a simple nudge. If that itself builds knowledge gap awareness, then what about intentionally designed failure in problem solving that students go through in Productive Failure? One would expect even greater awareness of knowledge gaps.

In 2014, Katharina Loibl and Nikol Rummel were the first ones to demonstrate how learning from Productive Failure builds an awareness of a knowledge gap. Using the same materials I had developed for my studies on teaching statistics (specifically, the concept of standard deviation described in Chapter 2), they gave one group of students explicit instruction on the concept of standard deviation, and then asked them to solve practice problems. Recall from Chapter 2 that I called this the Direct Instruction condition, or instruction followed by problem solving. The other group followed the Productive Failure model, where they solved the problem before receiving instruction.

The Direct Instruction group had all the information required to solve the problem, and therefore did not experience any impasse or failure. In contrast, the Productive Failure group was by definition designed to experience failure because students lacked the information required to solve the problems.

What did they find? Students in the Productive Failure condition reported significantly higher awareness of a gap in their knowledge than the group that received Direct Instruction.

As Figure 4.3 shows, failure made them aware of the gap in their knowledge. This helped them derive greater benefit from subsequent instruction especially when the teacher specifically contrasted and discussed the gap between their solutions and the correct solutions. And that led to deep learning.

Researchers such as Inga Glogger-Frey and colleagues have since replicated the effect of Productive Failure on knowledge gap awareness in two experimental studies reported in 2015. Although the experiments were designed to test a different hypothesis, both their experiments followed the Problem Solving followed by Instruction (PS-I) design that we discussed in Chapter 2. In both the experiments, the Productive Failure condition reported higher knowledge gap awareness than the other condition where students did not experience failure. Christian Hartmann and colleagues echoed similar findings in their 2021 study.

Collectively these studies demonstrate how an impasse of problem-solving failure helps build an awareness of a knowledge gap. In these studies, the experience of an impasse or problem-solving failure was sufficient, as can be seen in Figures 4.1 and 4.3. In both cases, an impasse or failure to solve a problem was sufficient for us to recognize and realize that there is a gap. And if at this time, the right explanation or instruction is provided, we learn better.

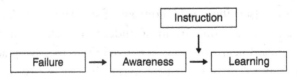

Figure 4.3 **How failure drives awareness of knowledge gaps and learning.**

But there are also times when we do not even know we have failed or made an error, let alone are aware of a knowledge gap. For example, sometimes we find ourselves in situations where our idea or thinking or answer makes such intuitive sense that we do not stop to think or even reflect that we could be wrong. In such cases, we first need to be given a chance to discover the error of our thinking, and only then do we become aware of our knowledge gap.

When Intuition Failure Builds Awareness

It is time to take a test. Try to answer the following three problems:

(1) A bat and a ball cost $1.10 in total. The bat costs $1.00 more than the ball. How much does the ball cost? _____ cents

(2) If it takes 5 machines 5 minutes to make 5 widgets, how long would it take 100 machines to make 100 widgets? _____ minutes

(3) In a lake, there is a patch of lily pads. Every day, the patch doubles in size. If it takes 48 days for the patch to cover the entire lake, how long would it take for the patch to cover half of the lake? _____ days

Before we get to the solutions, reflect on your thought process as you attempted the problems. Chances are that for each problem, your first answer was an intuitive one. For the first problem, you might have immediately thought of 10 cents as the answer, for the second you may have guessed 100 minutes, and for the third, the first answer that most people think of is 24 days.

All three answers are wrong.

The test, developed by Shane Frederick in 2005, was designed precisely to have such a property, that the first most intuitive answer that most people would think of would likely be the wrong one. He called it the Cognitive Reflection Test (CRT). If people succumb to their immediate intuitions, they will most likely get it wrong. If, however, they allow themselves a chance to reflect upon it, chances of getting the correct answer increase.

It is this property of the CRT that makes it a perfect candidate for examining if and to what extent we can learn from intuitive failure. These kinds of tests allow us to examine what happens when people are made aware that their intuitive answer is wrong, and whether they change their mind when a correct explanation is given immediately afterward.

In 2014, Emmanuel Trouche and colleagues carried out several experiments to test precisely this question. They also added several other problems like the ones below that have similar properties like the CRT. Give these problems a try as well.

> Julie puts her books on a shelf in her bedroom. She realizes that her favorite book is the 33rd from the left and the 44th from the right. How many books does Julie have on her shelf? _____ books
>
> Paul is looking at Linda and Linda is looking at Patrick. Paul is married but Patrick is not. Is a person who is married looking at a person who is not married? Yes / No / Cannot be determined

Trouche and colleagues asked participants to solve items like those in the CRT and the ones above. As expected, many got them wrong. Then participants were given written explanations of the answer, with some being correct and others incorrect, and were told that these explanations were produced by their peers in a previous experiment. Therefore, participants knew that these were not expert explanations, which also means that they had no way of knowing if the explanations were correct or not.

Imagine yourself in this experiment. You get a question, you solve it intuitively, you think you got it right when in fact you are wrong. You are then randomly presented with either a correct or an incorrect explanation given by someone like you from an earlier experiment. You do not know for sure if they are correct or not. You can only rely on your ability to discern. The question is, would you change your mind if you come across an explanation that runs counter to your reasoning and answer? Would a counter-explanation and answer be sufficient to make you aware of the fault in your reasoning?

It turns out, 45% of the time, people did change their mind. Having gotten it intuitively wrong, the mere presentation of a counter-explanation and answer was sufficient to make them aware that their reasoning was faulty. Without the counter-explanation, that may not have happened at all. Even if at first we do not know we are wrong, we have the ability to discern and correct ourselves provided the counter-explanation is given right after our answer.

Therefore, in contrast to Figures 4.1 and 4.3 earlier, Figure 4.4 shows that in such cases the explanation has to come in before, not after, the awareness of a knowledge gap, because people may not have even realized that they were wrong to begin with. An explanation then increases the probability that people realize their failure first, and then become aware of the knowledge gap. And that is when the explanation leads to learning.

Now you may say that 45% may seem like a small number, but this was also a much stricter test given that people did not know whether the counter-explanations were correct or not. The only thing they could see was that the explanation was counter to theirs. The contrast between their explanation and the counter was all they had to work with. Still, in the end, many changed their minds and adopted the correct answer.

That sets up the intriguing possibility: What if the counter-explanations were explained by people who know the right answer? Perhaps if someone who knows the right answer explains it to you, maybe the chances of you changing your mind would be even higher.

Trouche and colleagues tested this in their follow-up experiments. They tested people first individually and then in groups. So, this time, as a participant, you are given similar problems, but you first solve them individually, and then in small groups of three to five people until the group reaches a consensus. After that, you solve two new problems – transfer problems – requiring similar reasoning but in different contexts.

Once again, if there was at least one person in the group who had solved the problem correctly individually before the group, the group consensus almost always adopted this correct reasoning and answer. Even when there was exactly one group member with the correct answer, they too almost always managed to convince the group to adopt the correct answer.

It seemed group discussion allowed people to share their reasoning, compare and contrast with each other, and those with the incorrect

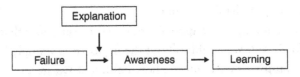

Figure 4.4   How failure drives awareness of knowledge gaps and learning.

reasoning could see where they were wrong, and therefore changed their mind. Without the opportunity to see the correct reasoning, people may not even have known that they were incorrect. But once such an opportunity presented itself, and in group discussions it often did, then correct reasoning was contagious.

Indeed, as depicted in Figure 4.4, it was correct explanations that made people check their own explanations and realize at once that they were wrong and become aware of their gap in reasoning. Group discussion allows for such explanations to be shared, making people aware of their errors, leading them to change their minds and adopt the correct answer.

And it was not merely that people adopted the correct answer. They actually learned the correct explanation to solve such problems in general. How do we know? Recall that people were individually asked to solve two new problems – transfer problems – requiring similar reasoning but in different contexts. On these problems, results showed that the people who changed their minds were also able to perform better on the individual transfer problems, demonstrating that they actually learned something from their errors thanks to the group discussion.

Once again, it turns out that even if at first we do not know we are wrong, we have the ability to discern and correct ourselves provided the counter-explanation is given right after our answer. We have the capacity to change our minds. It begs the question, however, whether such a capacity is more general across all contexts.

Clearly, strongly held beliefs are hard to change. It is hard to see anyone holding on to answers to the above problems in the form of hard belief one might have, say about other more personal, sensitive issues like abortion, vaccination, equality, rights and responsibilities, and many others. To be clear, findings from the studies above do not apply to strongly held belief systems, because the latter are not intuitive in nature; instead, they are beliefs we get enculturated into over many years, which is why we believe them strongly and they are hard to change.

The above findings only apply to intuitive answers, ones that we do not hold too closely. But we could still test the notion of a strongly held answer, even if it is intuitive, by examining how confident we are in it. Sometimes we hold on to an idea or a misconception because it makes such strong intuitive sense, and we are confident that we are right. It would be intuitive to conjecture that the lower the confidence we have in our intuitive answers, the easier we should be able to change our minds when a counter-explanation is provided.

Or is it? As we see in the next section, sometimes our overconfidence seduces us into thinking that our answer is so obviously true that a lesson in humility is needed.

Humbled By a Six Year Old

When my elder son Dev was six years old, he came back from kindergarten one day looking very upset. After much probing, he finally revealed the source of his anguish: "Papa, I want to be either pure Indian or pure Chinese. I don't want to be half-half," he admitted. You see, his mom is Singaporean Chinese, and I am ethnically Indian, so I replied, "Dev, that is not possible. Your mama is Chinese, and papa is Indian, so you are half-Indian and half-Chinese." He got even more upset, and much as I tried to comfort him, he would not accept my explanation. I was sure though that he would come around and finally accept the fact and the explanation for why he had to be half-Chinese and half-Indian. Instead, what he argued next blew my mind, retorting, "But papa, you are a boy and mama is a girl, but I am not half-boy and half-girl right? I am a boy!"

There are some moments in one's life when you know your argument or explanation has been utterly and entirely demolished and humbled. That was one of those moments. I was so confident of my explanation, perhaps even overconfident, that I thought surely there was no counter to it, and certainly not from a six year old. Yet, at that moment, Dev showed me the flaw in my logic, that sometimes A plus B can result in A or B and not necessarily a mix of both.

I have of course many wonderful memories from Dev's childhood, but there are a few that really stand out. This is one of them. Part of the reason for its standing out is that my six year old showed me the flaw in my logic. He made me aware of a clear gap in my thinking. I stood corrected, keenly aware of how and why I had failed. Another part had to do with the fact that I was perhaps overconfident of my logic to begin with, and that made my fall even more spectacular and memorable. And of course, the fact that a six year old did me in had a lot to do with it, too.

I suppose it seems intuitive that we should remember our failures, especially if we were confident of succeeding to begin with. But are the lower confidence failures easier to correct than higher confidence ones? One line of argument, as noted earlier, would be to argue that the lower the confidence we have in our intuitive answers, the easier we should be able to change our minds when a counter-explanation is provided. Another line of argument would predict exactly the opposite. The more confident we are that we are correct when in fact we are wrong, the greater the effect of the failure on our awareness and learning from the correction. The more money you put on a bet, metaphorically (or not) speaking, the more you would remember losing it.

Which of these arguments hold up to scientific scrutiny?

In 2001, Brady Butterfield and Janet Metcalfe designed a simple experiment to test precisely this idea, that is, if and how we learn from errors we make with high versus low confidence. The dominant theories of error correction at the time predicted that errors we make with low confidence would be easier to correct than those we make with high confidence. It would be easier to shake off something we were not sure of in the first place than something we held strongly.

To test their hypothesis, they had 19 undergraduate students answer general knowledge questions such as "What poison did Socrates take at his execution?" or "What is the capital of Canada?" and so on. Each student was shown one side of an index card with a question on it. They had to read the question aloud, write down their answer, and then rate how confident they felt about their answer on a scale from −3 (very unsure) to +3 (very sure). If they got the answer right, the experimenter would confirm it and move to the next question. If they got it wrong, they were shown the right answer on the other side of the card, and the experimenter also told them the correct answer. This went on until the student had at least 15 correct and 15 incorrect answers.

After this first round, they had to solve a distractor problem – a logic problem – that had nothing to do with the general knowledge questions. Recall from Chapter 3 that distractor tasks are often used in psychological experiments to keep the participant's mind busy so that they do not rehearse or think about the material that was just presented to them, in turn helping to capture the experimental effect more precisely.

After five minutes of working on the logic problem, the experimenter surprised them with a final test of general knowledge using the same 30 questions in a random order. Students read the questions to themselves, thought of not one but the first three answers that came to mind, wrote them down, rated their confidence in each just like before, and marked one of the three answers as their final choice. Only the final choice was scored as correct or incorrect.

Butterfield and Metcalfe found that high confidence errors were indeed better remembered than the low confidence errors, because these errors turned up in the three answers on the final test more often than the low confidence errors. That is, people were more likely to remember errors they made with high confidence than with low confidence. This would explain why they could recall them on the final test.

However, contrary to the predictions of the dominant theories at the time, these higher confidence errors were also more likely to be corrected. That is, even though high confidence errors showed up in the three choices on the final test, students still indicated the correct answer as their final choice, meaning that they were aware of both the incorrect and the correct answers. The same was not true for the low confidence errors.

It seems that the beneficial effects of corrective feedback that helps us learn from errors are stronger when we make these errors with high confidence. The reason is simple too. As Figure 4.5 suggests, when something we think we know with high confidence is corrected, we become even more aware of the gap in our knowledge.

Why? Because the error was made in high confidence, its correction and awareness make us more aroused and focused on the mismatch, and pay even more attention to and learn from the correction. Further studies, both behavioral and neuroimaging, by Metcalfe and colleagues, as well as recent integrative reviews have largely bolstered these findings and the underlying reasons as well (Butterfield and Metcalfe 2006; Metcalfe and Finn 2012; Metcalfe and Miele 2014; Metcalfe et al. 2012; Mera, Rodríguez, Marin-Garcia 2022; Metcalfe 2017).

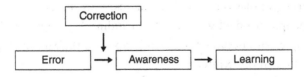

Figure 4.5 How high confidence error correction leads to learning.

Still, the above findings in the previous two sections apply to intuitively held explanations to simple problems or general knowledge questions. As concepts and ideas become more complex, mere awareness of a gap, whether brought on by an impasse or failure, or more forcefully by an explanation or a humbling correction, may not be sufficient for learning. We need stronger experiential or external stimulus to turn our awareness of the knowledge gap into learning.

The Warmth Above the Clouds

You know, I always thought mountains were synonymous with bitter cold, a place where even the Sun's embrace felt frosty. This belief was so ingrained in me that I would scoff whenever my close friend and colleague Pierre spoke of the warm, sunlit afternoons at his mountain chalet. "You have to experience it to believe it," he'd say, but I never took his word for it. That was until I found myself standing on his terrace, high above the clouds, my skepticism about to be turned on its head.

Pierre's chalet was nestled in the picturesque Swiss Alps, a setting straight out of a storybook, yet all I could think about was how many layers I would need to keep the cold at bay. One late morning, with the sun shining brightly, Pierre suggested we take our coffee outside. I remember laughing at the idea, bundling up as if preparing for an Arctic expedition.

But as I stepped out onto the terrace, a different reality hit me. The sun, unfiltered and resplendent, bathed me in a warmth that felt almost surreal. It was a stark contrast to the chill I had braced myself for. There I was, standing in just my t-shirt, basking in the gentle warmth, thinking how wrong I had been in my thinking: an awareness that one can feel only in such moments.

It took a spectacular demonstration of the failure of my beliefs for me to become aware of such an embarrassing gap in my knowledge about the warmth above the clouds. However, I am not alone in holding on to such misconceptions. People in general hold on to a lot of misconceptions. A notoriously popular one is about what causes seasons.

Most people, from all walks of life, including Ivy league students, think that we have seasons because the Earth is closer to the Sun during the summer and farther in the winter.

However, the truth could not be farther away. The real reason is that seasons are caused by the Earth's tilted axis. As the Earth orbits the Sun, this tilt causes different parts of the Earth to receive more direct sunlight at different times of the year. When tilted toward the Sun, we get more direct sunlight, longer days, and warmer temperatures; that is, we get summer. When tilted away, we get winter. Distance actually plays no role, especially in light of the fact that the Earth is closest to the Sun in the dead of winter, during the first week of January.

Understanding and correcting misconceptions in science is a crucial aspect of education and general knowledge. It is also a prolific area of scientific research on how best to address misconceptions. For example, the way I set up and refuted the "what causes seasons" misconception is an example of one strategy, called refutation texts.

The idea, as captured in Figure 4.6, is not just providing the correct information but also helping people recognize the gap in their own understanding. This involves setting up the misconception, explicitly confronting and refuting it so that it creates an awareness of a knowledge gap, and then correcting it in a manner that is easy to understand so that we can learn the correct knowledge.

Researchers have developed and deployed a range of methods, from textual materials and analogies to interactive simulations and visual mapping tools, all aimed at addressing scientific misconceptions. The 2023 meta-analysis by Cagatay Pacaci, Ulas Ustun, and Omer Faruk Ozdemir looked at evidence from more than 200 experiments with more than 18,000 students to show a strong effect of a range of methods.

Misconceptions can be addressed, and effectively so. Sometimes one has to actually experience the refutation or conflict on a sunny day at a friend's chalet in the mountains to become aware of one's ignorance. Other times, it is best to be more pragmatic, and thankfully, research gives a host of highly effective methods.

The methods vary, but invariant across the methods are the critical features of their effectiveness: engage students actively, confront existing

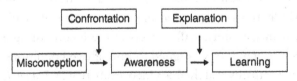

Figure 4.6 How misconceptions can be addressed.

misconceptions, create an awareness of a gap, and present scientific concepts in a more accessible and relatable manner. Without confronting and
knowledge gap awareness, the efficacy of the correct explanation is com-
promised. Much like in tutoring, correct explanations have an impact only
when one is stuck and aware of their own ignorance. The same goes for
correcting misconceptions.

We saw how the awareness that results from impasses prepares us to
learn from a well-timed explanation. We saw how a similar dynamic unfolds
when we engineer impasses, for example, in Productive Failure. But when
we are not aware of our impasse or failure, we need to be counter-explained
or corrected, and in the case of misconceptions, even more systematic con-
frontation and explanation are necessary.

Taken together, it may seem that impasses, failures, errors, and misconceptions are necessary for us to become aware of our knowledge gap. At
least that may well be the impression that comes through. If so, then I must
correct it. Impasses, failures, errors, and misconceptions are sufficient, but
not necessary. If failure happens or is designed for, it can create an awareness
of a gap. It is sufficient. But it is strictly not necessary. If it were necessary,
then only failure could create awareness of the knowledge gap. That is not
true. There are other things that also make us aware of our knowledge gaps.

In Awe of Awe

In a world brimming with mysteries, what if the key to unlocking our
thirst for knowledge lies not in the answers we find, but in the awe we feel
for the unknown? It was not until recently in 2019 that the first studies
testing the effect of awe on awareness of ignorance came out, revealing
how that spine-tingling sensation of encountering something vast and
beyond our understanding – awe – can be a powerful catalyst for learning,
particularly in science (McPhetres 2019).

Imagine watching a mesmerizing video of Earth's natural wonders,
the kind that leaves you breathless, versus a light-hearted, humorous clip.
Jonathon McPhetres conducted a series of experiments with more than
1,300 participants, exploring the effects of these contrasting experiences.
Participants were randomly assigned to one of two conditions. In the awe
condition, participants watched a video from BBC's *Planet Earth*. In the
control condition, participants watched a humorous video from BBC's
Walk on the Wild Side.

After watching the videos, all participants responded to a seven-item measure of knowledge gap awareness (e.g. *I ask myself if I really understand how the natural world works; This activity makes me realize how much I don't know about nature, and so on*) and to an eight-item measure of science interest (e.g. *science magazines and stories are interesting*).

As predicted, those who witnessed the awe-inspiring scenes of nature consistently reported a heightened awareness of their own knowledge gaps. They realized there was so much more they did not know about the world around them. This realization was not tinged with frustration or defeat; instead, it sparked a deep, enthusiastic interest in science. In one of the studies, to gauge a better sense of interest, participants had to choose between tickets to a science museum or an art museum. Those bathed in awe from the natural world video overwhelmingly chose the science museum, as if the experience opened a door to a world of wonders waiting to be explored.

If, as Figure 4.7 suggests, awe can make us aware of our knowledge gap, and in turn increase our interest in bridging the gap, then providing information explaining the awe-inspiring phenomenon should reduce the interest to learn more. Perhaps not entirely, but once we have more information about the phenomenon, we might be a little less interested to learn more, because the thirst has been quenched somewhat.

Jonathan McPhetres tested this hypothesis in a follow-up study with more than 200 undergraduate students, using the immersive world of virtual reality. Students donned VR headsets and were transported to the mesmerizing dance of the aurora borealis, the Northern Lights. The awe was palpable, but this time some received information relevant to the awe-inspiring scene they just witnessed, while others were given unrelated information. The results supported the hypothesis: providing specific information about the awe-inducing event slightly diminished their burgeoning interest in science, suggesting that the mystery and the unanswered questions might be part of what drives our curiosity.

These studies paint a vivid picture: It is not just the beauty or grandeur of what we see that captivates us, but the realization of our ignorance and how much more there is to understand. So, the next time

Figure 4.7   How awe drives awareness and interest in learning.

you gaze at the stars, watch a nature documentary, or stand in the presence of something vast and incomprehensible, remember: it's not just a moment of awe; it's a doorway to endless learning and discovery. The path to knowledge begins not with what we know, but with the awe and awareness of all that we do not.

Key Takeaways

1. **Socratic Method.** The Socratic method underscores the importance of acknowledging one's ignorance, setting the stage for effective learning.

2. **Learning at Impasses.** We experience significant learning when we encounter impasses, as these moments highlight our knowledge gaps.

3. **Challenges and Productive Failure.** The combination of intentionally designed impasses and the concept of "Productive Failure" – tackling problems before formal instruction – helps us further recognize and address our knowledge gaps.

4. **Intuition Failure.** When we face situations where our intuition fails, it not only reinforces an awareness of these gaps but also pushes us to reevaluate and reconstruct our understanding.

5. **Influence of Awe.** Finally, even without any failure, experiencing awe can magnify our awareness of ignorance, encouraging a more profound interest in learning.

5

Affect

When Charles Dickens published *The Old Curiosity Shop* in serial form in his own weekly periodical, *Master Humphrey's Clock*, from 1840 to 1841, it was a commercial success. The story was so popular that readers eagerly anticipated each new installment. The character of Little Nell, in particular, captured the hearts of readers both in England and abroad. Readers became deeply invested in her story, and as the installments neared their end, speculation about whether Little Nell would live or die reportedly reached a fever pitch.

This anticipation was not limited to England. In the United States, where the novel was also extremely popular, the narrative reportedly sparked such intrigue that readers eagerly gathered at the docks of New York Harbor, anticipating the arrival of the ship from England carrying the magazine with the next installment of the series. And when it was revealed that Little Nell does indeed die, the public reaction was intense.

The widespread engagement with the serial and emotional response to Little Nell's death is a testament to Dickens's skill as a writer and the power of serialized storytelling.

It is also a testament to the power of cliffhangers – a key feature of serials – which is why they are used across various forms of media to create suspense and anticipation, compelling audiences to return for more. They are often seen in advertising, movies, TV shows, and games, where they serve to maintain audience engagement and interest by creating a sense of suspense and anticipation, leveraging our natural desire for resolution to keep us invested. By creating a sense of suspense and anticipation, they leverage our natural desire for resolution to keep us coming back for more.

A similar dynamic unfolds in Productive Failure. When we fail to solve a problem correctly in spite of trying multiple ways to solve it, it creates something like a cliffhanger – a cognitive and affective cliffhanger. Having invested in the problem, we are eager to discover the correct solution. This unresolved state can enhance memory retention and engagement, making the eventual learning experience more impactful. This is the cognitive benefit that we discussed in the earlier chapters.

But it also has an affective benefit.

Cognition and affect are distinct yet coupled aspects of human experience. Cognition refers to the mental processes involved in acquiring knowledge, understanding, and reasoning. It encompasses perception, attention, memory, language, and problem solving.

On the other hand, affect pertains to emotions, interest, desire, motivation, moods, and feelings. It involves the subjective and experiential aspects of human emotions, influencing one's attitudes, preferences, and responses. While cognition focuses on thinking and understanding, affect emphasizes the emotional and evaluative dimensions of human experience. Both cognition and affect play crucial roles in shaping human behavior and decision-making.

When we fail to solve a problem correctly in spite of trying multiple ways to solve it, the unresolved issue sparks interest and a desire for resolution, where failure can become a powerful motivator, driving the learner to persist in the journey, and wanting to learn knowledge and achieve understanding, turning the learning journey into an engaging narrative of discovery. Here the emotions, interest, motivations, and feelings reign, in other words, affect comes into play.

Let us unpack how affect comes into play in Productive Failure.

The Zeigarnik Effect

Imagine you and your friends are taking part in a trivia quiz. There are a variety of categories and multiple-choice questions, and you are all racing against the clock to answer as many questions correctly as you can.

Some questions are easy for you. You quickly recognize the answers and feel a sense of satisfaction when your responses are confirmed as correct.

These questions, the ones you have confidently answered, represent completed tasks. But there are some tricky questions where you just can't decide between the options. The timer is ticking down, and you finally make a guess, but you are not sure if it is right. These are the "cognitively incomplete" tasks, the ones you are unsure about.

After the quiz, if you were to try to recall the questions, which ones would you recall more: the completed or the cognitively incomplete ones?

You will likely find that the unanswered or incomplete ones stick out more in your memory than those you swiftly answered. You may even find yourself pondering over those questions, maybe even looking up the answers later.

This is the Zeigarnik effect, a psychological phenomenon named after the Russian psychologist Bluma Zeigarnik, who discovered it in 1927. The story goes that Zeigarnik was in a restaurant, where she observed an interesting phenomenon: waiters could remember complex orders, including specific meal requests and drink preferences, while they were in the process of serving them. However, once the order was delivered and the bill was paid, they struggled to recall the same details.

To test her restaurant observations, Zeigarnik conducted controlled experiments, asking participants to complete 20 simple tasks, for example, creating words from letters or writing city names that start with the letter "L." The catch was that half of these tasks were intentionally interrupted, leaving them incomplete. After finishing all tasks, participants were asked to recall as many tasks as they could. She found that they remembered the interrupted tasks much better: 68% of the incomplete tasks were recalled compared to just 43% of completed tasks.

A similar thing may happen if you are in the middle of a great book, only to be interrupted, and then find that the unfinished story keeps nagging at you. Or after an exam, you are more likely to remember the tougher or unanswered questions more than the ones you could solve. Or perhaps you are halfway through cleaning your garage when a friend calls, and even during your chat, your thoughts keep drifting back to the unfinished cleaning task. These are everyday examples of the Zeigarnik effect at work. Unfinished business leaves you wanting somewhat.

Although the Zeigarnik effect is cognitive in nature, that is, better memory of incomplete tasks, the underlying mechanism is more affective in nature. This stronger memory of uncompleted tasks is usually attributed to what we commonly refer to as a "need for closure," a concept derived from Gestalt psychology. In simple terms, once we start a task, we have an urge or a drive to finish it. You can think of it as a mental pop-up reminder that keeps nudging you about a task you have started but have not finished.

One of Zeigarnik's contemporaries, Maria Ovsiankina, studied the effect of interruptions on our ability to get things done. In 1928, Ovsiankina discovered that people feel a more intense desire to finish tasks that have been started and then interrupted, rather than those tasks they have not yet begun. When a task is completed, it satisfies our goal, and we stop thinking about it. On the other hand, if a task is not finished and our goal remains unachieved, we lack closure. This lack of closure coupled with our need or desire for closure keeps our brain somewhat engaged in the task, helping us retain the task details in our memory. Of course there are individual differences that come into play; the urge or drive varies from person to person and depends upon the context among other things.

The human need for closure is obviously much more general than the Zeigarnik effect. Experiencing unpleasant or challenging events in life, such as a heated argument, receiving bad news, or confronting failure, often leaves us with an uncomfortable, unresolved feeling. We have all experienced the echoes of an unresolved argument lingering long after the heat of the moment, or the failure continuing to haunt us until we learn from it or find a way to succeed. As beings who thrive on patterns, predictability, and resolution, we naturally seek a sense of completeness, particularly after difficult situations. We yearn for understanding, clarity, and, above all, closure, to help us move on from the distressing experience. Our brain's commitment to completing the incomplete motivates and moves us toward resolution and closure.

What if we could turn this human need for closure into less of a distress and more of a safe way to design for and learn from failure? That is indeed what Productive Failure strives for. Failure to generate the correct solution, even after trying multiple ways, leaves one with an awareness of a gap, as indeed we saw in the previous chapter. The desire to bridge this gap drives learners to explore new strategies, challenge their understanding, and ultimately gain a more robust grasp of the subject. The "unfinished business" of failure propels the learner toward achieving closure from instruction that follows.

The Need for Closure

We like to achieve closure. In this sense, we like to complete things we have started. In fact, we derive a strong affective boost for completing things we have put effort into. There are four levels of such affective boosts, each Affective Boost Level (or ABLe) targeting a different aspect of our need to close. I unpack each in turn.

Affective Boost Level 1 (or ABLe 1): Avoiding Loss

Our tendency for closure is usually so strong that we tend to persist even if persisting is rationally not the best choice for us. In behavioral economics, it is called the *sunk cost fallacy*.

This is why you might be motivated to continue watching a television series because you have already invested time in it even if it is not a particularly good one, or stay in a career you are not entirely happy with because you have spent years studying and training for it, or stay in a relationship even if it is not working out so well. The basic idea is that we are more likely to continue with something we have invested effort and time and resources into, even if continuing is not the best decision.

And one of the reasons we tend to do this is because we want to avoid wasting our effort, time, and resources that we have already put into it. Nobel Laureates Daniel Kahneman and Amos Tversky called it *loss aversion*, which is a key concept in their 1979 work on Prospect Theory. We do not treat losses and gains equally. Instead, we focus more on avoiding losses than realizing gains. Inertia that comes from having started something can make us go far, sunk cost and loss aversion can make us go dangerously far.

However, in the context of learning, we can turn sunk cost and loss aversion into a positive force. Not finishing a task or failure to solve a problem can of course be perceived as a loss, but if it can also be more productively and intentionally framed as an awareness of a knowledge gap, it can motivate us to persist with and complete the task – a dynamic that we carefully design for in Productive Failure. Failure to solve a problem after trying multiple ways of solving it could lead to Unproductive Failure if we give up and do not go on and learn from instruction that follows. Loss aversion can come into play, making us seek completion to avoid loss of utility of our failed efforts.

This is Affective Boost Level 1 (or ABLe 1), the basic motivation to avoid loss.

Affective Boost Level 2 (or ABLe 2): Endowed Progress

ABLe 1 can be easily turned into ABLe 2. How?

By simply framing the failed problem-solving efforts as progress – progress in terms of preparation for learning from instruction that would follow. In that sense, such progress itself can be motivating and help us persist in our efforts. We can see the progress we have made, and the gap, which sets up the motivation to pursue and complete goals. In fact, what motivates us to pursue goals is a rich area of research in the broader literature on the science of human behavior, or the behavioral sciences.

Suppose you go to a car wash, perhaps your regular car wash, and you are given a loyalty card that gives you a free wash for every eight paid washes. Each time you buy a wash, you get a credit stamp on your card. Now imagine your friend also goes to the same car wash but they are given a loyalty card that has ten washes, with two already credited and stamped. Rationally, both of you have to buy eight washes to get the free wash, but your card makes you go from zero to eight, whereas your friend's card goes from two to ten. Who do you think would be more likely to avail the free wash?

In 2006, Joseph Nunes and Xavier Dreze actually carried this out as a randomized experiment with customers of a real car wash company. They found that your friend would not only be more likely to buy the remaining eight washes and avail the free wash, but also do it faster than you. They called it the *endowed progress effect*, where even an artificial endowment of progress (e.g. in the form of two credit stamps) made people more motivated to pursue the goal and do so faster than others who did not have such an endowment.

What more then, when the endowment is not artificial, but real?

Think of Productive Failure as a learning method where each failed idea, representation, or solution is a credit stamp on your mental progress card toward the goal of learning something new. Each stamp is valued, and the effort celebrated. The learner realizes they do not start from scratch, that they have relevant prior knowledge, but it needs to be activated, extracted, and endowed on their mental progress card. In this way, not only does such prior knowledge activation help you cognitively, as indeed we saw earlier, but the endowed progress effect suggests that it also motivates you and helps you persist toward your learning goals.

It gives your cognition an additional affective boost to level 2, or ABLe 2. But wait, it gets better. It turns out the boost gets stronger the closer you get to the goal, which takes us to ABLe 3.

Affective Boost Level 3 (or ABLe 3): Goal Gradient

Suppose you plan to swim 20 laps in a swimming pool, would your motivation to get to 20 laps after 16 laps be greater than after 10 laps? Asked another way, if you have completed 16 laps, will you be more motivated to get to your goal if your goal was 20 laps than if it were 30? It turns out the closer we get to the goal, the more motivated we are, and the harder we find we can work toward it.

More formally, our increased desire to complete a task the closer we are to completing it is known as the *goal-gradient effect*. First proposed by Clark Hull in 1932 when he was studying the behavior of rats searching for food in a maze, he found that the closer rats got to the food, the faster they ran toward it. When pursuing the goal, rats' effort was not uniform throughout. It varied like a gradient: the closer the goal, the greater the effort.

It turns out humans do the same, too. In 2006, Ran Kivetz and colleagues extended Hull's findings to human behavior. No, they did not have people run around looking for food in a maze. But they demonstrated evidence for the goal-gradient effect in a variety of contexts. For example, they found people participating in a coffee loyalty card program purchased coffee more frequently when they were closer to earning the free coffee. I think most of us can relate to this. Or people who participated in rating songs in return for a reward worked harder when they were closer to the reward, and so on. Basically, as in the swimming pool, the affective boost gets stronger, and so does our behavior, as we get closer to our goal.

In other words, this is ABLe 3.

As happens often in science, their influential paper spawned several lines of inquiry trying to replicate the findings and uncover the boundary conditions for how the effect works, when it works, for whom it works, under what conditions and contexts, and so on (Koo and Fishbach 2008). For example, in 2011, Andrea Bonezzi and colleagues beautifully demonstrated that the goal-gradient effect depends upon how people frame their progress. Do we compare our progress with the initial state and focus on how far we have come, or do we instead compare with the goal state, that is, how far we need to go? And does it matter which state, initial or goal, we use as the point of reference?

Suppose you want to read a 100-page book. Your initial state is 0 pages, as this is where you start. You want to get to 100 pages, that is your goal state. Now suppose you have read 20 pages already, which is your current state. You have 80 more to go. What Andrea Bonezzi and colleagues demonstrated is that it is easier to go from page 20 to 21 if you compare your progress with the initial state (0 pages), because you gain 1 in 20. However, if you compare with the goal state (100 pages), reading one more page is merely gaining 1 in 80, which is much less motivating. The reverse is true if you are close to finishing. It is easier to go from page 80 to 81 if you compare your progress to the goal state; only 20 pages to go, and reading one page gives you a gain of 1 in 20. However, now if you compare with the initial state, then you gain merely 1 in 80, which is not as motivating.

Therefore, depending upon where you are in the process, and whether you focus on how far you have come or how far you still need to go, the goal-gradient works differently. The classic gradient discovered by Clark Hull in rat behavior, and Ran Kivetz and colleagues in human behavior, seems to be valid only if progress is compared with the goal state. That is, as long as we maintain our focus on the goal, and compare our progress with the goal state, the closer we get to the goal state, the greater our motivation to reach it.

To top it off, when we are really close to completing, we get an additional, final boost, ABLe 4.

Affective Boost Level 4 (or ABLe 4): Completion Itself

Be it the last lap in the pool or the last hundred meters of a long race, or the last few sit-ups or the last few pages of the book, we find an additional drive when the goal is near and clear in sight. Here, completing in and of itself becomes its own and an additional reward. In 2023, Benjamin Converse and colleagues showed that we tend to prefer to work on a task that is almost complete to ones that are, say half-way done, even if the latter is more fun or offers a higher reward. There is something about completion that we are highly attracted to so much so that we value completion in and of itself, or ABLe 4.

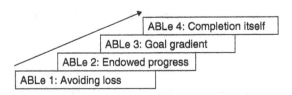

Figure 5.1 Affective boost levels 1 – 4.

In short, the four affective boosts form a staircase, each building on the previous one (see Figure 5.1). ABLe 1 focuses on avoiding loss, which is a powerful motivator. ABLe 2 focuses on progress already made, which motivates us to persist. ABLe 3 derives its force from the goal gradient: the more progress we make, the more motivated we get. And finally ABLe 4 kicks in when we are delightfully close to our goal, when we are almost there, and the joy of completing itself pushes us through to reach our goal.

Inventing solutions to a challenging problem that requires knowledge you have not learned yet is hard. Not one but several solutions. Especially when the solutions end up being suboptimal or incorrect. This is where we need the affective boost levels to come into play. They get you started, keep you motivated, supporting you all the way as you generate multiple ways of solving the problem, one after another, until you are ready, ready for the final step.

You're at your cliffhanger of learning, your interest and curiosity piqued, which gives you an additional affective charge on top of the need for closure.

Situational Interest and Curiosity

Figure 5.2 shows 10 matchsticks arranged in the following order from 1 to 4. Here's a challenge: move exactly one matchstick so that order is reversed, that is, from 4 to 1. Take a minute or so to figure out that one move.

Most people find this problem hard, and chances are you, like me, will not be able to find the solution. But you certainly will be able to try a number of moves, because the problem lends itself to trying multiple moves, only to find that it is really hard to find out the correct move.

Suppose, as expected, after having tried several ideas, you fail to figure out the solution. At that moment, how interested and curious would you be to find out that elusive move? Chances are you would be curious and highly

Move <u>exactly one</u> matchstick to turn the 1,2,3,4
arrangement into a 4,3,2,1 arrangement

Figure 5.2   Matchstick arrangement puzzle.

interested in learning the correct move. And if you want to find out, just google it, and once you find out, try to notice how you felt, for we shall need to visit that later in the chapter.

In the learning sciences, we call this situational interest. In contrast to more stable interests that you may have, situational interest is triggered in the moment, when something in the environment piques you. It is by definition temporary, fleeting even, and bound to the immediate context or situation within which you find yourself. In that moment, you become interested in exploring the problem, and if you are unable to solve it, your curiosity spikes and you become interested in finding out the solution.

The question is: What triggers such situational interest and curiosity in people? And how can we harness those triggers for deep learning?

The Curious Child

Long before scientists started to study curiosity experimentally, the Swiss psychologist Jean Piaget in the 1930s proposed that children use curiosity in their play to construct knowledge through interactions with their environment (Piaget 1936). When faced with something they do not fully understand, children's curiosity is piqued and they use their play to reduce that uncertainty. However, Piaget did not have strong experimental evidence to back his claims.

But sometimes you do not need experimental evidence, especially if you have experienced it yourself. Ask my mother. She would wholeheartedly agree with Piaget. She would be quick to share one of the ways I would frustrate her when I was a child. Why? Because I wanted to break all my new toys. Whether it was a shiny new car, a speedy airplane, or a whistling engine, I was always more curious about what was inside rather than what was on the surface. No sooner would I get my hands on a new toy than I would start taking it apart, piece by piece, because, for me, the joy was not just in possessing a new toy but also in discovering how it worked. And for that I had to break it open.

Experimental evidence has since caught up with Piaget and my parents' experience. As science now suggests, I was not abnormal; it was my young mind's way of understanding the world around me, one toy at a time. Almost a hundred years on since Piaget's proposals, research has gathered ample evidence to suggest that children's play often serves a significant function: it helps reduce their uncertainty about the world and enables them to uncover its underlying causal structures, that is, how and why things work the way they work.

Scientists who study the effects of uncertainty do so by manipulating uncertainty in different ways, and study its effects on curiosity and behavior.

Elizabeth Bonawitz and colleagues have done an amazing set of studies to demonstrate that children exhibit a preference for toys that defy their expectations. For example, as a child my elder son Dev used to be fascinated with magnetic toys. The idea that you could move things without touching them defied all his expectations. He found it incredibly intriguing.

What Bonawitz and colleagues found was that this increase in curiosity is not only present in formal educational settings where children are given explicit instructions, but also when they have no explicit instruction to go on.

Remember Groups 1 and 2 from Chapter 1? In one such experiment, Bonawitz and colleagues (2011) gave children an unfamiliar toy to play with. Children who were not given any instructions about the toy's function actually spent more time with it and discovered more of its features than those who were explicitly instructed about the toy and its features. Instead of playing with the toy that was clear and unambiguous in what it did, they were more curious about the toy that was ambiguous.

Uncertainty made them curious, which in turn drove their behavior; that is, they acted to explore ways to reduce or manage that uncertainty.

It is not simply that children act in and explore ways to reduce uncertainty when they find themselves in such situations, but that they actually prefer situations where there is more uncertainty. They seem to actively seek uncertainty.

Imagine a toy involving boxes and two levers, with only one of the levers being actually responsible for the toy's behavior (say, make a sound, or some sort of movement, and so on). Is a child more likely to play with the toy where she knows exactly the lever that makes the toy go, or the one where it is not clear which lever is responsible?

In 2007, Schulz and Bonawitz carried out a similar experiment and found out that, given a choice, children preferred to investigate the toy where it was not clear which lever controlled the outcome than the one where it was crystal clear. Children were more inclined to interact with toys for which it was *not* clear how the toy worked compared with toys that were unambiguously clear. They actively sought uncertainty.

Actively seeking toys with uncertain behavior is all good, but how do children play with such ambiguous and uncertain toys? Do they play with it randomly, or are there any patterns in how they play and explore with the toy?

In a follow-up study in 2011, Cook, Goodman, and Schulz presented children with a toy music box, which played tunes when certain beads were placed on it. Some beads made the toy play music, others did not. One group of children were shown clearly which beads made the toy play music, and which ones did not. For another group, this remained unclear.

Despite the ambiguity in the causal variable (i.e. which bead made the toy play music), children in the second group were astonishingly adept at designing simple experiments to identify the beads that made the toy play music. Those who were shown clearly tended to play with the toy indiscriminately without trying to figure out which beads were responsible. After all, they already knew. However, children for whom it was not clear selected and designed little experiments, functioning almost like little scientists engaged in generating and testing hypotheses as they played with the toy.

For years, we have underestimated the capabilities of children, and it is quite remarkable that children go about their play not in some random fashion but are more deliberate and systematic. What is even more remarkable is that their systematicity resembles how we go about doing science.

It is of course hard to imagine children as little scientists going about their work of making sense of the world. Another of my parents' favorite stories about my childhood was about one such hypothesis-testing behavior of mine. I have absolutely no memory of this, but this story has been told so many times that I almost feel it is my own memory. When I got my first tricycle, I was absolutely thrilled, and enjoyed riding it. One evening, when my dad came home from work, he found me in the garden all covered in mud. Nothing unusual there, except I had dug a large hole and buried my tricycle in it. He could tell that I had done so because only the handlebars were sticking out. When he asked me to explain what I was up to, I told him I wanted more tricycles, and thought that if I could sow the tricycle, perhaps I could get a tree of tricycles. I was curious, and it was a hypothesis worth testing. If only tricycles grew on trees.

Once again, I was not abnormal, for this kind of hypothesis-testing behavior in children is well-documented in developmental psychology literature (Gopnik, Meltzoff, and Kuhl 1999; Schulz, Gopnik, and Glymour 2007). They not only demonstrate an ability to unravel variables when causality is unclear but also make effective use of available information to comprehend correct causal structures (Gopnik and Schulz 2007). For her groundbreaking research in understanding children's long underestimated cognitions and capabilities, the psychologist Alison Gopnik was awarded the 2023 Rumelhart Prize, widely considered as the Nobel Prize in Cognitive Science (Gopnik 1996; Gopnik 2016; Gopnik, Griffiths, and Lucas 2015; Gopnik, Meltzoff, and Kuhl 1999; Gopnik 2009).

In a nutshell, we now know that children tend to spend more time figuring out toys that are ambiguous, and if given a choice, they actually prefer to play with toys that seem ambiguous. Ambiguity and uncertainty drive their curiosity. As if this alone were not remarkable enough, we now also know that when such curiosity turns into action, it does so in a systematic way. Children play in a way that helps them figure out how cause-and-effect relationships work in their world.

Uncertainty drives curiosity. Curiosity acts to reduce uncertainty. And such action mirrors much like what scientists do.

The Curious Adult

It turns out older children and adults are not that different. The propensities may change but the pattern remains the same: uncertainty drives curiosity, and curiosity acts to reduce uncertainty and drives learning.

In a 2009 study with undergraduate students, Nicolas Campion and colleagues studied the effect of inconsistency in narrative texts on curiosity. They gave a group of students several short stories to read. In some stories, characters behaved consistently throughout, whereas in others, they did not behave in a manner that would be expected given the premise of the story. For example, if the premise of the story had Jack set up to be a computer scientist with no interest in dressing up nicely for work, then in the consistent version of the story Jack would behave by putting on something casual before going to work. In the inconsistent version, he would make an effort to put on fancy clothes and take care in styling and looking good before going to work, and in the neutral version, he would just carry on without any overt support for or deviation from the premise.

As students read through several of the three types of texts presented to them in a random manner, Campion and colleagues found that students spent more time reading the inconsistent texts, like the children who spent more time on uncertain toys. And just like those children, undergraduate students also reported more interest in the inconsistent texts than the consistent and neutral texts.

Inconsistent texts create an uncertainty, which toys with us; it provokes us, piques our interest, and makes us curious. It is not surprising therefore that a similar dynamic plays out in more formal learning contexts as well, such as when learning from Productive Failure.

In 2014, my colleagues Katharina Loibl and Nikol Rummel, I believe, were the first ones to demonstrate this in two classroom-based studies. Using the same materials I had developed for my studies on teaching statistics (specifically, the concept of standard deviation described in Chapter 1), and adapting them to the German context, they gave one group of students explicit instruction on the concept of standard deviation, and then asked them to solve practice problems. Recall from Chapter 1 that I called this the Direct Instruction condition, or instruction followed by problem solving. The other group followed the Productive Failure model, where they solved the problem before receiving instruction.

From the lens of uncertainty, the Direct Instruction group had all the information required to solve the problem, and therefore they experienced little or no uncertainty. In contrast, the Productive Failure group was by definition a high uncertainty condition because students lacked the information required to solve the problems.

What did they find? Students in the Productive Failure condition reported significantly higher curiosity to learn from instruction than the group that received direct instruction.

Think of it this way. Suppose you are going into a lecture on a new topic, and the teacher starts by asking you how interested you are in learning that topic. Compare this with the situation where the teacher throws you in an uncertain situation first by asking you to solve a problem, a problem that is designed in a way that you would not be able to solve correctly, and then asks you how interested you are in learning the topic. In which case would you be more interested, more curious? Intuitively, you might say the latter.

What Loibl and Rummel showed was that your intuition is supported by experimental evidence, that uncertainty in the Productive Failure condition even though it initially led to failure made students more curious to learn from subsequent instruction than those who were given that instruction right off the bat.

What was even more remarkable was that Productive Failure students remained more curious even after receiving instruction. Even though their thirst for knowledge was quenched after learning the correct solution, they remained more curious than their counterparts, which is an amazing finding from an educational point of view. After all, who does not want to design learning in ways that not only invoke curiosity but also maintain it beyond learning?

But wait, it gets better. Wouldn't it be even more spectacular if there was a direct link between curiosity and learning, that uncertainty not only drives curiosity but also predicts learning? For this, we turn to a fascinating set of studies by my colleagues Marianna Lamnina and Catherine Chase.

In 2017, Lamnina and Chase worked with community college students learning about one of the more difficult concepts in physics: moment of inertia. The goal of the lesson was to teach students how the mass, radius, and length of a cylinder determine how fast it rolls down a ramp. They set up several demonstrations where cylinders of different mass, radius, and length were placed on a ramp and allowed to roll as the ramp was raised, systematically varying only one of the three variables (mass, radius, length) at a time.

However, the experimental trick was not in the demonstrations but what happened *before* students watched these demonstrations. They divided them into two groups. As before, one group received direct instruction from the teacher about the concept, where the teacher explained the order in which cylinders would go down the ramp and why. These students were given all the information to understand the demonstrations, and therefore experienced low or no uncertainty. The other group was first asked to predict the order in which the cylinders would go down the ramp, and only then observe what happened in the demonstration. These students made predictions *before* watching the demonstration, making them inherently more uncertain.

Afterward, all students took a quiz where they had to solve problems on the targeted concept. As expected, they found that the inherently more uncertain learning condition led to greater curiosity compared to inherently more certain direct instruction. And more importantly, students who reported being more curious learned more. Two years later in 2019 in a follow-up study, Lamnina and Chase replicated and extended these findings to high school students learning two other concepts in physics.

Overall, therefore, be it children playing with toys, or college students reading texts, or high school and college students learning various concepts in physics, these studies suggest that there are multiple ways in which we can manipulate uncertainty to trigger situational interest and curiosity, with the most recent evidence suggesting that students with higher triggered curiosity perform better on assessments of learning.

Although this body of work is small but growing, the pattern of effects across several age groups, contexts, and domains is remarkably consistent. Plus, as we shall see in the following section, evidence from neuroimaging studies is lending more explanatory weight to the pattern of effects.

The Curious Brain

Do you know which letter was the last one to be added to the English alphabet? Or which instrument was invented to sound like a human singing? Or what is the name of the galaxy that our planet Earth is part of?

I had no idea about the answers to the first two questions. I found the questions themselves so intriguing, which obviously made me highly curious about the answers. As for the third question, I was less curious as I could answer it easily.

In 2009, Min Jeong Kang, Colin Camerer, and colleagues were among the first ones to study how our brains respond to trivia questions like these, not because they liked trivia per se (they may well do), but more because they wanted to study the levels of curiosity such questions invoke, and the parts of the brain that are recruited in the process. They wanted to see what happens in our brain when we feel curious.

To do this, they ran a brain imaging study using an fMRI machine. FMRI stands for Functional Magnetic Resonance Imaging, and an fMRI machine allows researchers to see which brain regions are activated as people engage in mental activities like seeing, thinking, selecting, and so on.

Kang and colleagues selected 40 trivia questions on a diverse set of topics designed to make people feel either curious or not that curious at all, just like what the questions above did to me.

Once participants were inside an fMRI machine, the 40 trials began. For each trial, participants were shown a trivia question, and asked to silently guess the answer. After making a guess, they were asked to rate how curious they were about the actual answer. They were also asked to rate how confident they were about their own guesses. Then, each trivia question was shown again, followed by the correct answer so that participants could see whether their guess was correct or not. This procedure was repeated until all 40 trivia questions were exhausted. After coming out of the fMRI machine, participants were asked to recall and share their original answers to the questions.

They found that for questions for which participants had reported high curiosity, parts of the brain typically associated with anticipation of reward lit up. These areas usually light up when we are anticipating that something good or rewarding is about to happen. Imagine how you feel just before watching a concert or a movie you've been eager to see, or waiting for a meal at a restaurant you've been planning to eat at – that is the kind of anticipation that gets registered in this region of the brain.

This was how the brain behaved during the anticipation bit. Next, as you know, came the reveal.

When participants finally got the answers to the trivia questions, the parts of their brains that are typically associated with memory, learning, and understanding language became active. Even more telling was that these areas were more strongly activated when the initial guess was incorrect than when it was correct. In other words, if you had initially answered a trivia question wrong, areas associated with memory and learning were activated more strongly when you finally saw the correct answer than if you had answered it correctly to begin with. There was greater learning in the brain from failure than success.

Simply put, what these findings suggest is that curiosity sets up an anticipation of a reward (for the correct answer), and once we receive the reward (the correct answer), the brain acts to consolidate our memory so that we learn the correct answer. And this learning is stronger if we had initially failed than succeeded.

And such learning from failure is also stickier. Even after 10 days, Kang and colleagues found that participants could remember the correct answers to the questions they had initially guessed incorrectly, showing that failure can make us curious to learn the correct answer, and once we learn it, it sticks for longer as well.

In 2014, University of California, Davis, scientists Matthias Gruber and colleagues extended Kang and colleagues' findings to incidental learning. They followed the same trivia-style method of examining brain behavior using fMRI. But with a clever twist. In the time between showing them the trivia question and its answer, they inserted pictures of random peoples' faces, a task that had nothing to do with the trivia questions. They simply wanted to see if and how well participants would remember these random faces later. The result? Participants remembered the faces better when they were shown after trivia questions they were more curious about than those they were less curious about. In other words, the more a trivia question made someone curious, the more likely they were to remember a random face shown to them before the answer was revealed.

It seems that in a heightened state of curiosity, we not only learn that which we are curious about, but also other things incidentally in our environment that we may pay attention to or take note of. When we are curious, our brain gets into a super-absorptive state; we tend to learn better what we are curious to learn, but also things we are not curious about.

While research programs led by scientists such as Min Jeong Kang and Matthias Gruber are paving the way to better understandings of how curiosity plays out in the brain, and the pathways by which it results in better memory and learning, there is still a lot of work to be done in understanding the underlying mechanisms. However, it is also becoming increasingly clear that these brain imaging studies, along with the behavioral studies discussed earlier, are pointing to the importance of stimulating curiosity to bring about deeper learning.

Learning methods that stimulate interest and curiosity set us up for learning. Productive Failure does exactly that.

It turns out the letter J was the last letter to be added to the English alphabet, and the violin was invented to sound like a human singing, and now that I have found these out, I am sure I will not forget them for a long time to come. The Milky Way is the name of our galaxy, something I already knew and it too will probably stay with me.

Mastery Orientation

One of the ways curiosity sets us up for learning is by changing our orientation toward instruction. Scientists have studied how we orient toward learning opportunities by examining the kinds of goals we bring into learning situations.

Imagine two high school students: Alex and Jamie. Both are assigned a number of math problems, some easy, others hard. Alex dives into the hard problems, intrigued by their complexity, seeing them as an opportunity to learn and grow. He is not afraid of not being able to solve them correctly, enjoying the challenge itself. Jamie, on the other hand, is more focused on ensuring he does not appear stupid or less competent than his peers. So he decides to tackle easier problems instead. The question is: Given the same task, why do Alex and Jamie approach it so differently?

Based on the seminal works of scientists such as Carol Dweck, John Nicholls, Andrew Elliot, and Judith Harackiewicz, the answer lies in their respective goals, often called *achievement goals* (Dweck and Leggett 1988; Elliot and Harackiewicz 1996).

Achievement Goals

Achievement goals are the goals we bring into a learning situation, and guide our behavior in that situation. They play a pivotal role in shaping how we approach, engage in, and reflect upon learning tasks. If we adopt Alex's goals, we are more focused on learning and mastery. The goal there is to really understand and grow, so we do not mind, or even invite, challenges and struggle to deeply understand and learn something. Such goals are called *mastery goals*. We could also call them quite simply learning goals. If, however, we adopt Jamie's goals, we are more likely to focus on demonstrating some successful performance, to at least not be worse than our peers, and if we can perhaps outperform others. Such goals are called *performance goals*.

Several studies, including meta-analyses, suggest that students with a mastery goal orientation tend to favor learning strategies that promote deep understanding of the material (Hulleman et al. 2010; Wirthwein et al. 2013). These are the students who would tell you, "I really want to get to the essence of this topic, not just memorize facts." They are typically confident, less anxious, genuinely interested in learning, and more likely to show resilience in the face of challenges, often seeing setbacks as opportunities to grow. They are also good at adjusting their strategies when things get tough. Their intrinsic motivation – the drive that comes from genuine interest or enjoyment – often remains high because their goal is to truly understand deeply, not just skate by.

Not surprisingly therefore, mastery goal students shine especially bright when taking on challenging problems. In other words, they tend to outperform performance goal students especially when things get difficult or challenging, suggesting that wanting to deeply understand something not only helps in learning but also in applying that knowledge to new, challenging situations.

Performance goals need not be all bad, however. It really depends upon what kinds of performance goals one has (Elliot and McGregor 2001). Although performance goals students are basically motivated to show that they are competent, the degree to which they pursue these goals could differ. One student may want to show competence by wanting to outperform others. They want to be the best performer or top scorer in the class. Another student might simply be content with not doing more poorly than others. They want to avoid poor performance or low scores, especially compared to their peers. The former wants to approach the upside, the latter wants to avoid the downside. That is why they are called *performance-approach* and *performance-avoidance* goals, respectively.

It should not be surprising that performance-avoidance students often do not fare well in their studies (Hulleman et al. 2010; Wirthwein et al. 2013). They tend to feel negative emotions like test anxiety and a lack of interest in the subject. So, rather than being driven by a love for learning, they are driven by the fear of failure. Research is solid on this front.

In contrast, Elliot and Harackiewicz (1996) found that performance-approach students often do well in terms of grades. But, there was a catch. Even though they may do well on tests and exams, they often deploy and rely on surface-level learning tactics – like memorizing rather than deeply understanding. The goal is to perform, not necessarily to learn. Moreover, they might avoid asking for help when they need it or even resort to tactics that make things look good on the surface (like not tackling challenging problems) to maintain their status.

So, which types of goals are best to adopt? Historically, it has been clear that we should adopt mastery goals and not performance goals. This is intuitive and should not come as a surprise. Recent years have seen this more hotly debated, however, largely because of evidence suggesting that sometimes performance approach goals can be good to have, too.

For example, in a study tracking university students from their first semester to graduation, Harackiewicz and colleagues (2002) found that a combination of both mastery and performance-approach goals can be beneficial. Consistent with past findings, they found that students who adopted mastery goals were more likely to enjoy lectures, and express greater interest and engagement in their learning. On the other hand, students who adopted performance-approach goals received higher grades over the entire academic career. Mastery goals seemed to drive interest and engagement, performance-approach goals seemed to drive exam grades and overall GPA. But here's the key insight from their study: neither goal drove both interest and performance.

Given that success in college and university contexts depends on both performance and interest, Harackiewicz and colleagues argued that adopting both types of goals might be more beneficial to achieve complementary and synergistic effects on interest and performance. Balancing a genuine thirst for knowledge and mastery with the human instinct to excel among peers could be a better driver of learning than either of them alone.

The debate on the absolute size and relative effects of different types of achievement goals on academic outcomes continues, with the recent meta-analyses by Hulleman et al. (2010), Huang (2012), and Wirthwein et al. (2013), giving mastery goals an edge while also acknowledging the need for a dual goal – mastery and performance-approach – strategy.

As we go about our lives, we are capable of taking on different kinds of achievement goals. In school, we may have mastery goals for learning arts but performance goals for learning math, or vice versa. At work we may have performance goals; in our hobbies we may adopt mastery goals. Or even within a domain, depending upon the situation, we may switch from one goal orientation to another. Our achievement goals may vary over time as well. Achievement goals are therefore not mere checkpoints on a to-do list; they influence our motivation, strategies, and ultimately, the outcomes of our learning endeavors. Achievement goals are like compasses guiding our learning journeys. The directions we set, whether toward mastery or performance, can significantly influence our motivation, strategies, and eventual outcomes.

Against this backdrop of variability and adaptability in how we are able to adopt different types of goals, scientists have also started to ask the related, and perhaps a more powerful question: Can we design learning environments to make students adopt more mastery-oriented goals? The studies discussed thus far take the goal orientation of the students as a given, an incoming characteristic, like gender or prior knowledge or academic ability. In this view, there isn't much one can do about it. Some students are more productively goal oriented than others, and that's that. However, if we take the view that we can design the context and the learning environment to even temporarily change goal orientations, nudging them toward more productive orientations such as mastery goals, exploit the human capacity for adaptation, then maybe we can optimize learning even more. And because mastery goals are associated with deep learning strategies, inducing mastery goals is an important, exciting, and growing area of research.

Inducing Mastery Goals

This is where the work of learning scientists Daniel Belenky and Timothy Noakes-Malach (2012) comes in. In what was a first demonstration of the power of inducing mastery goals, they divided students into two conditions: Tell-and-Practice and Invention. The Tell-and-Practice condition was similar to the Direct Instruction method we have discussed in the earlier chapters. The Invention condition was similar to the Productive Failure method. Before, during, and after learning, they administered surveys on students' mastery goal orientation, asking questions like, "In this class, it is important for me to understand the content as thoroughly as possible" (adapted from Elliot and McGregor 2001). Three key findings emerged:

1. *The Wanting to Master Effect:* Based on the pre-survey, students who truly want to understand and master the material – in other words, adopted mastery goals – were more likely to apply what they learned. In fact, for every unit increase in their desire for mastery, they had a 45% better chance of successfully tackling new problems. Simply wanting to master material was powerful. Performance-approach goals did not have the same effect.

2. *The Invention Boost:* The Invention method led students to think more deeply about the problem and also made them care more about truly understanding their solution. In essence, the act of inventing made them more inclined toward adopting mastery-oriented goals, suggesting that the way we are taught can shape our learning goals. Invention induced a mastery orientation; Tell-and-Practice did not.

3. *Invention Meets Mastery:* The final twist? For students who already had a high mastery goal orientation, the type of instruction (Invention or Tell-and-Practice) did not matter much – they excelled either way. But for those *not* naturally inclined toward mastering material, the Invention method made a world of difference. Mastery goal induction helped them the most. These students were much more likely to successfully apply their knowledge to new problems compared to their counterparts who were just told the solution.

In a nutshell: if you already have the desire to master material, that is golden. But if that desire is not naturally strong, being encouraged to invent and explore on your own can bridge the gap. Learning methods like Productive Failure have the power of fostering a genuine desire for understanding and deep learning.

As we saw earlier, these learning methods not only give us powerful affective boosts but also stimulate interest and curiosity to want to learn from subsequent instruction. And if such interest and curiosity nudges us toward mastery goal orientation, it sets us up for deep learning.

But the journey is far from easy. Learning through Productive Failure is challenging. Emotions run high, but that may not necessarily be a bad thing for learning.

Emotional Rollercoaster

A rare thing happened after a recent keynote I gave at a conference in Switzerland. My talk was on Productive Failure, and as is typical, I took questions after my talk. After the session ended, one of the conference participants, who had already asked me a question, came up to me with a follow-up question. We discussed for a bit; after she was satisfied with my response, she thanked me, and started to leave. But after a few steps, she stopped, turned back and walked toward me. With the gentlest of voices, she said: by the way, there's one more thing; it's not carpenting, it's carpentry.

You see, in one of my slides I had used an example of a carpenter working with his apprentice to illustrate a key takeaway for the audience about learning. And I had repeatedly used the word "carpenting" to describe the activity of "carpentry" in the slide. I suppose I must have said "carpenting" several times. But it gets worse. I have used that slide in many of my talks and keynotes, so really I must have been saying the wrong word for two decades now. In my keynotes! Yet, no one, not once, ever has come up to me and said, it's not carpenting, it's carpentry.

So, when she so delicately corrected me, I remember being flushed, my pupils dilating, my heartbeat rising, yet outwardly I kept my calm as best I could manage. I knew she was right, but I couldn't help feeling embarrassed and ashamed, especially to think of all the years I had gone on making a fool of myself.

I stood corrected. I thanked her for it. It was a powerful moment of learning, and now I cannot imagine I will ever forget that it's not carpenting, but carpentry.

It was not simply the correction, but also the emotive charge attached to it. Had I read the same thing somewhere, I would have learned it, but the emotional dynamics that unfolded in that brief but powerful learning moment made sure that the lesson was deeply learned, and will never be forgotten.

That is the power of emotion, over and above cognition.

When we encounter emotionally charged situations – whether they're painful, joyful, or downright embarrassing – our feelings act like a highlighter pen, marking those moments as "important" in our memory banks. It's like your brain and emotions are tag-teaming to say, "This one's a keeper; let's remember it for next time!" Your emotions aren't just reacting to the situation; they're shaping how you respond, learn, and remember.

Simply put, how you feel deeply impacts how well you learn and remember things. When something grabs your emotional attention, your body and brain kick into high gear – making you more focused, enhancing your memory, and helping you make sense of what's happening.

If emotions can be so powerful, what if we could harness them, maybe they can be a secret weapon for supercharging your learning?

For the longest time, the study of emotions had not been the focus of scientists. Study of logic, reason, rationality, even irrationality prevailed. Study of emotions and feelings, not so much, as they were seen as phenomena that could not be studied scientifically. Thankfully, things have changed, and the momentum is growing toward understanding the critical role of emotions in human behavior in general, and learning in particular.

Emotions in the Brain

The human brain is particularly attuned to processing emotional stimuli. People are generally quicker to notice things filled with emotion, like a scared face, among other distractions, and indeed studies show that emotional events tend to form stronger and enduring memories. In fact, brain imaging studies show that emotional events cause stronger brain activity in areas related to our sensory perception. Sensory perception is of course not just limited to what we see but also what we hear, and all other senses, prioritizing the brain to process emotion-laden information, leading to a cascade of physiological and cognitive changes.

But how exactly do our brains prioritize, store, and recall emotional experiences so vividly? Enter the amygdala (the emotional epicenter), the frontoparietal network (the attention arbiter), and the hippocampus (the memory maestro), for it is a delicate coordination between the three that makes it all happen.

Amygdala: The Emotional Epicenter. Picture this: you are watching a thrilling movie, your heart thudding in your chest as the music swells and a character wanders through a dim, eerie hallway. That rush of emotion is processed by the amygdala, an almond-shaped cluster nestled deep within the brain. It springs into action, assessing the emotional weight of the experience, whether it is the fluttering excitement of a first date or the tense anticipation of a cinematic scare, or being corrected for using the wrong word. Traditionally linked with processing threats, recent theories propose a more extensive role for the amygdala in quickly determining the relevance of a stimulus for our emotional needs. This determination allows the amygdala to signal to the sensory cortex and frontoparietal network – the arbiters of attention – asking them to pay more attention to the emotionally charged event.

Frontoparietal Network: The Attention Arbiters. In our daily lives, we are constantly bombarded with a multitude of stimuli. Not all stimuli are treated or attended to equally. If they were, we would be overwhelmed. Thanks to the frontoparietal network located in the front and upper sides of the brain, not everything gets equal billing. Emotional events, like the suspenseful movie scene, are given priority, thanks to a timely nudge from the amygdala. Our focus then narrows, filtering out the mundane – the feel of popcorn in our hand or the hum of the refrigerator – centering our attention on the emotionally charged moment. The frontoparietal network and the amygdala work together to heighten our awareness and readiness to respond to the emotionally significant event unfolding before us.

Hippocampus: The Memory Maestro. The hippocampus is the brain's chief for memory and learning. Damage to the hippocampus often leads to amnesia, causing issues in recalling past memories or forming new ones. After the amygdala has processed the emotion and the frontoparietal networks have honed our attention, the hippocampus steps in to encode the experience, transforming the emotional event into a lasting memory. Think about that spine-chilling scene from the movie – it's etched into your memory, ready to be recalled in vivid detail thanks to the teamwork of the hippocampus and the amygdala.

Memory processing includes three stages: encoding (processing information when first perceived), consolidation (storing the information in the brain), and retrieval (recalling the information). Emotions influence each stage. As noted, our perception and attention are more focused on emotionally relevant information, leading to a preference in encoding this information, resulting in better memorization of the emotional aspects of a scene.

After encoding, memories are not immediately solidified; they undergo a consolidation process. Emotions influence this process, too. A strong emotional response triggers physiological arousal, allowing the amygdala to influence hippocampal activation and strengthen specific memory traces, meaning emotionally relevant events benefit from stronger consolidation, which in turn increases the chance of later recall.

In short, neurobiological evidence indicates that key cognitive functions such as attention, memory, and learning are deeply intertwined with emotional processes. The amygdala, frontoparietal network, and hippocampus perform an intricate and harmonious dance. The amygdala kicks things off, assessing and processing the emotional heft of an experience, and signaling to the frontoparietal network to steer our attention, spotlighting the emotional event amidst the clamor of everyday stimuli. Finally, the hippocampus encodes the experience, crafting a memory imbued with emotional resonance, ready to be retrieved and re-lived. This collaboration ensures that the more emotionally charged an experience, the more vividly captured, stored, and recalled it is, weaving a rich, emotional tapestry through the narrative of our lives.

That's why I will never forget being corrected so publicly that it is not carpenting, but carpentry.

The Emotional Spectrum

When exploring the role of emotions in learning, one might instinctively categorize emotions as either positive – such as wonder, joy, happiness – or negative, like shame, anger, and frustration. It is common to assume that fostering positive emotions and minimizing negative ones is optimal, associating negative emotions with adverse outcomes and positive ones with beneficial results. However, this may not always hold true.

That positive emotions can enhance learning and well-being is not in doubt. Several research programs converge on this effect. For example, when a teacher uses positive reinforcement, interactive activities, or engages students' interests, it fosters a positive environment that can lead to better memory retention and problem-solving skills. This aligns with the "Broaden and Build Model" developed by Fredrickson (2001), which argues that positive emotions expand one's awareness and encourage innovative thinking, while negative emotions limit and narrow one's focus. Essentially, feeling positive emotions like joy, interest, and contentment can help students to see the bigger picture and think more creatively, while negative emotions such as fear and anger can cause students to tunnel vision and miss out on potential solutions or connections. This is crucial in the learning process as it allows students to approach problems and new information with a more open and receptive mindset (Fredrickson and Losada 2005).

Educators and researchers are increasingly recognizing the significance of emotions in learning and are adapting teaching methods and classroom environments accordingly. However, the key factor may not be the emotions themselves, but rather the students' emotional responses to these feelings. This concept, known as meta-emotion – a feeling about a feeling – can involve obvious same-valence reactions, such as feeling positive about positive emotions or negative about negative ones.

Surprisingly, opposite-valence emotions can also occur. For instance, a student excited about a science project (positive emotion) might fear that their happiness could jinx the outcome, leading to failure (negative meta-emotion). Alternatively, a student struggling with math problems (negative emotion) might view the challenge as an opportunity for growth, feeling motivated to persevere (positive meta-emotion).

In summary, while it is natural to associate positive emotions with favorable outcomes and negative emotions with adverse consequences, the reality is more nuanced. Both positive and negative emotions, as well as the meta-emotions they trigger, play pivotal roles in the learning journey. Acknowledging and understanding these emotions can lead to more effective teaching strategies and learning experiences.

Emotions in Failure

The heavy weight of expectation is a peculiar thing; it can serve either as wings to soar or shackles that bind you to the ground. For Tanmay, a bright high school student from a small city in India, it felt like the latter when he failed to clear the Indian Institute of Technology entrance exams, the most prestigious engineering entrance test in India. The news was not only a blow to his self-esteem but also a disappointment to his friends and family who had sky-high expectations from him. The failure, coupled with the emotional turmoil of shame, suffocated him.

Tanmay found himself at a crossroads. He could either wallow in self-pity or channel those negative emotions into something constructive. He chose the latter. He embraced the discomfort he felt and channeled his negative emotions into engaging in meaningful projects. Over time, this led him to a doctoral degree at ETH Zurich, where he worked with me to explore, among other things, the role of emotions in learning from Productive Failure.

And who better than Tanmay then to put the full force of science behind it to study emotions as they unfold in Productive Failure.

Recall that Productive Failure involves two phases: a problem-solving phase followed by an instruction phase (see Figure 2.3). In 2022, Tanmay designed an experiment to study how emotions unfold as learners experience failure in the problem-solving phase of Productive Failure. He focused on the problem-solving phase, because this is the phase where learners experience failure in problem solving, making it a goldmine of temporarily induced emotions like shame, anger, confusion, frustration, surprise, interest, happiness, and so on.

As expected, he found that students went through an emotional roller-coaster during the problem-solving phase, experiencing complex and diverse sequences of positive and negative emotions. Emotions such as shame, anger, and disgust were frequently present in the problem-solving phase, as were emotions such as confusion, surprise, and happiness. The next question he asked was: How do these positive and negative emotions relate with the quality of solutions students produced during the problem-solving phase and also on three learning outcomes: the How (procedural knowledge), the Why (conceptual understanding), and the Apply (transfer to novel problems)?

He found that shame was positively correlated with the quality of solutions students produced during the problem-solving phase. That is, the more shame they experienced, the better the quality of solutions they produced, a result that is surprising and counterintuitive, but one has to remember that all of this is happening within the safe confines of Productive Failure. It turns out, shame can propel students to work toward their problem-solving goals. The same goes for other emotions like anger, disgust, and confusion, which can serve as triggers for persistence in problem solving, and in turn deep learning. Negative emotions such as shame, anger, disgust, and confusion can be good for learning, provided they are designed for in a safe and supportive environment such as Productive Failure.

At the same time, Tanmay found that positive emotions such as happiness do not necessarily lead to better learning outcomes. Happiness was positively correlated only with the How problems. Recall that these are the kinds of problems where students had to remember the recipe or the steps or the procedure to solve it. They had learned those procedures, and they used those procedures to solve the problems. However, happiness was negatively correlated with performance on the Why and Apply problems. In other words, happiness experienced during the problem-solving phase negatively influenced how well they understood the concepts (the Why) and their ability to transfer to novel contexts (the Apply). Again, a surprising and counterintuitive finding. Positive emotions such as happiness can be bad for learning, even when experienced in a safe and supportive environment such as Productive Failure.

Sometimes in life, bad can come from good, and good can come from bad. As it is in life, it is in learning. Positive or negative emotions, when experienced safely and appraised appropriately, can result in better learning outcomes.

In Chapter 3, we saw how the problem-solving phase of Productive Failure serves to activate prior knowledge even as students fail to solve the problem correctly. In Chapter 4, we saw how this failure is critical for building an awareness of a gap between what we know and what we need to know. In Chapter 5, we saw how awareness of the gap drives our affect – needs, interest, curiosity, motivation, and emotions – to learn from subsequent instruction. The problem-solving phase therefore works to set up the activation, awareness, and affect, making us ready for the instruction phase of Productive Failure.

We are now ready for assembly, where a teacher or an expert can bootstrap failure for deep learning. The science of assembly is therefore the focus of Chapter 6.

Key Takeaways

In Productive Failure, we recognize the power of failure, and design for it in a safe way, in a way that supercharges our affective selves in four ways:

1. **The need for closure.** Awareness of a gap drives us to bridge the gap. This is where the affective boost levels ABLe 1–4 come into play. They get you started, keep you motivated, supporting you all the way as you generate multiple ways of solving the problem, one after another, until you are ready, ready for the final step.

2. **Situational interest and curiosity.** The final step works like a cliffhanger. It piques your interest and curiosity, making you want to learn from subsequent instruction.

3. **Mastery orientation.** Situational interest and curiosity not only just make you want to learn but do so with a mastery goal orientation, where you really want to understand what worked, what did not, and learn deeply from instruction.

4. **Emotional rollercoaster.** But this journey is not easy. It is a complex dynamic that takes you through the ups and downs of positive and negative emotions. These emotions, when designed within a safe and supportive environment, draw on an emotive charge to drive deeper learning, where even negative emotions can be associated with positive learning outcomes.

6 | Assembly

Niji was a smart and motivated boy. From early on, he was driven to succeed, especially since he bore the weight of familial responsibilities after his father's untimely passing. This sense of responsibility drove him to study and work hard, do well in his exams, graduate as the top student in his high school back in Malaysia, and win a prestigious scholarship for undergraduate studies in engineering in Singapore.

However, upon entering university, overconfidence and the allure of hostel life led Niji astray. He neglected his studies, focusing instead on friendships, fun, and frolic. Not surprisingly, his academics suffered, and he failed five out of eight subjects in his first year, including the dreaded mathematics. As a result, his struggle with mathematics continued into the second year, where he failed the subject again, jeopardizing his academic future.

With only one more chance to retake the paper, he faced the grim prospect of being expelled from university. Fear and anxiety set in. He knew he had to find a way to pass the dreadful subject. Distraught and alone, he did not know what to do or whom to turn to. Once a star high-school student, now facing humiliating failure.

With luck, he found help from an unlikely source: a new friend, a freshman, who was good at two things: soccer and mathematics, two things that do not always go together. This freshman had himself only just started his first year of engineering studies, but he was willing to help Niji with second-year mathematics.

They had two months to go through the entire second-year mathematics curriculum. The modus operandi was simple: the freshman dedicating his mornings to learning second-year mathematics by himself, so that in the afternoons and evenings he could teach Niji what he had learned. By carefully working through Niji's knowledge gaps in a motivating and encouraging manner, the freshman was somehow able to help Niji not only get over his phobia of mathematics, but also understand and sometimes even enjoy the subject.

When the results came out, Niji's professor was utterly astonished, remarking that had Niji tackled the original math paper similarly, he would have easily gotten an A. Niji had turned failure into success, albeit with a little help. A turning point in his engineering studies, Niji never looked back, successfully passing all his subjects, and graduating as a civil engineer.

To this day, Niji gives a lot of credit to his freshman friend, but he is himself too humble to recognize that a big part of why he could turn things around was precisely because his failures had made him ready to learn. He recognizes that now, which is why he shared his story with me.

After repeatedly failing at mathematics, Niji not only became acutely aware of his knowledge gaps, but also motivated to bridge those gaps. All he needed was someone to help him. After all, his failure was not so much a lack of ability but effort, and as trying as failing was, it prepared him for learning. He was ready to learn. The freshman turned up at the right time, and put things together for him. In other words, assembly.

That is not to say assembly is easy. It is hard. We struggle with it. Take, for example, the various shapes and forms assembly comes in: explaining something hard to a friend or colleague, having a discussion or debate, tutoring someone, or formally training or teaching people. In all these situations, we need to assemble knowledge, yet we often struggle to do so. This is because explaining the correct concepts and ideas in clear and engaging ways is the easier part. The harder part is to first activate prior knowledge of the person(s) you are explaining something to or discussing with or teaching, make them aware of the knowledge gaps, motivate and engage them, and then bootstrap their own knowledge for learning. Good assembly therefore starts with identifying the parts of the activated prior knowledge resources, and then using them for learning. That is what makes assembly hard, which is why developing this skill is important not just for teachers but for all of us.

It's like building stuff with Legos, which is why I call prior knowledge resources the Lego blocks of assembly.

Identify the Lego Blocks

A few years ago, I was invited to speak at a physics education seminar on the role of Productive Failure in the teaching and learning of physics. The audience consisted mainly of university lecturers who took a keen interest in physics education. It was my first time in front of an audience almost entirely of physicists, and I would be lying if I said I was not intimidated. Physicists are known to be super-smart. And blunt; they tell you like it is. And I was not sure what they would think of Productive Failure.

I started my talk with a standard problem from an introductory physics course. Suppose you have a smooth ball sliding on a smooth surface, as shown in Figure 6.1; is there a force acting on the ball in the direction of its motion? Note that the word "smooth" in physics is code for frictionless. In other words, assume the surfaces are so smooth that friction can be neglected.

When I put this question to novices, students, or even lay people, who do not have a background in physics, the answer typically is "Yes, there is a force acting on the ball in the direction of its motion." How else would the ball be sliding otherwise? This answer and line of argument is well documented, and represents what is commonly known as the *force-as-mover* misconception. If you thought the same, then you are in the majority.

Ask any physicist, however, and the answer will be a resounding "No." And that is the correct answer indeed. Once the ball has been set sliding, there is no force acting in the direction of its motion.

And that is indeed how all the physicists in the audience also answered. The next question I asked them was: If your students answer, "Yes, there is a force. . .," how would you respond? How would you teach them the correct conception?

Figure 6.1 Ball sliding on a smooth (frictionless) surface.

After some discussion, the consensus view emerged: Students are clearly wrong in their thinking, they should be explicitly corrected, and why there is no force acting on the ball in the direction of its motion should be explained.

They said: that is good physics.

I asked them if there was anything in students' reasoning that could be used for teaching the correct concept. Their response? No. Students were completely wrong. I urged them to think harder, not as physicists but as teachers, that perhaps there was something in the students' reasoning that could be a resource, a useful resource for learning. Again, the response was no. The physics here was simple, they argued, and students were completely wrong.

I then asked them to consider the following possibility. What if, instead of telling students they are completely wrong, we tell them the following: Your intuition is correct in the sense that there is indeed something the ball has in the direction of its motion, but that thing is not force. It is momentum, which is the product of the object's mass and its velocity.

There was a moment of silence. The moment turned into many. I let it sink in. And as it did, I could see that they started to understand where I was going with it. Some started nodding, others restrained a smile even. That was already more than I could ever hope for from an audience of physicists. And then suddenly, someone in the audience started clapping.

When asked why he was clapping, he said: that is good teaching.

When I pressed him further to explain why he thought that was good teaching, he elaborated: We are quick to see what is wrong in students' answers and reasoning. We are quick to zone in on that which is incorrect, so that we can quickly and robustly correct it. What we are not good at is analyzing students' incorrect answers to see if there are elements in those answers, bits and pieces and components, that could be used as building blocks for helping them learn the correct concept.

And then he added: That is the difference between doing good physics and good teaching.

Good teaching involves identifying parts of a student's thinking or reasoning that can be used for learning. Think of these parts as Lego blocks. These parts can be big or small, and can come in all sorts of (metaphorically speaking) shapes and sizes.

Now think of concepts as a configuration of Lego blocks. Students may have some Lego blocks, but obviously not all. The teacher or the expert of course has all the Lego blocks. The trick is to identify students' Lego blocks and assemble them with the expert Lego blocks.

In the above example, the student's Lego blocks were:

1. The object has some physical property in the direction of motion.
2. The physical property is force.

The expert Lego blocks are:

3. The physical property the object possesses in the direction of its motion is momentum.
4. The rate of change of momentum is force.

All the teacher now has to do is to assemble these four blocks together. I will get to how this can be done in the following section, but for now, let us continue on this idea of prior knowledge resources as Lego blocks.

The Lego Blocks of Lived Experience

The inspiration for thinking of our prior knowledge resources as Lego blocks comes from the pioneering work of Andrea diSessa (1993), who was the first to propose such a notion.

Imagine your mind as a vast collection of Lego blocks, each representing a piece of prior knowledge or an intuitive understanding of the world around us. He argued that as we experience the world, we develop simple Lego blocks of knowledge: self-contained nuggets of knowledge derived from our everyday experiences. The force-as-mover misconception we just covered is a perfect example. Or "things fall when dropped," or "it gets hotter the closer we are to a heat source," or " bigger causes result in bigger effects," and so on. These basic observations from daily life, through persistent repetition, result in fundamental units of knowledge, so much so that such knowledge requires no further proof or explanation. He called them "p-prims" or phenomenological primitives.

P-prims, or phenomenological primitives, are the fundamental units of our intuitive understanding, formed from our direct experiences with the world. They are akin to basic "facts" or "rules" that seem self-evident based on our daily experiences. They are axiomatic. Andrea diSessa theorized that p-prims are in fact the initial building blocks of our knowledge, which we constantly use, refine, and reconfigure to build more complex understandings.

Although diSessa's work was derived in the domain of physics, the idea of p-prims applies more widely in a diverse number of domains:

1. **Physics:** Consider the concept of inertia. A foundational p-prim here is the observation that an object at rest stays at rest unless acted upon. This p-prim emerges from everyday experiences, like noticing a ball only rolls when pushed. To understand inertia in a physics context, this p-prim is combined with others, like the understanding that force affects motion, leading to a more nuanced grasp of Newton's First Law of Motion.

2. **Mathematics:** In algebra, the concept of solving for an unknown variable can be traced back to simpler p-prims. One such p-prim is the basic understanding of balance, like balancing weights on a scale. This idea, when coupled with the p-prim that operations can reverse each other (like addition and subtraction), helps in grasping how to isolate variables in equations.

3. **Biology:** Understanding the food chain in biology starts with basic p-prims like "animals eat other living things to survive." This p-prim, combined with the observation that some creatures eat plants while others eat animals, helps form a more complex understanding of ecological relationships.

4. **History:** In history, understanding causality in events involves p-prims. For example, the idea that "complex events often have multiple causes" is a p-prim that can be used to understand complex historical events like wars, where economic, political, and social factors interplay.

5. **Literature:** In analyzing literature, a p-prim might be the understanding that "characters' actions reflect their motivations." This basic understanding helps in deeper literary analysis, allowing readers to infer themes and plot developments.

6. **Art:** In art, a p-prim could be the recognition that "colors evoke emotions." This foundational understanding is crucial in appreciating and creating art that resonates emotionally.

The theory of p-prims offers a fascinating lens to view learning as a dynamic, building-block process. Simple, intuitive pieces come together to build more complex understandings. Each domain has its own set of p-prims that we intuitively use and reconfigure to understand the world around us, much like how diverse structures can be built from Lego blocks, where you initially build with simple blocks of different shapes, sizes, and colors, but then start to experiment and create new structures (advanced concepts) by rearranging the blocks (p-prims) in novel ways.

The process of learning, therefore, involves not just identifying and accessing these Lego blocks, but also reconfiguring them to fit new contexts and expert understandings. Identifying and accessing Lego blocks comes from activating prior knowledge resources. Indeed this was a key realization I had during my doctoral studies: the first job of teaching is actually not to teach, but to prepare the novice to see, to prepare the learner to receive expert knowledge. And failure-based activation is remarkably good at identifying and accessing these Lego blocks of knowledge. And only after that can assembly take place, where the Lego blocks can be reconfigured, combined, and recombined with expert knowledge to achieve deeper, more comprehensive understandings.

We are now ready to see how we can assemble.

Assemble the Lego Blocks

Let us return to the physics example earlier in this chapter. Recall that in that example, the student's Lego blocks were:

1. The object has some physical property in the direction of motion.
2. The physical property is force.

And the expert Lego blocks were:

3. The physical property the object possesses in the direction of its motion is momentum.
4. The rate of change of momentum is force.

How do we assemble these Lego blocks together? One way an expert teacher may assemble for their students is as follows: Yes, your intuition is correct in the sense that the object does have a physical property in the direction of motion (Lego block 1). However, whereas you thought this physical property is force (Lego block 2), it is in fact a related property called momentum (Lego block 3). What you intuitively thought of as force is actually momentum. Now, the object has momentum, which on a frictionless surface will not change; that is, the object would continue to slide without losing speed. Given that force is the rate of change of momentum (Lego block 4), and momentum is not changing, the rate of change of momentum is therefore zero. That is, there is actually no force on the object in the direction of its motion.

Such assembly is not easy. What is easy is to dismiss students' answers and explanations as abjectly incorrect. What is easy is to explain the correct concepts and explanations. But this is not teaching at its finest. For that, one needs to develop the skill set to first resist the impulse to dismiss students' explanations as wrong, and instead to mine them for Lego blocks. And then figure out a way to use these Lego blocks together with expert knowledge to help students build deep knowledge and understandings.

This is precisely what makes Productive Failure such a powerful learning method. When designed well, it activates the Lego blocks, making them visible to both the learners and the teachers. To see this more tangibly, let us return to the mathematics class on the concept of standard deviation in Chapter 2. Recall the basketball players problem in Figure 2.1. Also recall the kinds of solutions students typically generate to solve that problem. Before proceeding further, it would be good to revisit the description of these solutions, so that the assembly will make sense.

If, however, you already remember the problem and the various solutions, then you would recall that students typically generated totals, averages, range, graphs, and varied calculations of game-to-game changes. While all the solutions are highly intuitive, they are either incorrect (e.g. totals, averages, range), or at best suboptimal (graphs, range, game-to-game changes). None of these solutions are correct from a canonical standpoint, which is calculated using the formula for standard deviation – the targeted concept for the lesson.

But these solutions are perfect for mining for Lego blocks. Here is a list of Lego blocks that one can easily find in students' solutions:

1. All data points should be used
2. Calculate the total

3. Calculate the average
4. Fluctuations in the points has something to do with consistency
5. There is something about differences between the data points (e.g. range, game-to-game differences) that tells us about fluctuations
6. Positive and negative fluctuations should not cancel each other
7. Individual fluctuations can be summed up to calculate total fluctuation
8. Dividing by the number of fluctuations gives the average fluctuation
9. The larger the average fluctuation, the greater the inconsistency

If you know your mathematics, then you would know that these Lego blocks represent almost all the components needed to assemble the correct formulation of standard deviation. And if you do not know this concept or have forgotten it, then let us assemble it step-by-step using the nine Lego blocks. My goal here is merely to give you the gist of the process of assembling the Lego blocks 1–9; the mathematics itself does not matter as much. I first describe each step, and then show the accompanying mathematical form.

1. The first step is indeed to use the Lego blocks 1–3 to calculate the mean.
   Amy's Total = 11 + 12 + 13 + 14 + 14 + 14 + 15 + 16 + 17 = 126
   Therefore, Amy's Mean = 1269 = 14
   Ben's Total = 12 + 14 + 17 + 15 + 11 + 16 + 12 + 13 + 16 = 126
   Therefore, Ben's Mean = 1269 = 14
2. Lego block 4 is insightful: we do need to calculate fluctuations.
3. Lego block 5 attempts at some ways of calculating these fluctuations, but not the canonical way, which is to calculate fluctuations as the difference between each point and the mean. So, instead of calculating game-to-game differences, all one needs to calculate is the difference between the points in each game and the mean.
   Amy's differences from the mean = $(11-14)$, $(12-14)$, $(13-14)$, $(14-14)$ ...
   Ben's differences from the mean = $(12-14)$, $(14-14)$, $(17-14)$, $(15-14)$ ...
4. Lego block 6 is a critical one. As some points will be above the mean and others below the mean, some differences will be positive and others negative, and adding them would mean the positive and

negative ones will cancel each other out. One way to avoid the cancellation effect is to consider only the magnitude of the difference, not whether it is positive or negative. This would ensure all differences are positive. And by the way, we call these differences deviations. Just a norm.

Amy's magnitude of differences from the mean = 3, 2, 1, 0, 0, 0, 1, 2, 3
Ben's magnitude of differences from the mean = 2, 0, 3, 1, 3, 2, 2, 1, 2

5. But that raises the possibility of other ways of making the deviations positive. How about squaring each deviation? We know that squaring a number always returns a positive number. Therefore squaring would make all the deviations positive.

Amy's squared differences from the mean = 9, 4, 1, 0, 0, 0, 1, 4, 9
Ben's squared differences from the mean = 4, 0, 9, 1, 9, 4, 4, 1, 4

6. Lego block 7 can then be used to sum all the squared distances.
Sum of Amy's squared deviations = $9+4+1+0+0+0+1+4+9 = 28$
Sum of Ben's squared deviations = $4+0+9+1+9+4+4+1+4 = 36$

7. Lego block 8 can be used to calculate the average of the sum of squared distances. What one ends up with thus far is the variance function.
Average of Amy's squared deviations = 28/9
Average of Ben's squared deviations = 36/9

8. The final Lego block comes from the expert. By taking the square root of the variance function, we get the standard deviation. Square rooting somewhat reverses the squaring of the distances, and brings the final measure in the same units as the data points.
Amy's standard deviation = 28/9 = 1.76
Average of Ben's squared deviations = 36/9 = 2

9. Lego block 9 closes the assembly: Ben's standard deviation is 2, which is greater than Amy's 1.76. Hence, Amy is the more consistent of the two.

There you have it. The entire canonical procedure for calculating standard deviation built almost entirely using the prior knowledge resources, or Lego blocks, generated by novices who do not even know the concept.

One could of course just explain the canonical steps, but when the canonical solution is built upon student-generated Lego blocks, it connects with their prior knowledge, making for deeper understanding and transfer.

However, the expert or the teacher has a big role to play in ensuring deeper understanding and transfer, and this comes from a process of comparing and contrasting that helps students see what is critical and what is not.

Comparing and Contrasting

Some of my favorite memes on social media are ones on punctuation, like the ones below.

I love cooking my family
  and my dog.
I love cooking, my family,
  and my dog.

I'm giving up drinking
  for a month.
I'm giving up. Drinking
  for a month.

It is time to eat friends.
It is time to eat, friends.

I'm sorry I love you.
I'm sorry. I love you.

In each pair of statements, everything is the same, except for the placement of the comma or the period. And how drastically, and hilariously, the meaning changes. Now you can teach someone about the importance of getting your punctuation right, or you can show contrasting statements like the above, and they will get the point immediately.

That is the power of well-designed contrasting cases. Research shows that we do not learn as well from single examples or cases, but when presented with (typically) two cases at once, cases that are similar and different in interesting ways, we tend to learn and transfer a lot better.

Mary L. Gick and Keith J. Holyoak (1983) were probably the first ones to systematically demonstrate how we fail to learn from single cases or examples, and why two cases are better than one. They started by having undergraduate students solve a problem called the radiation problem. You might want to try it too.

The Radiation Problem

Suppose you are a doctor faced with a patient who has a malignant tumor in his stomach. It is impossible to operate on the patient, but unless the tumor is destroyed the patient will die. There is a kind of ray that can be used to destroy the tumor. If the rays reach the tumor all at once at a sufficiently high intensity, the tumor will be destroyed. Unfortunately, at this intensity the healthy tissue that the rays pass through on the way to the tumor will also be destroyed. At lower intensities the rays are harmless to healthy tissue, but they will not affect the tumor either. What type of procedure might be used to destroy the tumor with the rays, and at the same time avoid destroying the healthy tissue?

In several of their experiments, the base rate of solving the radiation problem was about 10%; that is, one in ten undergraduate students were able to produce the most effective solution to the problem. One in ten. Meaning that the problem is quite a challenging one to solve.

Gick and Holyoak thought of helping students by giving them an analogous case and its solution in the form of a story. Therefore, prior to solving the radiation problem, they had students read a story, *The General*, about a military general who wanted to overthrow a dictator. Students were told they would be asked to recall the story after reading it, but they were not prompted to use the story for solving the radiation problem.

The General

A small country was ruled from a strong fortress by a dictator. The fortress was situated in the middle of the country, surrounded by farms and villages. Many roads led to the fortress through the countryside. A rebel general vowed to capture the fortress. The general knew that an attack by his entire army would capture the fortress. He gathered his army at the head of one of the roads, ready to launch a full-scale direct attack. However, the general then learned that the dictator had planted mines on each of the roads. The mines were set so that small bodies of men could pass over them safely, since the dictator needed to move his troops and workers to and from the fortress. However, any large force would detonate the mines. Not only would this blow up the road, but it would also destroy many neighboring villages. It therefore seemed impossible to capture the fortress. However, the general devised a simple plan. He divided his army into small groups and dispatched each group to the head of a different road. When all was ready he gave the signal and each group marched down a different road. Each group continued down its road to the fortress so that the entire army arrived together at the fortress at the same time. In this way, the general captured the fortress and overthrew the dictator.

You can probably make the connection between the story and the radiation problem. They share the same underlying principle: Just like the general divided his army into small groups and had them converge on the fortress from different directions, so too can the doctor divide the rays into lower intensity rays and have them converge on the tumor from different directions.

If students could spontaneously see this connection – the underlying principle – they should be able to transfer it from the story to the problem. Recall that transfer refers to our ability to learn something in one context (the story) and apply it in a novel context (the radiation problem). And that is exactly what happened. Reading the story followed by solving the radiation problem improved the percentage of students who could solve the radiation problem. The needle moved from 10% to about 30%. Giving students an analogous story, which was different in context but similar in the underlying principle, did improve problem-solving success. Although it tripled it from one in ten to three in ten, still, if you think about it, 30% is quite dismal.

Spontaneous transfer is hard.

Gick and Holyoak thought that perhaps most students were unable to see the underlying principle, which was necessary for spontaneous transfer to occur. So they took the logical next step, and made the principle explicit by adding the following sentence at the end of the story: "The general attributed his success to an important principle: if you need a large force to accomplish some purpose, but are prevented from applying such a force directly, many smaller forces applied simultaneously from different directions may work just as well."

Surely now students would be able to see the underlying principle and transfer it to solve the radiation problem. After all, making the principle explicit is almost like giving away the solution. Clearly, this ought to work. What did they find? Disappointment. The needle did not budge. Not a bit. Making the principle explicit did not significantly improve the solution rate. The needle stayed at 30%. Explicitly stating the principle had no effect.

This must be shocking, and if not, at least surprising. After all, much of Direct Instruction proceeds along a similar manner. Give students worked examples and clearly explain the underlying principles and explanations, and then have them solve problems. As intuitive as this method sounds, it is unfortunate that we are unable to spontaneously abstract the general principle from one example, even if it is stated explicitly for us.

If we cannot abstract from one example, then perhaps two examples are better than one? That was indeed the logic of the next set of experiments by Gick and Holyoak. They gave students two stories to read, each analogous to *The General*. After reading the stories, students solved the radiation problem. No other prompt, hint, or explicit principle was given. Students read the two stories and then solved the radiation problem.

This time the needle moved. Forty-five percent of the students could spontaneously transfer from the two stories to solve the radiation problem. And when the underlying principle was also explicitly stated after the two stories, students could make sense of the principle and use it to solve the radiation problem.

As we have seen throughout this book, merely giving a formal principle or a law is usually not effective because novices do not see what experts see. Here again, we find a similar pattern. Reading one analogous story followed by the underlying principle was not effective. Reading two analogous stories, however, was better at preparing students to see and understand the underlying principle. The effectiveness of stating the underlying principle is not in its provision but in the preparation preceding it. Two analogous stories plus the underlying principle helped 60% of the students solve the radiation problem, almost double the 30% rate of just the story and the problem, and almost six times the base rate of 10%.

Thus far, all the experiments focused on spontaneous transfer from either one story or two stories, with or without the underlying principle being made explicit. At no time were students explicitly prompted to use the story to solve the radiation problem. But when they were prompted to use the story to solve the problem, almost 80% of the students could solve the problem. When a prompt directed students to use the story, it aided transfer. Lacking that direction, transfer was hard.

In summary, Gick and Holyoak demonstrated that spontaneous transfer from one case or an example is exceedingly hard. Spontaneous transfer from two cases or examples is easier. Making underlying principles explicit has no effect when transferring from one case or example. The same is more effective when transferring from two cases or examples, because two cases allow for comparison and contrast. These contrasts help us notice what is similar and different, and facilitates the seeing of the underlying principle. Finally, a direct prompt to use the case or example to solve problems further facilitates transfer. Directed transfer is easier.

Good assembly should therefore take advantage of the power of comparison and contrast and directed transfer.

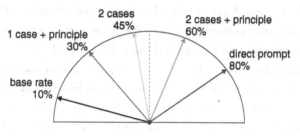

Figure 6.2 The dial of effects of one vs two cases on transfer.

Gick and Holyoak are not alone in demonstrating the power of learning from comparing cases. Much work has been done since their seminal studies, in laboratory experiments as well as in classrooms, and in a range of domains. Thirty years on, in 2013, Louis Alfieri, Timothy J. Nokes-Malach, and Christian D. Schunn conducted a meta-analysis of 57 such studies exploring more than 300 experimental effects, and found a robust and strong effect of learning from comparing cases over learning from single cases and traditional instruction, among others.

In the context of Productive Failure, learners generate multiple solutions to a challenging problem prior to instruction. I described one such set of solutions in detail in Chapter 2, and also earlier in this chapter when identifying the Lego blocks. A natural variation in the kinds of solutions students produce sets up opportunities for comparison and contrasts; these solutions can be compared with each other to see what is similar and different, what works and what does not.

However, as we have seen in the studies above, just because there are opportunities for comparing and contrasting does not mean that students spontaneously engage in them. At least it does not happen often enough to be an effective strategy. They need to be explicitly prompted. Therefore, a critical role of the teacher during assembly is to directly prompt students to compare and contrast their solutions with each other, and also with the correct solution. If the pattern of effects demonstrated by Gick and Holyoak and the meta-analysis above is true also for Productive Failure, then we should conjecture that such explicit prompting to compare and contrast should help students see the underlying principles and features of the targeted concept.

Katharina Loibl and Timo Leuders tested precisely this conjecture in their 2019 study on Productive Failure with 200 fifth graders learning fractions. As per Productive Failure, all students engaged in problem solving first. The experimental manipulation happened after the problem-solving phase, that is, in the instruction phase, as shown in Figure 6.3. Students were assigned to one of three conditions in the instruction phase: they studied only the correct solutions, or the correct and incorrect solutions, or the correct and incorrect solutions plus prompts for comparing and contrasting them. All students then took a posttest to test how well they had understood the concept and could transfer what they had learned.

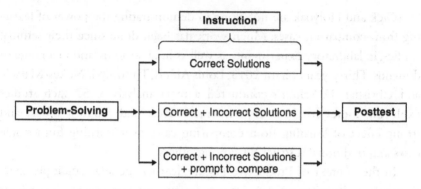

Figure 6.3   Adapted from Loibl & Leuders 2019 experimental design.

Consistent with the pattern of effects seen in the meta-analysis, Katharina and Leuders found that students in the prompted condition out-performed the rest on learning. The mere provision of correct and incorrect solutions was not enough; students had to be explicitly prompted to compare the two, to figure out what worked and what did not, and only then did they learn better.

To illustrate the power of comparisons, let us return to the solutions students produced to the basketball problem in Chapter 2, and examine a few comparisons that the teacher could direct students' attention to:

1. By comparing the means of Amy and Ben, we can see that they are the same, yet clearly if you eyeball or compare with the graphical solution, the ways the points are distributed around the mean are different. This comparison helps students see that using all the data points is critical, which, as you will recall from earlier, is Lego block 1.

2. The same goes for comparing the ranges of Amy and Ben, where we can see that the range is the same, yet the points are distributed differently in between. Again, this comparison helps students see that using all the data points is critical, that is, Lego block 1.

3. By comparing the game-on-game changes for Amy and Ben, we can see that positive and negative changes tend to cancel each other out, which may not be desirable. This comparison helps students see that positive and negative fluctuations should not cancel each other, which helps students see Lego block 6.

4. By comparing the game-on-game changes with and without taking the signs of the changes into account, one can see how it is important to consider only the magnitude of the change, and not its sign, again pointing to Lego block 6.

5. By comparing the magnitude of the game-on-game changes with the magnitude of game-to-mean changes (or squared changes, as in the correct solution), one can see how the latter is not sensitive to the sequence or order in which the data points are arranged. This comparison is a new Lego block that students can see only when comparing with the canonical or correct solution.

6. By comparing the total magnitude of game-to-game changes with the average magnitude of game-to-game changes, one can see how the latter is not sensitive to sample size, allowing one to compare across different sample sizes. This comparison helps students see the importance of dividing by the sample size, that is, Lego block 7.

When designed well, Productive Failure provides many possibilities for comparison and contrast. The trick in good assembly is to choose comparisons that help students see the underlying principles or key features. In doing so, comparison and contrasts solve one of the major problems of learning, that is, the failure to see critical features. And as we saw in Chapter 1, without seeing the critical features and connecting them with prior knowledge, deep understanding is unlikely. Deep understanding requires that we are able to see what is critical and connect it with our prior knowledge. That is the goal of assembly. A good teacher would assemble by directing these comparisons, helping students see the critical features as part of the assembly process, facilitating deep understanding of the concept.

And because this way of assembling new knowledge actively bootstraps students' own prior knowledge resources, or as we call it Lego blocks, it also helps students see not only why whole solutions work or do not work but also how the various components are assembled, and how a different assembly works or could work differently, each with its pros and cons. This is precisely what cognitive flexibility is all about, and as we shall see, one needs it in high dosage for creative problem solving and transfer.

Fitting a Square Peg into a Round Hole

In 1970, Apollo 13's journey to the moon turned perilous when an explosion wreaked havoc on board, making the three astronauts move from the command module to the lunar module. However, the lunar module was built for two, not three astronauts. A third astronaut would therefore, by merely breathing, strain the air filtration system, building up lethal levels of carbon dioxide, and threaten the astronauts' lives.

They had to find a way to filter carbon dioxide in the lunar module. The problem, however, was that they did not have any backup filters in the lunar module, and the backup filters from the command module could not be used. Why? The lunar module used cylindrical scrubbers while the command module used cubic ones. To be able to plug the command module scrubbers into the lunar module ones was like fitting a square peg into a round hole.

Back on Earth, at NASA's mission control in Houston, a frantic race against time began. They faced a daunting challenge: devise a fix using only what the astronauts had on board the spacecraft. The solution had to be ingenious yet simple enough for the astronauts to carry out in the cramped, zero-gravity confines of their damaged spacecraft. In a stroke of brilliance, they concocted a makeshift filtration device using items on board such as hoses from the astronauts' spacesuits, tube socks, card stock, and the ever-versatile duct tape. This was engineering at its most resourceful – they managed to fit a square peg into a round hole, both literally and figuratively. This improvised contraption worked remarkably, scrubbing the deadly carbon dioxide from the air and safeguarding the astronauts' lives until they safely returned to Earth.

Creative problem solving at its finest. They managed to identify parts on board that could be used for solving the problem, even parts that normally do not go together, and assembled these parts flexibly into one contraption to solve the problem.

Now think of "parts on board" as the Lego blocks of prior knowledge that students have. The various solutions that students generate during the problem solving phase of Productive Failure contain some of these parts; let's call them components, and some solutions contain more of these components than others. For example, in the basketball problem in Chapter 2, when students calculate the range, they are using the component of taking the difference between two points, and applying this component on the two extreme points. In contrast, when students calculate the game-to-game changes, they are also using the same component. but this time they apply it to all the points. The same component is used more or less frequently to assemble two different solutions.

Equally, different solutions contain different assemblies of these components, helping the learner see the various ways in which a component can be used as part of an assembly, and not just the one way as in the canonical solution. For example, the component – taking the difference between two points – can be applied to calculate the game-to-game changes, as well as game-to-mean changes. In the former, the component operates on all the points, and in the latter, the component operates between all the points and the mean of the points. The same component is used in two different ways to assemble to different solutions.

The ability to see any solution as an assembly of components, while recognizing that the components can be flexibly repurposed, recombined, and rearranged to assemble solutions for some other, often novel, context, is important for transfer. And as we saw in Chapter 2, students who learned from Productive Failure outperformed their counterparts in Direct Instruction on both deep understanding – the *why* – as well as transfer – the *apply*. They did so because their knowledge was assembled more deeply and flexibly.

Let's see if you can. Try solving the following problem.

Who's the better champion?
An equal number of students competed in the 100m sprint and 100m swim finals. The timings (in seconds) of the champions of the 100m sprint and 100m swim are shown below, as are the average timings, Mean (M) and the Standard Deviations (SDs) of the finalists in the two competitions.

	100m sprint	100m swim
Champion	11s	40s
Mean, M	12s	45s
Standard Deviation, SD	1s	10s

Assuming all else being equal, who is the better champion?

If you look at just the difference between the timing of the champion and the mean of the finalists, the sprint champion is 1 second faster than the average, whereas the swim champion is 5 seconds faster than average. So, one may argue that the swim champion is the better champion. But this is the wrong answer. One also needs to take into account the standard deviation, which is a measure of how the finalists were spread out. If the finalists were more spread out, the SD will be high, and vice versa. It is a relatively easier feat for the champion to be faster than the average if the finalists are more spread out than not. Therefore, to solve this problem, one has to take the difference between the champion and the mean, and divide it by the standard deviation of the finalists. The sprint champion is exactly 1 SD faster than the mean, whereas the swim champion is 0.5 SD faster than the mean. Therefore, the sprint champion is the better champion.

This was one of the transfer questions that I used in my experiments, when I compared the transfer effects of Productive Failure versus Direct Instruction. Recall that after students learn the concept of standard deviation either through Productive Failure or Direct Instruction, they are tested to see how deeply they understand the concept and how well they can transfer it. For someone to solve the "Who's the better champion?" transfer problem, they need to know the following components:

1. The mean, and how to calculate it.
2. The difference between a point and the mean.
3. The standard deviation, and how to calculate it.

Students in both the conditions know these components, because on procedural knowledge, both groups of students performed equally well; that is, they could calculate the SD of a given data set and solve problems based on it. And, as I showed earlier in this section, to calculate the SD, one has to know the three components.

So, in spite of knowing the three components equally well, why did Productive Failure students transfer better than Direct Instruction students? After all, to solve the transfer problem, all they had to do was to take the difference between the champion and the mean, and divide this difference by the SD.

It was because knowledge of the components is necessary but not sufficient. To solve the transfer problem, the three components needed to be assembled in a new way, a way they had not seen or encountered before. So, even if both groups of students had the same components, learning through Productive Failure resulted in a more flexible assembly of the components than Direct Instruction. As we saw in Chapter 2 in the case of children being told how to play with toys, Direct Instruction somehow limits the flexibility with which children play with the toy. In other words, Direct Instruction increases the likelihood of functional fixedness (Duncker 1945). Productive Failure, in contrast, affords flexible assembly and allows students to reassemble the components in a new way to solve a much harder problem, much like how Houston put together hoses from the astronauts' spacesuits, tube socks, card stock, and duct tape to assemble a filtration system.

The Danger of Learning the Wrong Things Is. . .

Overestimated.

One question I am asked quite often when giving talks on Productive Failure and the underlying mechanisms is: Is it not dangerous to activate misconceptions, errors, and failed answers or solutions because they may stick, and worse, interfere with learning the correct knowledge? Another way to put the underlying argument would be that it could be counterproductive to retrieve incorrect knowledge, for it could strengthen those very retrieval paths that we need to avoid so that these paths do not interfere with the retrieval paths to the correct knowledge.

Fortunately, we have nothing to worry about. For two diametrically opposite reasons: pruning failure and promoting failure.

Pruning Failure

We now know from multiple studies that our brains have an amazing capacity to prune as we learn and grow. In his pioneering work in 1979, Peter Huttenlocher demonstrated how our brains develop a dense web of neuronal connections during the first two years, much like an overgrown garden. However, as we age and learn, our brains begin to prune away the unused or unnecessary connections, while strengthening those that have proved beneficial, much like a gardener might prune unwanted weeds and such over time. It has become generally accepted that such pruning in the brain starts around age two and is completed during adolescence. In 2011, however, Petanjek and colleagues further showed that pruning in fact continues beyond adolescence well into our late twenties before stabilizing.

Our brain's ability to prune suggests that just because there is a connection, a retrieval path, it does not mean it cannot be suppressed or erased over time. What is needed is appropriate feedback to learn from. Use it or lose it is one feedback mechanism; that is, if you do not use the connection, you are giving feedback that you do not need the connection. Over time, therefore, you lose it.

Another feedback is corrective, where you are told the correct answer or explanation, as we have seen in several studies earlier. And John Hattie's 2009 meta-analysis robustly shows that feedback is one of the most powerful mechanisms for learning. Here, you learn that the connection is encoding an error, or is faulty, and that there is another connection that is more productive or useful or correct. The contrast between the failed path and the successful path is necessary, making it quite plausible that activating incorrect knowledge or errors, which in turn activate those unwanted retrieval paths, is actually necessary for pruning to take place.

Obviously, pruning cannot proceed if there is nothing to prune. Some things that get pruned are generated naturally through our daily learning and living. Others, especially if you are learning something new, may need to be intentionally generated in service of deep learning. Failure-based generation can therefore be seen as a way to intentionally generate errors, and then suppress or prune them with feedback, making future recall of the correct paths easier.

Promoting Failure

Another way is to think exactly the opposite. Far from pruning, perhaps failures need promoting, for promoting failure can aid learning by providing opportunities to learn from the failure.

Indeed, the first line of evidence comes from analysis of students engaged in learning from Productive Failure. Although on average, students generate many solutions during the problem-solving phase, some students generate more than others. In fact, the design (as we shall see in the next chapter) is such that it actively encourages students to generate as many solutions as they can, even if what they generate is suboptimal or incorrect.

The variation in student production allows us to ask an important question: Do students who generate more failed solutions also learn more from subsequent instruction? In several studies, the answer to this question, directly or indirectly, has been yes. Students who generate more, on average, learn more from subsequent instruction and perform better on deep understanding and transfer than those who generate less. If generating failed solutions were problematic, these incorrect solutions would have turned up on the posttest. But they did not.

One way to explain this is that if by generating failed solutions, we strengthen their retrieval paths, then we are also strengthening the retrieval paths of the correct solutions. When the teacher or an expert engages in comparing and contrasting the incorrect and correct solutions, they not only help students understand what works and why, but that feedback also helps students hone their selection and discrimination capabilities. That is, precisely because of generating failed solutions, students have the opportunity to learn to discriminate between the correct and incorrect solutions, and select the correct procedures for solving the problem. Without the failed solutions, the development of these functions would not be possible.

There's a reason why I will always remember that the correct word is *carpentry*, not *carpenting*. Remembering the incorrect option actually aids my memory of the correct one. For the same reason, I remember the failure of additive logic with my son, as it facilitates the memory of the correct logic. In other words, far from pruning failure, comparing and contrasting coupled with feedback can actually result in retrieval paths to incorrect and correct knowledge in a way that facilitates recall. This is called *mediated recall*. Incorrect knowledge can serve as a mediator, connecting the question with the correct answer. Sometimes you have to go through the incorrect knowledge to get to the correct knowledge, and there is nothing to worry about that.

But correlation is not causation. Just because those who generated more solutions also learned more, does not mean promoting failure causes learning. All it shows is failure is associated with learning. For causation, one has to manipulate the failure and success rates experimentally.

One simple way to manipulate failure rate experimentally is to provide guidance during the problem-solving phase, as shown in Figure 6.4. Imagine two groups of students, both learning from Productive Failure. In the problem-solving phase of Productive Failure, one group is given the challenging problem (e.g. the basketball problem in Figure 2.1) and asked to

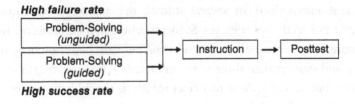

Figure 6.4   Guided vs. Unguided Productive Failure.

generate as many solutions as they can. No further help or support is given other than encouragement. And as we saw in Chapter 2, students are not able to generate the correct solution. They generate several solutions but none of them are correct. This is therefore a high failure rate condition. Now imagine for the other group, we provide prompts and hints as students generate solutions. The prompts and hints are designed to help them get to the correct solution. And these prompts and hints reduce the failure rate, or equally, increase the success rate.

If both groups of students were then given instruction on the targeted concept, who would learn more? Will it be the first group who had a high failure rate in the problem-solving phase, or the second group who had a high success rate in the problem-solving phase? Answering this question was part of my 2011 study, and I found out it was the high failure rate group that learns more: they outperformed the high success rate group on deep understanding and transfer on the posttest.

Encouraging or promoting failure facilitates learning. Reducing failure hurts learning. A simple causal demonstration why promoting failure is good for deep learning and transfer.

Another way to promote failure without having students generate it themselves is to design opportunities for students to learn from others' failed solutions. Instead of generating multiple solutions in the problem-solving phase, all of which are suboptimal or incorrect, what if we simply gave students the opportunity to study the failed solutions that their peers generated? I call this learning from vicarious failure. In a 2014 study, I carried out experiments with three conditions as shown in Figure 6.5.

Two of the conditions were exactly the same as in the original experiments comparing Productive Failure and Direct Instruction (see Figure 2.5). I added a third condition called Vicarious Failure into the mix. As the name

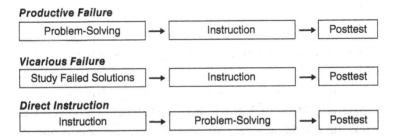

Figure 6.5 Comparing Productive Failure, Vicarious Failure, and Direct Instruction.

suggests, students were asked to study the typical (and incorrect) solutions that their peers generated during the problem-solving phase. They did not have to generate any solutions. They were given the opportunity to learn vicariously from the typical failed solutions of their peers. After that, they received instruction.

On the posttest, I found that all three conditions did equally well on the procedural knowledge items. However, on deep understanding and transfer, Productive Failure students performed the best, followed by Vicarious Failure, and then Direct Instruction students. What these findings suggest is that we learn more from our own failed solutions than if we merely study others' failed solutions, but absent the opportunity to generate our own, we are still better off learning from others' failed solutions than simply being told the correct solution through direct instruction.

Combining evidence from correlational and causal studies, as well as evidence from learning from Vicarious Failure, we see that promoting failure during problem solving, when carefully designed for, has strong effects on deep learning and transfer. Far from worrying about it, we need to intentionally design for it, in a safe and supportive way.

Note that the power of Productive Failure cannot be realized without assembly. You can activate all the prior knowledge you want, create heightened awareness, build the right affective state, but without a proper assembly, all of it goes to waste. Assembly, done well, brings it all together and turns what seems initially to be exploration and failure into something that makes for deep learning.

Key Takeaways

1. **Lego Blocks of Prior Knowledge.** Good teaching involves identifying parts of a student's thinking or reasoning that can be used for learning. Think of these parts as Lego blocks.

2. **Teacher's Role in Knowledge Assembly.** Teachers play a vital role in the knowledge assembly process, by connecting new information with their prior knowledge, guiding them to reconfigure known elements, or Lego blocks, to learn new concepts.

3. **Comparing and Contrasting for Deeper Understanding.** Good assembly incorporates comparing and contrasting of cases, examples, solutions, and so on to help the learner see and discern key features of concepts, enhancing their understanding and capacity to apply knowledge in varied contexts.

4. **Cognitive Flexibility and Transfer of Knowledge.** Good assembly also ensures cognitive flexibility, that is, the ability to see any concept or solution as an assembly of components, while recognizing that the components can be flexibly repurposed, recombined, and rearranged to assemble solutions for some other, often novel, context. Flexibility drives transfer.

5. **Concerns About Learning the Wrong Things.** Pruning and promoting failures both ensure that the chance of learning the wrong thing is low. Failed solutions create a contrast with correct solutions, helping us distinguish and select correct knowledge over incorrect knowledge.

III | Designing for Productive Failure

Oscar Wilde once remarked, "Experience is the hardest kind of teacher. It gives you the test first and the lesson afterward." These words capture the essence of life's unpredictable school, where the tests often come unannounced, leaving us to glean the lessons in their wake. Sometimes these lessons are manageable, other times so painful that they take a toll on us. Still, the importance of learning from these tests is necessary.

But what if we could design these experiences, these tests, without the pain and suffering, in a way that still challenges us but within a framework that's safe and supportive? This is where Productive Failure comes into play, in a way transforming Wilde's observation into a principle that not only educates but does so in a safe and assuring manner. Unlike life's harsh tests, Productive Failure is a deliberate design where challenges are set within boundaries that encourage risk-taking without the fear of devastating consequences. It's akin to practicing tightrope walking with a safety net below; the fall is not the focus, the learning from each misstep is. By engaging in tasks that are designed to push our limits within a supportive environment, we learn resilience, creativity, and problem-solving skills more effectively.

The challenge is one of design. We understand the science behind Productive Failure, but how do we translate the science into design?

Imagine two cars: a sleek, lightning-fast Ferrari and a reliable, family-friendly Volkswagen. Though they may sit on opposite ends of the automotive spectrum, both must adhere to the same fundamental laws of science – mechanics dictate how they move, materials science ensures they're strong and durable, and thermodynamics govern their engines' efficiency. However, knowing these scientific laws isn't enough to design a car. If it were, every car might look the same and serve the same purpose. Instead, engineers rely on design specifications, a blueprint that tells them whether they are crafting a high-performance sports car or an economical family vehicle. These specifications guide the application of scientific laws, tailoring them to produce vastly different outcomes based on the desired features, performance, and audience.

Just as the laws of science underpin both the Ferrari and the Volkswagen, the underlying mechanisms of Productive Failure – the 4As of Activation, Awareness, Affect, and Assembly – are grounded in the science of how we learn. However, understanding these mechanisms is just the starting point, much like knowing physics and materials science is for car design. To effectively implement Productive Failure, educators and designers need a set of "design specifications." These are not physical blueprints. Instead, they are a set of principles that help us design a Productive Failure experience, for others and for ourselves.

The next two chapters take on these very two questions: How do we design Productive Failure experiences for others to learn deeply in a safe way? And how do we design such experiences for ourselves so that we can accelerate our growth without waiting for life's tests to happen?

7

Designing for Others

One of the common but unfounded criticisms of Productive Failure is that maybe it is not for everyone. Perhaps Productive Failure is better suited for those with higher abilities, motivation, and resilience. Because those without these attributes may get frustrated and give up, making failure unproductive.

I argue that when we attribute a quality like "motivation" to an individual, such as when we say Julie is motivated but John is not, we are making an error. Motivation is not something an individual possesses in fixed quantities, like having green eyes or black hair. The same is true for ability or resilience. These qualities are not something an individual possesses but instead are best viewed as an interaction between the individual and the learning environment. In a well-designed learning environment, more people will appear resilient and motivated. If these concepts are conceived as interactions, the burden is then on the designer to design the learning in a way that motivates students, develops their abilities, and helps them build resilience. And this is precisely what the design principles of Productive Failure aim to do.

But what are design principles in the first place?

When I first started out as a professor in 2006, I was lucky to have a great set of colleagues, and among them, one of my early mentors, Kate Bielaczyc. After one of my presentations on Productive Failure, where I presented my research and findings, she asked me a simple question: "Manu, if you were to ask a teacher to design a lesson using your theory of Productive Failure, what exactly would you tell them they should do, and

167

how they should go about doing it?" This simple question sparked a series of conversations and discussion about the core features that make Productive Failure Productive Failure, much like what makes a Ferrari a Ferrari and not any other car. What are its distinguishing and defining features that make it a Ferrari?

In the same way, what are the distinguishing and defining features of Productive Failure in the way the activities are designed, and students are engaged, how they participate and interact, and the kinds of norms and expectations that drive their learning in the classroom? It took Kate and me almost a year to pin down the key features and characteristics of Productive Failure, and describe them in a way that a teacher could use to design a Productive Failure lesson. We called these defining features and characteristics the design principles of Productive Failure, and published them in our 2012 paper (Kapur and Bielaczyc 2012).

You might have noticed that several times in the earlier chapters, I have qualified my claims with caveats like "when designed well," "well curated," "based on Productive Failure principles." I did this to signal that Productive Failure has its own set of design principles, and only when learning is designed based on these principles can we call it Productive Failure, and expect powerful learning outcomes. Figure 7.1 presents the three-layered design framework for Productive Failure.

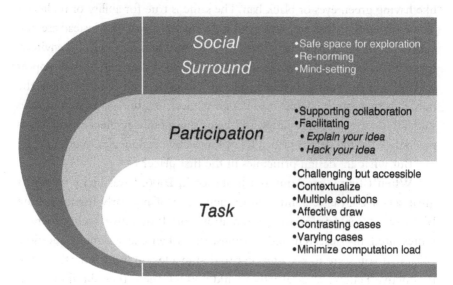

Social Surround
- Safe space for exploration
- Re-norming
- Mind-setting

Participation
- Supporting collaboration
- Facilitating
  - Explain your idea
  - Hack your idea

Task
- Challenging but accessible
- Contextualize
- Multiple solutions
- Affective draw
- Contrasting cases
- Varying cases
- Minimize computation load

Figure 7.1   Three layers of the Productive Failure design.

The three-layered design framework specifies principles for designing the *task*, which is nested within the *participation*, which in turn is nested within the *social surround*:

1. *Task.* A Productive Failure task is not just any hard or challenging task. A good task has certain properties and features, and the task level principles provide a set of specifications for how to design these properties and features.

2. *Participation.* How students participate in the task designed for them is also key. Here again, there are specific ways to structure how students interact with each other and engage with the task. Participation structure principles provide a set of specifications for how to design such features.

3. *Social surround.* Learning does not take place in a vacuum. It is a cultural activity, and designs such as Productive Failure work well when we create a safe space for students to fail and learn. How do we design such safe spaces? What properties and features do such spaces have? Social surround principles specify the values, norms, and expectations of such safe spaces, and ways to build such spaces.

Finally, one has to go through several cycles of iterative design process that help calibrate the design to the particular contexts within which it is to be used or implemented.

Designing the Task

Let us re-examine the Productive Failure task illustrated in Chapter 2 (Figure 2.1). It is a problem-solving task in mathematics, but it has certain features or properties that make it a good task, independent of the domain of mathematics. What are these features or properties, and can we distill them so that we use them to design such tasks in any domain? Can we articulate a blueprint that any designer in any domain could use to design? That is the aim here.

One of the effective ways to distill the features of a good Productive Failure task is to contrast it with a bad one. An example contrasted with a non-example. Figure 7.2 presents this contrast between a good task (which is the same as the one in Chapter 2, Figure 2.1) and a bad task.

Good Task

Amy and Ben are two basketball players in a league. The table shows the number of points they scored in the 9 games they played. Invent as many ways as possible to determine who the more consistent player is. Just be creative, without worrying about getting it right or wrong.	Amy	Ben
	11	12
	12	14
	13	17
	14	15
	14	11
	14	16
	15	12
	16	13
	17	16

Bad Task

Here are the number of points Amy scored in 9 games of Basketball Calculate the Standard Deviation of Amy's scores.	Amy
	11
	12
	13
	14
	14
	14
	15
	16
	17

Figure 7.2   A good vs. bad Productive Failure task.

Before reading further, it might be good if you spent some time comparing and contrasting the good and the bad tasks, and generate your own list of features that you deem make the good task good and the bad task bad. Remember the goal of these tasks is for novices to generate and explore solutions that will prepare them for learning from subsequent instruction. It is against this preparatory goal that the two tasks ought to be compared. Once you have generated about five to seven features, read on.

To be effective, Productive Failure tasks should include the following seven features, which often take two to three iterations to develop:

Feature 1: Keep It Challenging but Accessible

For someone who does not know the concept – standard deviation – to solve the problem, both tasks are challenging. However, the bad example is not accessible because the novice may not have even heard of the term *standard deviation*, let alone know what it is. Hence, they are likely to simply give up and not produce anything. In contrast, the good task remains accessible because there is no mention of technical or formal terms, and instead relies on a layperson's language and understanding of the meaning of the word *consistency*. And this provides an "in," it gives the novice a chance to interpret and generate ideas for solving the problem.

Feature 2: Contextualize

Comparing the good and bad tasks, we can also see that the good task contextualizes the problem better than the bad task. It sets up a relatable context of comparing two athletes, and situates the need for using mathematics to solve the problem. Giving a proper context or a situation often helps learners make better sense; it anchors their learning. A good task should be a problem or challenge or something that needs resolution, and even better if something the learner can relate to (in this case, sporting contexts). By contextualizing the challenge, learners explore more aspects of the problem and are given tools to evaluate their progress.

Feature 3: Admit Multiple Solutions and Representations

Notice how the bad task invites one solution, implicitly the normative solution. In contrast, the good task explicitly invites novices to generate multiple ways of solving the problem. Not just one way as in the bad task, but multiple ways. To facilitate students' understanding of the target concept and its relationship with related concepts, tasks should invite a variety of solutions or representations. If you design a task that you think invites multiple solutions, yet most students are unable to generate more than one solution, then you need to redesign the task. A good task allows students to take baby steps, even if they are unable to find the correct solutions. They should be able to make gradual progress toward meaningful approaches to solving the challenges. This multiplicity is critical because, as we saw earlier, even though students' solutions are in general typically erroneous, they often include valid features and ideas – the Lego blocks – that can be bootstrapped for learning. Another reason why multiplicity is critical is that it allows for wider activation of relevant prior knowledge. As we saw in Chapter 3, research shows that a wider activation prepares the learner to learn from subsequent instruction.

Feature 4: Create an Affective Draw

To encourage people to persist in these challenging problems the tasks should be engaging, and draw the learner in. The good task does that better than the bad task, and it does so in several ways that were collectively termed *collative properties* by psychologist Daniel Berlyne in the 1950s, who was one of the leading scientists in the study of curiosity (Berlyne 1954, 1960).

These properties include but are not limited to novelty, intuitiveness, uncertainty, and conflict, which come together to create a powerful affective draw, fuel situational interest and curiosity, making the learner engage and persist in the task:

1. *Novelty.* A good task should feel as if you have never seen something like this before; it feels new, something unfamiliar, even unconventional, which piques interest.
2. *Intuitiveness.* Using intuitive language and inviting intuitive and informal ways of reasoning motivates novices to engage with the tasks. As we already noted, avoid technical terms; instead use more layperson language that closely approximates the intended meaning.
3. *Uncertainty.* Although there are many ideas or solutions one could explore, it should not be immediately obvious which ones would work. This sense of uncertainty can spark the novice's curiosity, making them more interested in finding the right solution, and curious about the correct one.
4. *Conflict.* A good task creates a conflict or an incongruity. For example, one might initially think of a certain idea or a solution, but then when you actually try it, you realize that it doesn't work. You reach an impasse or a failure, creating a knowledge gap, as well as an awareness of that gap. In addition to the cognitive benefits of awareness of the knowledge gap, a good task also provides the affective benefit of stimulating your interest and keeping you in the game. It pushes you to reassess your approach and try different strategies.

Feature 5: Use Contrasting Cases

The bad task uses only one case, that of Amy, and the novice has to make sense of one set of numbers to solve the problem. As you can imagine, it is hard to make sense from just one case or example. Imagine you do not know what a chair is, and I show you one picture of a chair to understand what it is. Now compare this with being given two pictures, one that is a chair, and one that is not a chair, say a stool. Surely, you will be able to discern what makes a chair a chair better by comparing than by looking at just one example. For the same reason, I am using two examples – good and bad – of Productive Failure tasks to distill features of what makes a good task. I am practicing what I am preaching. And this is why a good Productive Failure task uses at least two cases or examples that novices can compare and contrast. Ideally, good tasks should include contrasts that can be intuitively, and even better if perceptually, seen, compared, and examined, which allows learners to evaluate their own solutions. As we saw in Chapter 6, research shows that we do not learn as well from single examples or cases, but when presented with (typically) two cases at once, cases that are similar and different in interesting ways, we tend to see things, and learn and transfer a lot better.

Feature 6: Vary the Cases

Just having multiple cases or examples is not sufficient. A good task varies certain features between the cases while keeping others invariant, which affords students the opportunities to focus on the critical features. Variation helps people see things, and if one of the problems of learning is seeing the critical features, then designing the tasks to include variation becomes key. There is no one way of doing this. For example, in the good task, we kept the central tendencies and the range the same. Once students noticed this, it afforded them and even implicitly nudged them to focus on the distribution of the data. Alternatively, such variant – invariant relations can be designed on structure and stories, for example, keeping structure constant but changing the stories as we saw in the radiation problem and the general problem in Chapter 6, or vice versa. The same could be done with multiple representations, for example, giving the same information but in different representations such as drawings, tables, text, simulations, and so on. All of these must be carefully designed to keep some features constant and others variable. Having only one case or example does not afford such variation, and therefore is not a good Productive Failure task.

Feature 7: Minimize Computational Load

Students should focus on designing ideas and exploring their properties, rather than on calculating or applying solutions. Keep the text simple, the numbers easy to compute, graphs or pictures easy to discern, and so on. Lower the computational load so that students can focus on the critical aspects of the problem and its solutions.

Chances are if you did your own list, comparing your own with the list above would in and of itself have been a learning experience. Note also how the features do not contain any information or specificity about the domain itself; that is, the features are not tied to mathematics or any other domain. They remain domain general, meaning that they can be used to design Productive Failure tasks in any domain.

Designing the Participation

Once the task has been designed, we need to design how learners go about working on the task. Here, as a designer, we need to answer two questions:

a) Do learners work alone or together in small groups?
b) How do we facilitate their problem-solving process?

Working Alone or Together

Thus far, studies show that Productive Failure is effective in both configurations, whether learners work individually or in small groups, typically two to three people. For example, Claudia Mazziotti and colleagues showed in 2019 that whether students worked alone or in small groups, there was no difference in their learning from Productive Failure. However, my 2021 meta-analysis led by my then–doctoral student Tanmay Sinha found that working together during the generation phase of Productive Failure had an overall significant effect on learning. Because a meta-analysis aggregates findings across multiple studies, it is more reliable from an evidentiary standpoint than a single or a few studies, lending support to the principle for designing for collaboration rather than not.

The advantage of collaboration is that people bring their individual knowledge and perspectives to the table, which can be incredibly beneficial. They can learn from each other and build upon each other's ideas, much like the puzzle solvers combining their pieces to get a more complete picture. In this way, collaboration supports the mechanism of *activation* of prior knowledge, as individuals recall and share information they already know, which can be new or enlightening to others. It also helps in the *awareness* of gaps, as working with others can highlight areas of the problem at hand that are missing or need more attention, in turn building the positive *affect* for working together to bridge the gap. Three of the 4As – Activation, Awareness, and Affect – get directly invoked in this process, thereby setting the learners up for the fourth A – Assembly – later on.

However, collaboration also comes at a cost. While each person brings their own set of knowledge and perspectives, not everyone may be skilled or experienced in working as part of a team. Not everyone knows how to collaborate. And not everyone wants to collaborate either, for all sorts of reasons. And even if one wants and knows how to collaborate, collaboration is intrinsically hard. One has to coordinate understandings with others, and this takes time and effort. Some might struggle with communicating their ideas, or they may be used to working independently and find it difficult to integrate their approach with others. Collaboration, in this sense, is not just about bringing multiple ideas and perspectives together; it is also about effectively communicating, coordinating, and understanding each other's contributions.

Therefore, when using collaboration as a way of participation, we need to make sure that we help people *learn to collaborate* so that they can *collaborate to learn*.

Another variant that often works well is not to choose between working alone *or* together. Instead, one can work alone and *then* together. This allows everyone to generate their own ideas and solutions first, and then come together as a group to share and build upon each other's ideas.

Facilitating the Problem Solving

The benefits of generating ideas and solutions can be amplified if learners can be supported with effective facilitation. If you want to know what good facilitation looks like, look no further than the Socratic dialogue in Chapter 4. That is a masterful level of skill, and as you might have guessed, a level that is good to aim for but hard to achieve. Therefore, in working with hundreds of teachers and trainers implementing Productive Failure, I have designed a simplified two-step facilitation scheme that one can use for facilitating learners as they engage in generating ideas and solutions: a) explain your idea, and b) hack your idea.

Explain Your Idea For every idea or a solution that the learners generate, a great way to support them in their thinking is to ask them to explain their idea to you or their peers. It is one thing to generate an idea, it is quite another to be able to explain it. This simple prompt forces the learner to find ways to communicate to another person their thinking and reasoning in a way that the other can understand.

For example, for the basketball problem in Chapter 2, Figure 2.1, when students try to use the averages to solve the problem, asking them to explain their solution and why they think using averages is a good idea for measuring consistency forces them to articulate their reasoning. And when they do that, two things happen. First, the preparation to explain itself has cognitive and affective benefits. It motivates one to select, organize, and think of structuring the information in a way that will make it easier to understand. This is a cognitively demanding task. Therefore, even without actually explaining, the preparation alone leads to deeper understanding of the idea itself. If you have tutored, mentored, taught, or prepared a presentation, you can probably relate to this. Just the preparation alone helps us deepen our understanding of the content, even before we deliver it. Second, the act of delivery in and of itself has cognitive and meta-cognitive benefits. Engaging with the others' questions triggers reflection on our own knowledge, resulting in greater interrogation and deepening of our own knowledge.

Several reviews of research studies and meta-analyses broadly support the principle that on both counts – preparation and delivery – asking people to explain their ideas helps them deepen their own knowledge of the ideas. Of course, sometimes such explanations may not come easy for learners, in which case, and as it was with collaboration, it is good then that we help learners learn how to explain so that they can explain to learn.

Hack Your Idea   When we generate an idea or a solution, we generate it for a given context or situation of the problem we are trying to solve. We tend to focus so much on that particular situation or context that we might miss examining the generalizability or robustness of our idea. That is, we may overlook the potential weaknesses or limitations that only become apparent when the idea is tested in different, often unexpected, scenarios. Thus, generating ideas is not enough. We need to learn how to hack our own ideas to see how robust they are.

Does the idea work only for the given context or situation? Or can it work for other contexts and situations? Is there a context or situation when the idea or solution would not work? Asking questions like these forms the second step in the facilitation process. Helping learners hack their ideas can help them think more broadly about their ideas and solutions.

For example, for the basketball problem in Chapter 2, Figure 2.1, when students try to use the range (maximum minus minimum) to solve the problem, asking them to think of a situation where their own solution would not work or would break down really stretches their thinking. Deliberately seeking the counterfactual – the situation where the idea does not work anymore – forces them to consider if two players can have the same range, yet different consistencies, and the even more interesting situation where a player with a smaller range may in fact be more inconsistent.

Thinking across different contexts and situations demands a deep dive into the structure of the problem and the solution. Without it, we cannot test the generalizability of our ideas. And if we should find counterfactual contexts and situations where our ideas break down or do not work, then that is powerful for learning. Therefore, as soon as someone generates an idea, and has been given the opportunity to explain it to others, a good follow-up is to ask them to consider the limits of their ideas and solutions. It is in the limits – the crucial step – that we actively seek and identify the situations where the idea or solution might fail – essentially, testing for the counterfactual.

Think of how a company might employ a hacker to test their cybersecurity system. The hacker's job is not to validate that the system works under normal conditions, but rather to find conditions under which it doesn't – to think like an adversary and exploit any vulnerabilities that the system's designers might have missed.

Both in the realm of idea generation and in cybersecurity, this approach of deliberately seeking the counterfactual serves a dual purpose. First, it identifies the boundaries and limitations of the current solution or system, providing valuable insights into areas that require improvement or reinforcement. Second, it fosters the development of more resilient and adaptable solutions or systems that can withstand a wider array of challenges. Just as a hacker tests a security system to find its breaking points and improve its defenses, we must help learners develop the habit of rigorously testing their ideas and solutions against potential failure scenarios to ensure they are robust, versatile, and applicable in a variety of contexts. This process of challenging and questioning leads to better ideas, deeper understanding, and better preparation for subsequent learning from instruction.

Explaining your own idea. And hacking your own idea. Two simple steps that give large returns on learning. The more we can get learners to cultivate the habit of explaining and hacking their own ideas, the more they will learn from Productive Failure. If learners can develop these habits, then the benefits go beyond Productive Failure as well, for these are good habits for learning and life in general.

Designing the Social Surround

In traditional classroom settings, the norms and expectations often revolve around the acquisition of correct answers and the avoidance of mistakes. Students are often rewarded for quick, accurate recall of information and penalized for incorrect responses, leading to a fear of failure and a reluctance to take on challenges and intellectual risks. Such an environment – I call it the *social surround* – can stifle creativity, discourage deep understanding, and inhibit the development of critical thinking skills.

Productive Failure stands in stark contrast. It adopts new norms and expectations that embrace the value of failure and mistakes while taking on challenging tasks, the importance of effort, and the process of learning itself becomes essential in fostering a more effective and engaging educational experience. This shift requires a fundamental change in how students perceive what is expected of them, their role in the learning process, and how they interpret their successes and failures.

If we want learners to take on challenging tasks, explore widely, be creative, not worry about failure or mistakes, and work with each other, we need to design a social surround within which they find it safe to explore and learn.

Enter *psychological safety*, a concept first coined by Carl Rogers in the 1950s. Psychological safety refers to the idea that a supportive and non-judgmental environment is critical for people to feel comfortable expressing themselves and taking risks without fear of negative consequences. Management scholars such as Amy Edmondson (2018) have popularized the concept for organizational learning and innovation, where it translates to creating an environment where people feel included, able to express their ideas, make and admit mistakes, ask questions, engage candidly and authentically, and contribute their best. Likewise, in the training or education contexts, this translates to making learners feel safe to share their thoughts and ideas, ask questions, make mistakes, and see them as opportunities for learning.

To design for such a social surround in line with the principles of Productive Failure, two things need to be done: a) re-norming, and b) mind-setting.

Re-norming

To implement Productive Failure effectively, it is crucial to establish clear expectations and norms from the outset. Students should be encouraged to engage in open-ended exploration and to take intellectual risks without the fear of being penalized for incorrect answers. The emphasis should be on the effort put forth and the generation of diverse ideas. In this environment, every answer that can be explained and reasoned out is considered valuable, with fuller explanations seen as indicators of deeper understanding. Emphasizing the value of effort and the generation of diverse ideas, even if incorrect or suboptimal, is essential.

An integral part of setting these expectations is preparing students for the inevitable struggles and frustrations they will encounter. Educators must communicate that experiencing difficulty and dealing with frustration are normal aspects of the learning process and are in fact indicators of meaningful learning taking place. This approach helps students develop resilience and persistence, qualities that are essential for long-term academic and personal growth.

To reinforce these expectations and norms, they must be emphasized consistently throughout the learning process. Consistently reinforcing these expectations and norms throughout helps students internalize the new didactic contract, shifting their focus from traditional success metrics to a broader view of learning as an exploratory process. The effectiveness of Productive Failure is greater in contexts that are in alignment with the new norms and expectations.

Another critical aspect of Productive Failure is fostering a classroom culture that values effort and resilience. Educators can model this by sharing their own experiences with failure, such as rejected papers or challenges they have faced in their professional journey. By making themselves vulnerable and demonstrating how they overcame obstacles, educators can help students see failure as a natural and valuable part of learning.

Mind-setting

Learners' mindsets about learning and intelligence significantly impact how they respond to mistakes and challenges. The concept of a growth mindset, developed by psychologist Carol Dweck (2006), has garnered significant attention in educational psychology. A growth mindset is the belief that intelligence and abilities can be developed through effort, perseverance, and learning from mistakes. In contrast, a fixed mindset is the belief that these traits are innate and unchangeable.

Dweck's research suggests that individuals with a growth mindset, who view intelligence as a quality that develops through effort, are more likely to see mistakes and failure as opportunities for learning and improvement. Conversely, those with a fixed mindset, who believe intelligence is a static trait, may view mistakes and failure as a reflection of their inherent lack of ability. Encouraging a growth mindset therefore helps students view challenges as steppingstones to greater understanding and competence.

Research shows that a growth mindset can positively impact academic outcomes and more. In 2019, David Yeager and colleagues carried out probably the largest study on the effectiveness of a growth mindset intervention with about 13,000 secondary school students from more than 60 schools in a nationally representative sample in the United States. They found that even a short (less than an hour) online intervention focusing on the key message that intellectual abilities are malleable led to improved academic outcomes. Specifically, it raised the grades of lower-performing students and improved the overall enrollment in advanced mathematics courses.

Crucially, the effectiveness of the growth mindset intervention was contingent on the existing norms in the school. When these norms were supportive of taking on challenges, then the intervention worked better, showing the importance of establishing the supportive norms and expectations as described above. This is a critical point in intervention research. Interventions do not occur in a vacuum, but they are carried out in the context of preexisting norms and cultures that may or may not be aligned with the underlying assumptions and ethos of the intervention. Therefore, part of implementing learning interventions is to explicitly examine the existing norms and actively realign them if needed.

Still, no matter how good or representative a study is, it is important to not rely only on one or a few studies. One has to look at patterns across a large number of studies, which is what a meta-analysis is for. Luckily, there are a number of meta-analyses that have been carried out. Most notably, a 2023 meta-analysis by Jeni L. Burnette and colleagues used the most modern analytical methods (Tipton et al. 2023) to provide evidence supporting the benefits of growth mindset interventions on academic outcomes, mental health, and social functioning. Although the effects varied across different samples and contexts, growth mindset interventions were found to be especially effective for learners who needed it the most, typically at-risk learners.

The message seems to be clear. Growth mindsets matter. And they matter especially when the norms are aligned and consistent with the key message. Norm alignment is critical. Therefore, when designing for Productive Failure, it is not sufficient just to emphasize the mindset message, but to actively realign the norms that support the message as well.

In summary, an effective social surround requires one to design a safe space within which learners can explore and learn. This in turn requires re-norming to the norms and expectations of Productive Failure, and mind-setting, to enable a growth mindset to help learners frame their learning in ways that allow them to persist in spite of the challenges, struggles, and even failure, and see them as drivers for learning. Together, they not only enhance learning but also build the adaptability and resilience needed to navigate the complexities of life.

Iterate and Calibrate

Designing for Productive Failure is not easy. Like any design process, it requires generation of ideas, testing them, learning from testing, and redesigning them until the design works for your context. It is a process of iterating and calibrating as you go along:

1. **Identify Learning Goals:** Start by defining clear learning objectives. Productive Failure is good for learning things that you need to deeply understand and transfer to novel situations. If, however, the learning goals are more procedural (e.g. going through a protocol, following a procedure, rote memorization), then you do not need to learn using Productive Failure. Unless of course you need to understand why the procedure is the way it is. Therefore, having clarity about the learning goals within the design team, and sharing this understanding with the learners, is critical so that everyone knows the need for it.

2. **Create Initial Design:** The design space is vast. The design principles for designing the task, participation, and social surround constrain this space by specifying the kinds of features and strategies that the various components need to embody, without which the

design is unlikely to be aligned with Productive Failure. Even with this constraint, the design space remains sufficiently open for your imagination and creativity to flourish. Once you have an initial design, use the design features for the three layers as an analytical tool to check if you have designed for each feature. It is normal to iterate even within this phase, which may sometimes lead to drastically different designs.

3. **Implement:** Once you have settled on an initial design, it is time for implementation. Given the importance of the social surround, start by explaining to the learners what the goals are, why you are using Productive Failure, what the new norms and expectations are, and so on. As noted in the design features, this is a discussion that needs to be had and persisted with over the course of the implementation so that learners understand what is being done and why.

4. **Gather Data and Feedback:** During implementation, gather data on each layer of the design. For the task, observe how learners interpret the task, and the kinds of ideas and solutions they generate. For the participation, observe how they work together, and if there are any ways to support them so that they can work together better. For the social surround, observe if they feel that they are in a safe space to explore and learn, and if not, gather feedback from them about why they feel that way, and what could be done to make them feel safe.

5. **Analyze and Reflect:** Once you have the data, analyze it to identify patterns, successes, and areas for improvement. This is a domain-specific exercise, and you need to bring in your domain expertise to understand learners' ideas and solutions, reflect on how well the tasks met the learning goals, and how you can design assembly and facilitate Productive Failure.

6. **Revise and Adapt:** Based on the analysis, make necessary revisions to the design, and calibrate for each of the three layers. Go through the features of each layer to improve alignment with them. The greater the alignment, the better the fidelity of the design, the higher the learning outcomes.

7. **Repeat:** Implement the revised tasks and repeat the cycle as many times as necessary. Typically, two to three iterations are needed for the design to work well for a particular context. Do not be

surprised if you find yourself going through Productive Failure as well. After all, you are engaging in an iterative design process and chances are parts of the design will initially not work as well, forcing you to learn from them, and adapt and refine the design. As a designer, you need to be comfortable to be in this "beta" mode of design, constantly focusing on what is working and what is not, and adapting and improving as you go along.

I have applied this cycle in multiple contexts, ranging from formal educational settings like schools and universities, to corporate training programs and adult education. It works. And it works in a diverse set of domains as well, such as mathematics, science, engineering, psychology, language, writing, accounting, business, and even in artistic and creative fields. There is nothing in the design that is specific to a particular domain. By going through this cycle of design, implementation, evaluation, and revision, you can create more impactful learning experiences that leverage the power of Productive Failure.

Key Takeaways

The three-layered design framework for Productive Failure specifies an iterative calibration process for designing the *task*, the *participation*, and the *social surround* within which learning takes place:

1. **Task design.** Effective tasks should be challenging yet accessible, provide contextual relevance, allow for multiple solutions and representations, create an affective draw, use contrasting cases, vary cases, and minimize computational load.
2. **Participation design.** Facilitate problem solving through individual or collaborative work, and support it with effective facilitation methods such as explaining ideas and "hacking" them to test robustness.
3. **Social surround design.** Create a safe space for learning by fostering psychological safety, re-norming expectations toward embracing failure and mistakes, and mind-setting to encourage a growth mindset.
4. **Iterate, iterate, iterate.** Self-explanatory.

8
Designing for Self

Self-doubt is quite normal. More than most people will readily admit, most of us struggle with imposter syndrome at some points in our lives. In April 2012, I was a visiting professor at Tokyo University, and my dad, who lived in India at the time, came to visit. During dinner one evening, I shared with him that I was feeling out of my depth at work, struggling at times, that maybe I wasn't good enough. He listened intently, as he always did, and said, "Manu, one's ambition should always exceed their talent." He meant by this that what I was feeling was a good thing, as I was pushing myself to grow and learn.

A Russian psychologist, Lev Vygotsky, embodied this wisdom in his theory of cognitive development. He called it the *Zone of Proximal Development*. I will call it simply the Zone. Vygotsky's idea was that development and growth happen in the Zone where you are trying to learn something that is beyond your current abilities. In the wisdom of the generations, what you want to learn – your ambition – must exceed your current abilities – your talent.

How do we use the Zone for our own growth and learning? Well, first, you must enter it. And failure happens to be at the core of this dynamic.

Entering the Zone

The Zone of Proximal Development (ZPD) refers to a metaphorical zone of the difference between what someone can do without help and what they cannot do without help, but can achieve with guidance and encouragement from a skilled partner (see Figure 8.1). It emphasizes the potential for growth and development by focusing on tasks that we cannot do alone but can accomplish with some assistance. According to Vygotsky, this Zone represents the area where the most significant learning takes place, as it pushes us just beyond our current abilities, requiring us to stretch our capabilities.

How does one enter the Zone? By definition, you enter the Zone when you are taking on something that you cannot do as yet. If you try something, and you can do it successfully, then you are not in the Zone. If you take on something harder, and you are somehow able to do that too, you are still not in the Zone. So, you keep notching it up to harder and harder things. Only when you reach the level where you are no longer able to do the task successfully, that is, you fail, then you know you have entered the Zone.

We often think success is more useful than failure. Success makes us feel good, assures us, motivates us to go further. All good things. But when it comes to learning new things, failure is more important. For it is failure that gives you the necessary information about whether or not you are in the Zone. And if you are not in the Zone, you are not learning and growing as much.

And that is precisely why, in Productive Failure, we deliberately design for failure so that only by engaging in challenging tasks, tasks in which we are initially expected to fail, can we enter the Zone. And in the Zone is where we give ourselves the best opportunity for deep learning. As we have seen in the earlier parts of this book, engaging with tasks that we cannot solve independently forces us to confront our limitations and gaps, motivating the need for instructional support or collaboration with more knowledgeable others to bridge the gap in our understanding.

The initial failure is not only acceptable but desirable for learning. It sets up the need for *scaffolding* – providing the right kind of support at the right time – after we have had the chance to explore and struggle with the problems. This approach ensures that the subsequent instruction, help, or

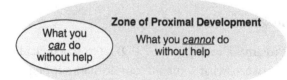

Figure 8.1   The Zone of Proximal Development.

support is more targeted and effective, as then it has a better chance of addressing the specific areas of difficulty identified through our attempts and failures, thus facilitating deeper learning and growth.

Without the initial failure, none of this would be possible. Without the subsequent instruction or scaffold, even the initial failure would be unproductive. Consistent with the two-phase design of Productive Failure, one needs both: the initial failure that gets you into the Zone, and then the appropriate support that helps you learn.

Clearly, we need to learn to fail. If we do not learn to fail, we will fail to learn. Fail not for failure's sake, but fail because we actively seek tasks and challenges that are just beyond our current skill sets and abilities.

What drives us to take on such tasks and challenges? Perhaps it is ambition, as was the case with me. Perhaps motivation, be it internal or external. Perhaps curiosity, perhaps some other need. Or some combination of all of them. Regardless of what the driver is, a common denominator across them is the need to be better than where we are – a discontentment with our current state. But this is not the bad kind of discontentment that holds us back. It is of the good kind that pushes us forward. I call it *productive discontentment*.

Practicing productive discontentment is the first step in learning to fail. If we remain content with where we are, we will likely not grow and learn much. Productive discontentment makes us seek to work on things that are beyond our current ability and skill set. And when we do that, we will struggle, and we might fail, but we will also give ourselves the opportunity to grow and learn.

Finding what drives you, be it one thing or many, to practice productive discontentment is the first step toward growth and learning. It sets you up to harness failure and learn from it. The design principles of Productive Failure that I described in the previous chapter can now be used for our own learning, to drive our own growth and development.

Harnessing the Productive Failure Design Principles

When designing learning experiences for oneself using the three layers – task, participation, and social surround – of Productive Failure, it is crucial to approach the process holistically, considering how each layer interacts with the others to enhance the learning experience. As shown in Figure 8.2,

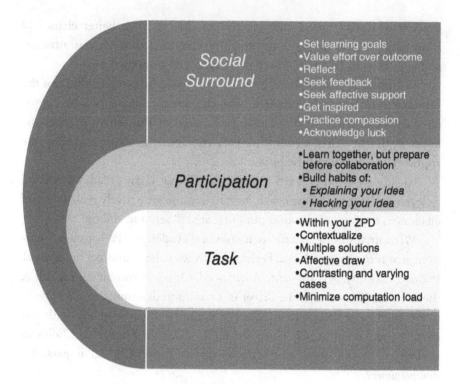

Figure 8.2 Three layers of the Productive Failure design.

designing your own challenging task should push the boundaries of current understanding, prompting exploration and inquiry. Designing your participation involves actively seeking feedback and collaboration opportunities at the right time, even if you are the primary learner. Finally, designing your safe space involves creating an environment with the right norms and expectations, and building a growth mindset.

Individually, each layer has a positive effect on learning and growth. However, the real magic lies in the synergistic effect of employing these principles together. For example, when tackling a challenging task you might initially struggle, but through active participation in a supportive community after you have tried on your own, you can gain insights and approaches you had not considered. This process not only aids in overcoming the immediate challenge but also reinforces a positive learning mindset. The integration of these principles leads to a richer, more engaged learning experience where resilience, critical thinking, and adaptability are developed. Learning becomes not just about acquiring knowledge but evolving one's approach to challenges and failures, ultimately fostering a lifelong learning journey.

Therefore, although I will describe and illustrate how you may use each layer, and the principles within the layers, one by one, the idea really is to learn to use them together. That said, you do not have to take an all-or-nothing approach. Take baby steps if you like, try one principle at a time, gradually incorporate the others, as they become part of your habits. All of this will take time of course, for it takes time to learn and become a deep learner. But it is well worth the journey.

Let us start with designing your challenge.

Designing Your Challenge

Keep It Challenging but Accessible When you are learning something new, it is counterintuitive to make things challenging. Often the impulse is to start with something simple. Now, that is fine as long as the simple task still gets you in the Zone. If not, you need to enter the Zone. It is essential for personal and professional advancement, as it pushes us to tackle more complex problems and learn new skills. Here are a few examples:

1. **Learning a musical instrument:** Starting to learn a complex piece that seems slightly beyond your current skill level can push you to refine your techniques and understand music more deeply.
2. **Physical fitness:** Trying a new, more demanding workout routine or sport can improve your physical condition and endurance, encouraging your body to adapt and grow stronger.
3. **Professional development:** Taking on a project at work that requires skills you're not fully comfortable with yet, such as leading a team, managing a more complex project, or learning a new technology, can significantly enhance your competence and confidence.

In each case, because you are in the Zone, you will struggle and even fail, but remember that this is precisely the locus of powerful learning. Struggle and even failure are a feature, not the bug. Of course, the challenge should not be so hard that you completely give up. Nor should it be harmful in any way (the principle of safe space applies). Finding the sweet spot is key.

One general strategy to get in the Zone that works across domains and skills is called *retrieval practice*. Recall the failed generation effect from Chapter 3? That was the idea that attempting to answer questions about an unfamiliar topic before learning improves learning of that topic even if the initial answers were incorrect, and the effect holds whether you are learning words, reading texts, or learning from videos. What this means is that anytime you are trying to learn something new or practicing a skill, always remember to test yourself first before jumping in. Be it revising for an exam, remembering a recipe, playing a new piece, or learning a new concept, test yourself first, and only then access the necessary information. Practicing retrieving information, even if we recall nothing or incorrect information, sets the stage for learning from the correct information. And only then should we access correct information, thereby completing the two-phase design.

Contextualize   When learning something new, contextualizing learning by relating new information to real-world situations or familiar concepts helps in understanding and retention. Recall from Chapter 1 that context matters. It matters where you learn something and how you learn something. The place matters, the situation matters, the practices matter. We encode information of not just the content we are trying to learn but also the context. Therefore, if we want to be able to learn something and apply it in the context of daily life, then we must contextualize our learning in the first place.

Suppose you want to or have to learn a new project management software. A decontextualized way of learning would involve consulting a manual or a series of generic training videos taking you through each functionality and feature. As intuitive as this way of learning may seem to be, it is not as effective as learning in the context of actual use. Imagine you are given a simulated project similar to their real tasks and asked to manage it using the new software. You might struggle initially, trying to figure out how to apply the software's features to your project. And once you have done that (your problem-solving phase), if a trainer then explains the software (the instruction phase), directly linking its features to the challenges you faced during the project management simulation, you will better relate each function of the software to your real work needs, enhancing your understanding and retention of how to use the software effectively.

The same logic applies in other areas too, such as learning a new language. You can learn language in a decontextualized manner by studying vocabulary and grammar rules through drills and textbook exercises. Or, before delving deeply into grammar and vocabulary, you can throw yourself into everyday situations – simulated or real – such as ordering food, asking for directions, and so on. This is your problem-solving phase. You will make mistakes and struggle to communicate effectively at first, but this is precisely what sets up the opportunity to learn from your mistakes. And then if you consult formal sources for grammar and vocabulary, or get just-in-time feedback in that situation – your instruction phase – you will learn language more meaningfully and retain it better. Context gets encoded, and this is why immersion works miracles. Design your own approximate immersions, simulated and real.

It does not matter what it is you are learning. Always contextualize in a way that the context of learning overlaps or is aligned with the context of use.

Multiple Solutions and Representations

To learn something means you can think about it in different ways, explain it in different ways, represent it in different ways, all connected with each other. Therefore, embracing multiple solutions and representations encourages diverse problem-solving approaches, enhancing understanding and creativity. Indeed, as noted in earlier chapters, research strongly supports that prior knowledge activation is key for learning, and problems that allow you to activate your knowledge more widely would therefore be better for your own learning.

Suppose you are trying to solve a complex problem at work. Engage in brainstorming sessions with colleagues from different departments or backgrounds. Encourage each participant to present their viewpoint or solution based on their expertise. For example, when addressing a customer service issue, include team members from sales, technical support, and product development in the discussion. This fosters a collaborative environment where multiple perspectives and solutions are considered, increasing the chance of more creative and effective outcomes. It also enhances your ability to work in diverse teams and appreciate different perspectives.

Equally, you may consider volunteering for or initiating projects that require collaboration across different functions of the organization. Working on such projects exposes you to various aspects of the business and different ways of thinking. This experience not only increases your under-standing of the business but also helps you develop a holistic approach to problem solving, improving your ability to contribute to complex projects effectively.

Tackling a mathematical problem using both algebraic and geometric methods can illuminate different aspects of the problem, offering insights into its structure and potential solutions. Or, if you are working on data analysis, try using various techniques to model the same data, for each may make different aspects or patterns in the data more salient. Or use different software tools like Excel, R, Python, SPSS, to find which offers the most insightful representations of data for your needs. By becoming proficient in multiple techniques and tools, you can choose the most effective one for each task, improving your work quality and efficiency.

The same goes for cooking. Preparing a dish with various techniques or ingredients, like baking vs. frying, offers insights into culinary science and nutrition. And financial planning. Comparing budgeting methods, such as the envelope system vs. digital apps, reveals the advantages of different financial strategies. Or continuous learning. Pursue learning opportunities in various formats, such as online courses, workshops, webinars, and books, covering a range of topics relevant to your field. By understanding concepts from multiple perspectives, you not only broaden your knowledge base, but also become more adaptive and innovative.

Design for multiplicity can be done after learning as well, especially through reflective practice. Regularly reflect on your learning experiences, challenges faced, and how you approached them. Consider what alternative strategies could have been employed. Keeping a journal or blog to document these reflections can be beneficial. Make it a habit to ask: Is this the only way? Could there be another way? Could I be wrong? How would someone else approach this? And so on. Such a habit encourages continuous improvement and helps you become more aware of the multiple approaches you can take to solve problems, increasing your efficiency and effectiveness over time.

Affective Draw   The principle of affective draw emphasizes engaging with topics that ignite curiosity and passion. When learning something new, choose contexts or topics that intrigue you, keeping motivation high. Find levers, anchors, inroads that you find interesting. This emotional connection enhances motivation and deepens learning.

Choose to learn about something you are passionate about, such as photography, gardening, or coding for personal projects. To get physically fit, pick a sport or a physical activity that you like instead of ones that you do not. Select books or articles in genres or topics you love, thereby increasing engagement and comprehension. Focus on professional skills or knowledge areas you are genuinely interested in, leading to more fulfilling career growth.

Even so, many of us struggle to get motivated to actually do the things, even the ones that we like or are curious about. All of us can use a boost from time to time, from getting us started, to keeping us going, to completing it. To help us, let us try to derive some hacks using the evidence-based Affective Boost Levels (ABLes) we encountered in Chapter 5.

1. *The first-lap hack:* The idea here is to get started. Sometimes the first step is itself the hardest. For example, my main exercise comes from swimming. I love swimming, but sometimes I struggle with my motivation. The idea of swimming for half an hour seems daunting at times, so I tell myself I will do just one lap, and that is it. Just one. That is my goal, and if I can do that, then I will have achieved my goal. That invariably gets me into the pool, and gets me started. After all, one lap is doable. The magic, however, happens after I have completed the first lap. Because once I get the first lap under my belt, I am already in the pool, and so I go for the second, then the third, ultimately completing my full set of 20 laps. Hence, the name: the *first-lap hack*. Take the first step. It gets you an "in." And an "in" gets you a "buy-in," much like the *endowed progress effect* or ABLe 2 discussed in Chapter 5. You are endowing your own progress, and hacking your way to getting started.

2. *The looking-back hack:* Even after getting started, the motivation to keep going needs a boost at times. It is quite easy to look at the goal and find it too far away. The trick, however, is not to look at the end, but instead the beginning. It helps to use your starting point as the reference point for your initial progress. Early in your journey, focus on how far you have come, and not on how much there is still left. Taking on a challenging task is hard, but if you get started and then focus on comparing your early progress with the initial state, you can hack your way into getting going and building momentum. Hence, the name: the looking-back hack, a direct

implication of the *endowed progress effect* or ABLe 2. It does not mean losing sight of the big goal, but hacking the process to stay the course.

3. *The move-the-goalpost-nearer hack:* Now that you have had a start and you are well underway, another way to hack your motivation is to break a big task into smaller chunks because smaller chunks bring the goalpost nearer, making the goal closer, which in turn could increase motivation. Move the goalpost, and you move the motivation. The *first-lap hack* is the special case of this, but we need more. For example, as I am writing this book, I do not want to think about the 70,000 words I contracted to write. That is daunting, a goal that seems far away, and not the most motivating I'd say. It's like writing another PhD thesis. So, I break my writing into daily goals, sometimes even a morning goal and an afternoon goal, intentionally moving the goalpost nearer to hack my motivation. And as I do, I leverage the *growth-gradient effect* or ABLe 3; that is, the more I write, the closer I get to the finish line, the more motivated I am to keep on writing. And it works for the most part, as I have now settled on a slow-and-steady 500 words daily. I call it the *move-the-goalpost-nearer hack.*

Contrast and Vary Cases   Contrasts help us see things. Don't just learn how to do something; also learn how else to do it, and perhaps how not to do it. Language learning is a perfect example. Do not just learn how to order a cup of coffee in a cafe, but even a slightly different way in which you can do that. Also learn the way in which you should not. These different ways create a variation, which in turn sets up comparison; each comparison helps you see what is critical in the meaning and use of language.

What is the capital of Switzerland? First of course, practice retrieval. Maybe you thought of one of the bigger cities such as Zurich or Geneva. You are wrong, but retrieval practice, even if it resulted in failure, has now set you up for learning. Now if you found out the capital of Switzerland, you will have learned which city is the capital, and which ones are not. The contrast is helpful for memory. And the next time you think about the capital of Switzerland, you might think of all the three cities, and know which one is and is not, but here is the thing: thinking about the ones that are not will guide you to the right one.

Therefore, as a rule, always learn from contrasts. If you are presented with only one case, then learn to ask for or generate other cases. Cases that are either variants, non-examples, or even counterfactuals. As we saw in Chapter 6, research shows that we do not learn as well from single examples or cases, but when presented with (typically) two cases at once, cases that are similar and different in interesting ways, we tend to see things, and learn and transfer a lot better.

Remember the museum study from Chapter 3? Research shows that the best way to understand an artist or a style is to learn it by comparing with other artists and styles. Comparing and contrasting is more effortful, even difficult, but as we have repeatedly seen in this book, such difficulty is desirable. Why? Because contrasting cases help you see by highlighting differences and similarities. Here are a few more examples:

1. **Comparing histories:** Delving into how different societies responded to similar challenges, such as economic depressions or political upheavals, provides a nuanced understanding of historical causality and human behavior. This approach can reveal patterns and influences that shaped societies' paths, offering lessons applicable to contemporary issues.

2. **Comparing products:** Investigating various products, like smartphones or investment plans, by comparing their specifications, user reviews, and prices helps in making informed decisions. This process not only highlights the strengths and weaknesses of each option but also educates the consumer about what features are most relevant to their needs.

3. **Comparing case studies:** Regularly study and analyze case studies from your industry, as well as from different sectors. This can provide insights into how various challenges are approached and solved, offering lessons that can be adapted to your own work context. For example, a marketer might study successful campaigns both from within their industry and from unrelated sectors, such as tech, fashion, and nonprofits, to glean diverse strategies and tactics.

4. **Comparing project management methods:** If you're involved in project management, explore different project management methodologies (like Agile, Scrum, and Lean) by applying them in various project types. This variation can help you understand the

strengths and weaknesses of each method in different contexts, making you more adaptable and skilled at choosing the most effective approach for each project.

5. **Comparing cultures:** Broaden your cultural understanding by exposing yourself to a variety of cultural experiences where and to the extent possible, such as through travel, literature, films, and cuisine from around the world. This exposure to diverse cases of cultural expression can enhance your empathy, communication skills, and global awareness, contributing to both personal growth and improved interpersonal relationships.

The idea is to never try to learn from a single case or example; always compare two or three. Not too many to keep it manageable, but also not just one. Ideally, simultaneously, side-by-side, so that you can perceptually see the similarities and differences, but also conceptually see features and underlying structure that are critical. And even if you fail to see at first, this failure is good, because we know that one of the ways failure helps us see is by naturally creating contrasts between our own failed prior knowledge and the correct knowledge.

Even when you are practicing something, for example, a topic in mathematics, a piece of music, shooting in basketball, preparing for an exam, and so on, it is good to change it up. The principle here is: do not amass practice. Design for variation. It is good to practice for a while, and then change it up. Do not just attempt one type of problem, but try different kinds that target the concept you are trying to learn. Do not stand in just one place and practice shooting basketball ad nauseum. Vary it. Try a few in one place, then another, and then another, each time adjusting and adapting to the angle, power, depth perception, and so on. Likewise, prepare a varied routine for exam preparation as well. Vary the topics, domains, places, and durations of study.

All this variation forces comparisons; comparison forces attention to critical features and adaptation, and prepares you to learn from feedback. Take one of the highest rated chess grandmasters, Magnus Carlsen, as an example. It is said he learned the game by playing multiple games simultaneously on the computer. He set up his own variation, each time adapting and learning from what worked, what did not, adapting constantly and accelerating his learning. Even though practicing with variation is difficult, such difficulties are desirable, as long as the mental load remains manageable.

Minimize Computational Load   The principle of minimizing computational load involves reducing the unnecessary complexity of tasks to focus on core concepts, facilitating deeper understanding. If the task involves numbers and computation, then keep the numbers simple and easy to calculate. Leveraging calculators or software for routine calculations allows more mental resources to be dedicated to understanding underlying principles and strategies. This way, the underlying problem can remain the same, but at least you do not have to suffer from overload. Sometimes, breaking a task down into sub-tasks and focusing on just those helps too. If there is too much technical language, try to get help from someone who can explain it in simpler language. By keeping computational load low without changing the underlying structure of the problem, you give yourself a better chance of learning it.

Design Your Participation

Alongside designing your challenge, you need to think about how you would approach it. Just like when designing the participation for others, you too need to think about the same two questions:

a) How and when would you work alone or with others?

b) How would you facilitate your own learning process?

Working Alone or Together   Regardless of what it is that you are learning, it is good to find or design a community around you, a group of peers and mentors who can support and guide you. For example, you may want to join thematic study groups, where you can engage in group discussions and activities to learn things together. The same goes for online forums to complement or supplement in-person groups, giving you access to peers and experts beyond your immediate circle. Attending workshops and events on the topic of your interest is also an excellent way of supporting and accelerating your growth.

However, as noted in the previous chapter, individual preparation for the group activity is key. You will derive greater benefit from the group if you go into it well prepared. By well prepared, I mean having explored a problem or a topic or a skill yourself first, so that your own knowledge is activated, you are aware of what you can and cannot do, and you are motivated to bridge the gap. This way, you will be ready for assembly.

And you can self-facilitate both your preparation and assembly by the same two strategies as in the previous chapter: a) Explaining, and b) Hacking.

Self-Facilitation via Explaining   I have given two TEDx talks thus far. The first one was in 2019 on Productive Failure and learning. The second one in 2023 was a broader take on Productive Failure in a number of domains. In both cases, I remember spending hours preparing for the talk, rehearsing it in the mirror, scripting parts of it if I needed to so that I could say what I wanted to say with economy, precision, and impact. It was not simply an exercise in transmission of what I knew to the audience. Even after 15 years of working on Productive Failure, I thought I could not possibly learn more, but I was surprised. Preparing for my TEDx talks helped me not only understand and improve my own content but also my confidence and capability in public speaking.

The point is not that you have to go searching for a way to give a TEDx talk. The point is that you can pretend that you need to. For example, after having read an article on climate change, or watched a video on longevity science, or heard a podcast on the French revolution, or learned a new concept in mathematics, you can pretend to explain all of it to a friend or family member with precision, economy, and impact. And rehearse it as much as it is possible to make it the best explanation you can give.

When you have to explain something to someone, you engage actively with the material, which places you high on the activation spectrum (Figure 3.1). Therefore, as already noted in the previous chapter, it is not surprising that research strongly supports the principle that when we prepare to explain something to someone and then actually deliver it, on both counts we benefit.

Do not worry if you do not fully understand the material. The whole point of preparing to explain and actually explaining is to help you learn better. When you have to break down the concept into simpler parts, create analogies, or even prepare mini-lessons or exercises, it forces you to organize your thoughts and make the subject matter clear in your own mind, highlighting areas you understand well and those you might need to revisit. The act of explaining something to someone else requires recalling the information, a kind of retrieval practice, which strengthens memory retention. And as you prepare to teach, you will likely discover gaps in your own understanding, providing an opportunity to fill these gaps before they become problematic.

Prepare for explaining as well as actually explaining early in and throughout your learning process, and you will see that it accelerates your own learning. And as it was for me, it also has the added benefit of boosting your confidence in your knowledge as well as improving your ability to communicate ideas succinctly and clearly, which is a valuable skill in work and life.

Self-Facilitation via Hacking   In 2019, I was invited to give a keynote at the biennial conference of the European Association Research on Learning and Instruction. It is the flagship conference of learning in Europe with attendees from around the world. Who's-who of research on human learning and education actively attend this conference. I was indeed honored to have been invited to keynote, and was asked to suggest a title and abstract for my talk. This was of course not my first keynote; I had done several before, most of them being about Productive Failure. I remember thinking at the time if I should give another talk on Productive Failure, or perhaps it was time for something else. Something new, something fresh.

It was then that I decided to hack Productive Failure. I told myself I should practice what I preach, so it only made sense to ask the question: When does Productive Failure fail? I had spent years trying to understand how and why Productive Failure works. It was time to ask the other question, and even more pointedly, when does it fail?

Answering this question required that we, my then–doctoral student Tanmay Sinha and I, undertake a systematic review and meta-analysis to gather all the experimental studies on Productive Failure, and try to detect a pattern across the various studies to understand "When Productive Failure Fails," which turned out to be the title of my keynote in the end.

We found a simple answer. Productive Failure fails when it is badly designed or implemented. Essentially suggesting that even if the science underlying it was sound and robust, Productive Failure could still fail if it was not designed well, much like a badly designed Ferrari would.

And we would not have found this out unless we had tried to hack it. The only way we could do so was by asking the failure question itself: When does Productive Failure fail? The answer we found to this question is how we started paying greater attention to the design principles of Productive Failure, specifying with greater clarity and precision exactly what goes into designing for Productive Failure.

Hacking Productive Failure told us that the science in Part II is sound, but that design is often where things go wrong. That is why Part III of this book is dedicated to design.

The same hacking principle can be applied to anything we want to learn, from the causes of war, to science, to literature, to strategy, to product development, and many others. Just when you think you have understood something, try to hack it, break it, make it fail.

Trying to make it fail requires that we separate the boundary of success from failure. This means challenging the idea by asking: Does the idea work only for the given context or situation? Can it work for other contexts and situations? Under what circumstances would the idea not work? This approach of hacking one's ideas fosters a mindset of continuous learning and improvement, essential for creating solutions that are robust.

In summary, I repeat what I said in the previous chapter. Explaining your own idea. And hacking your own idea. Two simple steps that give large returns on learning. The more we can develop these habits, the more we learn, even beyond Productive Failure, for these are good habits for learning and life in general.

Designing Your Safe Space

Creating a psychologically safe space for yourself involves fostering an environment where making mistakes is viewed as a part of the learning process, not a failure. It encourages taking risks and exploring new ideas without fear of judgment. Re-norming and mind-setting involve adopting a growth mindset, where challenges are seen as opportunities to improve and learn, rather than insurmountable obstacles. There is neither one way nor an exhaustive list of things you can do, but here are a few things you can do to create this space for yourself:

1. **Set learning goals:** Creating specific, achievable goals that encourage stepping out of comfort zones in a structured way. A lot of this depends upon cultivating productive habits such as reflecting, explaining, hacking your own learning, help seeking, collaborating, resourcefulness, and so on. Productive habits are goals in and of themselves. Learn these habits so you can use these habits to learn and grow. An excellent way to think about how you might go about doing this is to read James Clear's book: *Atomic Habits*.

2. **Emphasize effort over outcome:** Recognize and reward the effort and learning process, not just the final results. Recognize the first step, and as noted earlier, use it as an affective hack for persistent effort. Focus on doing small things every day that work toward building a system of productive habits that accelerate your learning and growth.

3. **Reflect:** Taking time, even briefly, to regularly journal about your learning experiences, focusing on growth, challenges, and lessons learned from mistakes, is a useful habit to cultivate. Regularly review personal progress and adapt your learning strategies, focusing on continuous improvement rather than perfection.

4. **Seek feedback:** Actively ask for feedback, not as a judgment but as a source of insights for growth. Exploration, struggle, making mistakes, failure, all of these, even if they happen in a safe space, will lead to nothing without feedback. Remember Productive Failure is a two-phase design: the first phase of exploration has to be followed by feedback or explicit instruction. Seek feedback, engage a mentor, find a knowledgeable other to guide you.

5. **Seek affective support:** Knowing what you need to do is the easy part. Actually doing it is harder. And if you are like me and most people, it always helps to have affective support from your peers, friends, family, colleagues who understand and embody the same spirit that feeling the ups and downs, the struggle, the emotions is just as important as the destination. Build a small circle around you. Do not wait for it to happen. Make it happen.

6. **Get inspired:** Reading, listening to, watching stories about how experts in a field overcame challenges helps reinforce the belief in growth through perseverance. These narratives provide valuable insights into the real-world application of skills, strategies, and resilience, a lived experience of setbacks as opportunities for learning and development rather than deterrents, and offer a roadmap for navigating obstacles and achieving success.

7. **Practice affirmation:** Using positive affirmations that focus on growth to reinforce a growth mindset toward learning and personal development. Using language that emphasizes effort and growth, such as "I'm not good at this yet" instead of "I can't do this," "I want to thrive outside of my comfort zone, pushing my boundaries," "If I am not struggling, I am not learning,"

"I embrace challenges as opportunities to learn and grow,"
"I celebrate my progress and achievements, no matter how small,"
and so on.

8. **Practice compassion:** Be kind to yourself and others. Practice
   mindfulness and self-compassion exercises to reduce self-criticism
   and anxiety about making mistakes. Everyone feels the same way
   when learning new things. Everyone feels a bit out of depth.
   Everyone feels some anxiety. Everyone fears failure. Practicing
   compassion for others and yourself is absolutely critical.

9. **Acknowledge luck:** Finally, amidst all of the above, one must
   acknowledge the important role luck plays. Learning and growth
   often involve a combination of preparation and luck. While we can
   diligently equip ourselves with knowledge, skills, and opportunities,
   unforeseen circumstances and chance encounters significantly
   influence our journey. Luck can manifest in unexpected
   opportunities, chance meetings, or fortunate (or unfortunate)
   events that are often not within our control. For example, it took
   me a long time to understand the role of luck, and when I did, it
   helped me finally overcome disappointment and despair after my
   knee injury abruptly ended my plans. Therefore, while preparation
   lays the groundwork for success, embracing the element of luck
   reminds us to stay open-minded, adaptable, and ready to seize
   unexpected opportunities that can propel us forward in our
   endeavors. Luck, as they say, favors the prepared.

The Whole Is Greater Than the Sum of the Parts

I started with the idea of *productive discontentment*. It gets us in the Zone, the
place where deep learning happens. But it is also the Zone where we might
struggle as we explore, and even fail as we generate ideas and solutions. It is
not a nice feeling to struggle or fail. It is okay to doubt ourselves from time
to time. But when you do, tell yourself it is okay to fail. Re-norming and
mind-setting are key. The more we embrace it, the more we will grow.
Embracing *productive discomfort*: the art of becoming comfortable with being
uncomfortable. All in the service of learning and growth.

And this is where Productive Failure comes in. Struggle and failure
alone do not guarantee learning. Even the healthiest of mindsets are not

sufficient on their own. To make failure productive for ourselves, we need to carefully design for it, be deliberate, intentional, and resourceful, seek out the right kind of expert help, work with people, and plug into and build a support community around ourselves.

Designing for and using all the principles in each of the three layers can seem daunting. Start small. Pick a few low-hanging fruits as they say. Pick one even. Work on it. Gradually, add more to the mix. Build it up over time. And as you do, you will start to see the synergistic effects of the principles as a system, where the whole is greater than the sum of the parts.

You have come this far with this book. You have already taken the first step. Recognize it, celebrate it. Now take the next one.

Key Takeaways

The three-layered design framework for Productive Failure specifies an iterative calibration process for designing your own *task*, your own *participation*, and your own *social surround* or *safe space* for learning:

1. **Designing your own tasks.** Effective tasks should be within your ZPD, provide contextual relevance, allow for multiple solutions and representations, create an affective draw, use contrasting and varied cases, and minimize computational load.

2. **Designing your participation.** Develop the habits of explaining and hacking your ideas. Structuring learning experiences to include feedback and collaboration at the right moments enhances understanding and supports the learner through challenging tasks.

3. **Designing your safe space for learning.** Be deliberate about setting specific learning goals, emphasizing effort over outcomes, actively seeking feedback, and building supportive networks. Learn to reflect, practice affirmation and compassion, get inspired, and recognize the role of luck.

4. **It takes time.** Self-explanatory.

Conclusion

When my elder son, Dev, was in kindergarten, he would make me lie down so he could sit on my stomach and play games. One of our favorites was the number counting game, which would go something like: If you have three toy cars and I gave you five more, how many would you have? His natural impulse would be to start counting using his fingers. He would count to three to denote the three cars he already had. And then count on five more to get to eight. At least that is what most kids would do – except this kid had me as his father, and I was testing my theory of how making things harder to the point that we fail can be beneficial for learning. Therefore, every time my son would start using his fingers, I would playfully grasp his hands and tell him he could not use them. He had to think without his hands. It was all fun and games, and there was no pressure or a reward to get it right.

Initially, I could see he was trying to figure it out. Over time, he got better and I could see he was counting in his head, but still couldn't get the right answers. And then a few weeks later, it all clicked for him, as if a phase transition had taken place, and he started giving the correct answers almost all the time.

What happened next surprised me even more. He started giving the correct answers at astonishing speeds. This meant that he was no longer literally counting, for such counting would have taken a longer time. Instead, he was performing mental arithmetic effortlessly, much to the surprise of many of his kindergarten teachers later. It seemed as if the initial difficulty I had put him through had worked out for him, even though in the short term he seemed to be flailing and failing. I do not suggest you start putting your children through this, but when you come to think of it, such a process is natural in a number of things a child learns, from learning to sit up, crawl, and walk to her first words and spoken language. Later on, a similar process may ensue when a child is learning to ride a scooter or a bike. In each case, initial trials often result in struggle and failure. Performance suffers, but it sets the stage for deep learning provided there is someone to guide and learn from at the right time.

Performance and learning therefore are not the same thing, but we often conflate the two.

In school, at work, in sports – wherever we strive for success – we focus on achieving the best results. This focus on performance success, however, can sometimes obscure a more profound, yet less visible facet of success – learning. Performance does not necessarily equal learning, and vice versa. High performance doesn't always mean high learning, and low performance doesn't necessarily mean low learning. Taking them as two separate, orthogonal scales creates four potential outcomes as shown in Figure C.1: Productive Success, Productive Failure, Unproductive Failure, and Unproductive Success (Kapur 2016).

Sometimes when we take on challenging problems, our performance suffers initially. The students who tried to solve the basketball problem

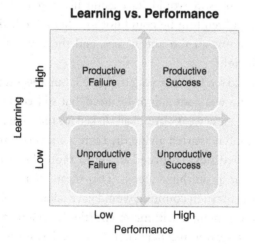

Figure C.1   Learning versus Performance: Productive Success, Productive Failure, Unproductive Failure, and Unproductive Success (Adapted from Kapur 2016).

(Figure 2.1) without first learning the concepts are a perfect example. They tried different ways to solve the problem but failed to get to the correct answer. From an objective standpoint of reaching the correct solution, their performance repeatedly ended in failure. But this does not mean there was no learning, or preparation for learning, happening. Sometimes performance and learning do not coincide initially; their convergence is delayed somewhat. Yet, under certain conditions, the paths can converge eventually if we can extract value from the initial failure. This, as you know by now, is Productive Failure.

What happens when performance and learning converge from the get-go? Imagine a seasoned musician engrossed in their craft, playing a challenging piece of music flawlessly. They are in a state of deep focus where they not only perform excellently but also derive new insights about the music and their technique. They are "in the zone," or a state of flow, as the late psychologist Mihaly Csikszentmihalyi (1975) called it. Another way to call it would be Productive Success. It is characterized by a sense of effortlessness, intense concentration, and enjoyment, and it usually leads to high performance in the activity. Productive Success is the sweet spot where high performance meets high learning, where the two are in perfect harmony.

On the other side of the spectrum, we have Unproductive Failure, where both performance and learning are low. This can be seen in using pure discovery learning to learn formal concepts, where students are given a problem and left entirely on their own to find a solution. Without any guidance, students often flounder, leading to both low performance and low learning. They neither solve the problem effectively (low performance) nor gain a good grasp of the underlying principles (low learning). Nobody wants this to happen, and we should avoid it.

That leaves us with the deceptive possibility of Unproductive Success – the illusion of learning in high performance. Performance is high, yet learning is low. Where performance seems to suggest that learning has taken place, but learning remains shallow, and transfer elusive. As we have seen so far, the classic example is rote learning or Direct Instruction, where students are spoon-fed information, which they memorize and regurgitate in exams, leading to high grades (high performance). However, the deeper understanding of concepts is often missing in this approach, leading to low learning. It is a hollow victory, where the apparent success masks a lack of genuine learning.

These examples illustrate that performance and learning are not always aligned. Performance can sometimes be a misleading indicator of learning, and it is essential to recognize the value of the process and the learning journey, not just the end result. Striving for high performance is not wrong, but we need to be aware that true learning – the kind that stays with us and shapes our understanding – does not always correlate with high grades, accolades, or applause. In embracing this nuanced understanding, we allow ourselves to celebrate not just the obvious victories but also the hidden ones embedded in our failures and struggles.

I now leave you with the four big-picture takeaways from this book:

Key Takeaways

1. **Failure as a mechanism.** Do not wait for failure to happen. Design for it, for yourself and for others. Productive Failure shows us how to deliberately curate our learning experiences, so that we can harness the power of failure for deep learning. If you are not deliberately designing for failure to learn something new, you are not optimizing learning and growth. The science behind it is robust; it tells us how, when, and why Productive Failure works.

2. **Failure as a signal.** Conversely, if you find that there is no failure, chances are you are not really pushing yourself, you are not really taking on hard problems, or operating at the cutting edge. Seen this way, failure, provided it is not because of stupidity, laziness, or incompetence, can be seen as a signal that you are in the zone of deep learning and innovation. Therefore, assess taking on new projects and challenges not just by the probability of their success but also the probability of their failure. If the failure probability is low, notch it up.

3. **Failure as a feature.** Build safe spaces for yourself, your family, your teams, and your organizations where tolerance for failure is a feature, not a bug. This does not mean we chase failure for failure's sake. Instead, when learning something new, taking on a new challenge, or solving a complex problem, you will find that failure is bound to happen. A safe space for taking on new learnings and challenges is essential.

4. Failure as a mantra. When the above three come together, the true power of Productive Failure is unleashed, for it is then that we begin to internalize Productive Failure as a way of thinking, knowing, and being in this world, helping us seek, design, and harness the other side of failure, on a regular basis, until it becomes a part of us in everything we do, and perhaps it ultimately becomes us.

References

Chapter 1

Bjork, R.A. and Bjork, E.L. (1992) A new theory of disuse and an old theory of stimulus fluctuation. *From learning processes to cognitive processes: Essays in honor of William K. Estes*, 2, pp. 35–67.

Brown, J.S., Collins, A. and Duguid, P. (1989) "Situated Cognition and the culture of learning," *Educational Researcher*, 18(1), pp. 32–42. doi:10.3102/0013189x018001032.

Chase, W.G. and Simon, H.A. (1973) "Perception in chess," *Cognitive Psychology*, 4(1), pp. 55–81. doi:10.1016/0010-0285(73)90004-2.

de Groot, A.D. (1965) *Thought and choice in chess*. The Hague: Mouton.

Godden, D.R. and Baddeley, A.D. (1975) "Context-dependent memory in two natural environments: On land and underwater," *British Journal of Psychology*, 66(3), pp. 325–331. doi:10.1111/j.2044-8295.1975.tb01468.x.

Jongman, R.W. (1968) *Het oog oan de Meester*. Amsterdam: van Gorcum.

Miller, G.A. and Gildea, P.M. (1987) "How children learn words," *Scientific American*, 257(3), pp. 94–99. doi:10.1038/scientificamerican0987-94.

Schoenfeld, A.H. (1988) "When good teaching leads to bad results: The disasters of 'well-taught' mathematics courses," *Educational Psychologist*, 23(2), pp. 145–166. doi:10.1207/s15326985ep2302_5.

Schwartz, D.L. and Bransford, J.D. (1998) "A time for telling," *Cognition and Instruction*, 16(4), pp. 475–522. doi:10.1207/s1532690xci1604_4.

211

Smith, S.M. and Vela, E. (2001) "Environmental context-dependent memory: A review and meta-analysis," *Psychonomic Bulletin & Review*, 8(2), pp. 203–220. doi:10.3758/bf03196157.

Webb, S., Uchihara, T. and Yanagisawa, A. (2023) "How effective is second language incidental vocabulary learning? A meta-analysis," *Language Teaching*, 56(2), pp. 161–180. doi:10.1017/s0261444822000507.

Chapter 2

Kapur, M. (2016) "Examining productive failure, productive success, unproductive failure, and unproductive success in learning," *Educational Psychologist*, 51(2), pp. 289–299. doi:10.1080/00461520.2016.1155457.

Kuhn, T.S. (1962) *The Structure of Scientific Revolutions*. Chicago, IL: The University of Chicago Press.

Sim, Z.L. and Xu, F. (2017) "Learning higher-order generalizations through free play: Evidence from 2- and 3-year-old children," *Developmental Psychology*, 53(4), pp. 642–651. doi:10.1037/dev0000278.

Sinha, T. and Kapur, M. (2021) "When problem solving followed by instruction works: Evidence for productive failure," *Review of Educational Research*, 91(5), pp. 761–798. doi:10.3102/00346543211019105.

de Jong, T. *et al.* (2023) "Let's talk evidence: The case for combining inquiry-based and direct instruction," *Educational Research Review*, 39, doi:10.1016/j.edurev.2023.100536.

Chapter 3

Bertsch, S. *et al.* (2007) "The generation effect: A meta-analytic review," *Memory & Cognition*, 35(2), pp. 201–210. doi:10.3758/bf03193441.

Bjork, R.A. (1994) "Memory and metamemory considerations in the training of human beings," *Metacognition*, pp. 185–206. doi:10.7551/mitpress/4561.003.0011.

Chi, M.T. (2009) "Active-constructive-Interactive: A conceptual framework for differentiating learning activities," *Topics in Cognitive Science*, 1(1), pp. 73–105. doi:10.1111/j.1756-8765.2008.01005.x.

Kang, S.H., Gollan, T.H. and Pashler, H. (2013) "Don't just repeat after me: Retrieval practice is better than imitation for foreign vocabulary learning," *Psychonomic Bulletin & Review*, 20(6), pp. 1259–1265. doi:10.3758/s13423-013-0450-z.

Kerr, R. and Booth, B. (1978) "Specific and varied practice of motor skill," *Perceptual and Motor Skills*, 46(2), pp. 395–401. doi:10.1177/003151257804600201.

Kornell, N. and Bjork, R.A. (2008) "Learning concepts and categories," *Psychological Science*, 19(6), pp. 585–592. doi:10.1111/j.1467-9280.2008.02127.x.

Kornell, N., Hays, M.J. and Bjork, R.A. (2009) "Unsuccessful retrieval attempts enhance subsequent learning," *Journal of Experimental Psychology: Learning, Memory, and Cognition*, 35(4), pp. 989–998. doi:10.1037/a0015729.

Pan, S.C. and Sana, F. (2021) "Pretesting versus posttesting: Comparing the pedagogical benefits of errorful generation and retrieval practice," *Journal of Experimental Psychology: Applied*, 27(2), pp. 237–257. doi:10.1037/xap0000345.

Pan, S.C. *et al.* (2020) "Pretesting reduces mind wandering and enhances learning during online lectures," *Journal of Applied Research in Memory and Cognition*, 9(4), pp. 542–554. doi:10.1016/j.jarmac.2020.07.004.

Potts, R. and Shanks, D.R. (2014) "The benefit of generating errors during learning," *Journal of Experimental Psychology: General*, 143(2), pp. 644–667. doi:10.1037/a0033194.

Richland, L.E., Kornell, N. and Kao, L.S. (2009) "The pretesting effect: Do unsuccessful retrieval attempts enhance learning?," *Journal of Experimental Psychology: Applied*, 15(3), pp. 243–257. doi:10.1037/a0016496.

Schwartz, D.L. and Bransford, J.D. (1998) "A time for telling," *Cognition and Instruction*, 16(4), pp. 475–522. doi:10.1207/s1532690xci1604_4.

Simmons, A.L. (2011) "Distributed practice and procedural memory consolidation in musicians' skill learning," *Journal of Research in Music Education*, 59(4), pp. 357–368. doi:10.1177/0022429411424798.

Slamecka, N.J. and Graf, P. (1978) "The generation effect: Delineation of a phenomenon," *Journal of Experimental Psychology: Human Learning and Memory*, 4(6), pp. 592–604. doi:10.1037/0278-7393.4.6.592.

St. Hilaire, K.J. and Carpenter, S.K. (2020) "Prequestions enhance learning, but only when they are remembered," *Journal of Experimental Psychology: Applied*, 26(4), pp. 705–716. doi:10.1037/xap0000296.

Toftness, A.R. *et al.* (2018) "The limited effects of prequestions on learning from authentic lecture videos," *Journal of Applied Research in Memory and Cognition*, 7(3), pp. 370–378. doi:10.1016/j.jarmac.2018.06.003.

Chapter 4

Acuña, S.R., García Rodicio, H. and Sánchez, E. (2010) "Fostering active processing of instructional explanations of learners with high and low prior knowledge," *European Journal of Psychology of Education*, 26(4), pp. 435–452. doi:10.1007/s10212-010-0049-y.

Butterfield, B. and Metcalfe, J. (2001) "Errors committed with high confidence are hypercorrected," *Journal of Experimental Psychology: Learning, Memory, and Cognition*, 27(6), pp. 1491–1494. doi:10.1037/0278-7393.27.6.1491.

Butterfield, B. and Metcalfe, J. (2006) "The correction of errors committed with high confidence," *Metacognition and Learning*, 1(1), pp. 69–84. doi:10.1007/s11409-006-6894-z.

Glogger-Frey, I. *et al.* (2015) "Inventing a solution and studying a worked solution prepare differently for learning from direct instruction," *Learning and Instruction*, 39, pp. 72–87. doi:10.1016/j.learninstruc.2015.05.001.

Hartmann, C., van Gog, T. and Rummel, N. (2021) "Preparatory effects of problem solving versus studying examples prior to instruction," *Instructional Science*, 49(1), pp. 1–21. doi:10.1007/s11251-020-09528-z.

Loibl, K. and Rummel, N. (2014) "Knowing what you don't know makes failure productive," *Learning and Instruction*, 34(1), pp. 74–85. doi:10.1016/j.learninstruc.2014.08.004.

McPhetres, J. (2019) "Oh, the things you don't know: Awe promotes awareness of knowledge gaps and science interest," *Cognition and Emotion*, 33(8), pp. 1599–1615. doi:10.1080/02699931.2019.1585331.

Mera, Y., Rodríguez, G. and Marin-Garcia, E. (2021) "Unraveling the benefits of experiencing errors during learning: Definition, modulating factors, and explanatory theories," *Psychonomic Bulletin & Review*, 29(3), pp. 753–765. doi:10.3758/s13423-021-02022-8.

Metcalfe, J. (2017) "Learning from errors," *Annual Review of Psychology*, 68(1), pp. 465–489. doi:10.1146/annurev-psych-010416-044022.

Metcalfe, J. and Finn, B. (2012) "Hypercorrection of high confidence errors in children," *Learning and Instruction*, 22(4), pp. 253–261. doi:10.1016/j.learninstruc.2011.10.004.

Metcalfe, J. and Miele, D.B. (2014) "Hypercorrection of high confidence errors: Prior testing both enhances delayed performance and blocks the return of the errors," *Journal of Applied Research in Memory and Cognition*, 3(3), pp. 189–197. doi:10.1016/j.jarmac.2014.04.001.

Metcalfe, J. *et al.* (2012) "Neural correlates of people's hypercorrection of their false beliefs," *Journal of Cognitive Neuroscience*, 24(7), pp. 1571–1583. doi:10.1162/jocn_a_00228.

Pacaci, C., Ustun, U. and Ozdemir, O.F. (2023) "Effectiveness of conceptual change strategies in science education: A meta-analysis," *Journal of Research in Science Teaching* [Preprint]. doi:10.1002/tea.21887.

Sánchez, E., García-Rodicio, H. and Acuña, S.R. (2008) "Are instructional explanations more effective in the context of an impasse?," *Instructional Science*, 37(6), pp. 537–563. doi:10.1007/s11251-008-9074-5.

VanLehn, K. *et al.* (2003) "Why do only some events cause learning during human tutoring?," *Cognition and Instruction*, 21(3), pp. 209–249. doi:10.1207/s1532690xci2103_01.

Funny talking animals: Walk on the wild side: BBC (2009) *YouTube.* Available at: https://youtu.be/EQ1HKCYJM5U (Accessed: 17 April 2024).

Planet Earth BBC. Amazing Footage. Montage. (2010) *YouTube.* Available at: https://www.youtube.com/embed/3voeYWCAE2s (Accessed: 17 April 2024).

Chapter 5

Belenky, D.M. and Nokes-Malach, T.J. (2012) "Motivation and transfer: The role of mastery-approach goals in preparation for future learning," *Journal of the Learning Sciences*, 21(3), pp. 399–432. doi:10.1080/10508406. 2011.651232.

Bonawitz, E. *et al.* (2011) "The double-edged sword of pedagogy: Instruction limits spontaneous exploration and Discovery," *Cognition*, 120(3), pp. 322–330. doi:10.1016/j.cognition.2010.10.001.

Bonezzi, A., Brendl, C.M. and De Angelis, M. (2011) "Stuck in the middle," *Psychological Science*, 22(5), pp. 607–612. doi:10.1177/0956797611404899.

Campion, N., Martins, D. and Wilhelm, A. (2009) "Contradictions and predictions: Two sources of uncertainty that raise the cognitive interest of readers," *Discourse Processes*, 46(4), pp. 341–368. doi:10.1080/ 01638530802629125.

Cook, C., Goodman, N.D. and Schulz, L.E. (2011) "Where science starts: Spontaneous experiments in preschoolers' exploratory play," *Cognition*, 120(3), pp. 341–349. doi:10.1016/j.cognition.2011.03.003.

Dweck, C.S. and Leggett, E.L. (1988) "A social-cognitive approach to motivation and personality," *Psychological Review*, 95(2), pp. 256–273. doi:10.1037/0033-295x.95.2.256.

Elliot, A.J. and Harackiewicz, J.M. (1996) "Approach and avoidance achievement goals and intrinsic motivation: A mediational analysis," *Journal of Personality and Social Psychology*, 70(3), pp. 461–475. doi:10.1037/0022-3514.70.3.461.

Elliot, A.J. and McGregor, H.A. (2001) "A 2 × 2 achievement goal framework," *Journal of Personality and Social Psychology*, 80(3), pp. 501–519. doi:10.1037/0022-3514.80.3.501.

Fredrickson, B.L. (2001) "The role of positive emotions in positive psychology: The broaden-and-build theory of positive emotions," *American Psychologist*, 56(3), pp. 218–226. doi:10.1037//0003-066x.56.3.218.

Fredrickson, B.L. and Losada, M.F. (2005) "Positive affect and the complex dynamics of human flourishing," *American Psychologist*, 60(7), pp. 678–686. doi:10.1037/0003-066x.60.7.678.

Gopnik, A. (1996) "The scientist as child," *Philosophy of Science*, 63(4), pp. 485–514. doi:10.1086/289970.

Gopnik, A. (2009) *The philosophical baby what children's minds tell us about truth, love, and the meaning of life.* New York: Farrar, Straus and Giroux.

Gopnik, A. (2016) *The gardener and the carpenter: What the New Science of Child Development tells us about the relationship between parents and children.* Farrar, Straus and Giroux.

Gopnik, A., Griffiths, T.L. and Lucas, C.G. (2015) "When younger learners can be better (or at least more open-minded) than older ones," *Current Directions in Psychological Science*, 24(2), pp. 87–92. doi:10.1177/0963721414556653.

Gopnik, A., Meltzoff, A.N. and Kuhl, P.K. (1999) *The scientist in the crib: Minds, brains, and how children learn.* William Morrow & Co.

Gopnik, A. and Schulz, L.E. (2007) *Causal learning: Psychology, philosophy, and computation.* Oxford University Press.

Gruber, M.J., Gelman, B.D. and Ranganath, C. (2014) "States of curiosity modulate hippocampus-dependent learning via the dopaminergic circuit," *Neuron*, 84(2), pp. 486–496. doi:10.1016/j.neuron.2014.08.060.

Harackiewicz, J.M. *et al.* (2002) "Predicting success in college: A longitudinal study of achievement goals and ability measures as predictors of interest and performance from freshman year through graduation,"

Journal of Educational Psychology, 94(3), pp. 562–575. doi:10.1037/0022-0663.94.3.562.

Huang, C. (2012) "Discriminant and criterion-related validity of achievement goals in predicting academic achievement: A meta-analysis," *Journal of Educational Psychology*, 104(1), pp. 48–73. doi:10.1037/a0026223.

Hull, C.L. (1932) "The goal-gradient hypothesis and maze learning," *Psychological Review*, 39(1), pp. 25–43. doi:10.1037/h0072640.

Hulleman, C.S. *et al.* (2010) "A meta-analytic review of Achievement Goal measures: Different labels for the same constructs or different constructs with similar labels?," *Psychological Bulletin*, 136(3), pp. 422–449. doi:10.1037/a0018947.

Kahneman, D. and Tversky, A. (1979) "Prospect theory: An analysis of decision under risk," *Econometrica*, 47(2), pp. 263–291. doi:10.2307/1914185.

Kang, M.J. *et al.* (2009) "The wick in the candle of learning," *Psychological Science*, 20(8), pp. 963–973. doi:10.1111/j.1467-9280.2009.02402.x.

Kivetz, R., Urminsky, O. and Zheng, Y. (2006) "The goal-gradient hypothesis resurrected: Purchase acceleration, illusionary goal progress, and customer retention," *Journal of Marketing Research*, 43(1), pp. 39–58. doi:10.1509/jmkr.43.1.39.

Koo, M. and Fishbach, A. (2008) "Dynamics of self-regulation: How (un)accomplished goal actions affect motivation," *Journal of Personality and Social Psychology*, 94(2), pp. 183–195. doi:10.1037/0022-3514.94.2.183.

Lamnina, M. and Chase, C. C. (2017) "Increasing curiosity through invention," paper presented at the Annual Meeting of the American Educational Research Association, San Antonio, TX.

Lamnina, M. and Chase, C.C. (2019) "Developing a thirst for knowledge: How uncertainty in the classroom influences curiosity, affect, learning, and transfer," *Contemporary Educational Psychology*, 59, p. 101785. doi:10.1016/j.cedpsych.2019.101785.

Loibl, K. and Rummel, N. (2014) "Knowing what you don't know makes failure productive," *Learning and Instruction*, 34(1), pp. 74–85. doi:10.1016/j.learninstruc.2014.08.004.

Nunes, J.C. and Drèze, X. (2006) "The Endowed Progress Effect: How artificial advancement increases effort," *Journal of Consumer Research*, 32(4), pp. 504–512. doi:10.1086/500480.

Ovsiankina, Maria (1928) "Die Wiederaufnahme unterbrochener Handlungen," *Psychologische Forschung*, 11, 302–379.

Piaget, J. (1936) *Origins of intelligence in the child*. Routledge & Kegan Paul.

Schulz, L.E. and Bonawitz, E.B. (2007) "Serious fun: Preschoolers engage in more exploratory play when evidence is confounded," *Developmental Psychology*, 43(4), pp. 1045–1050. doi:10.1037/0012-1649.43.4.1045.

Schulz, L.E., Gopnik, A. and Glymour, C. (2007) "Preschool children learn about causal structure from conditional interventions," *Developmental Science*, 10(3), pp. 322–332. doi:10.1111/j.1467-7687.2007.00587.x.

Sinha, T. (2021) "Enriching problem-solving followed by instruction with explanatory accounts of emotions," *Journal of the Learning Sciences*, 31(2), pp. 151–198. doi:10.1080/10508406.2021.1964506.

Wirthwein, L. *et al.* (2013) "Achievement goals and academic achievement: A closer look at moderating factors," *Educational Research Review*, 10, pp. 66–89. doi:10.1016/j.edurev.2013.07.001.

Zeigarnik, B. (1927) "Das Behalten erledigter und unerledigter Handlungen," *Psychologische Forschungen*, 9, pp. 1–85.

The old curiosity shop (2024) *Wikipedia*. Available at: https://en.wikipedia.org/wiki/The_Old_Curiosity_Shop (Accessed: 17 April 2024).

Chapter 6

Alfieri, L., Nokes-Malach, T.J. and Schunn, C.D. (2013) "Learning through case comparisons: A meta-analytic review," *Educational Psychologist*, 48(2), pp. 87–113. doi:10.1080/00461520.2013.775712.

diSessa, A.A. (1993) "Toward an epistemology of physics," *Cognition and Instruction*, 10(2–3), pp. 105–225. doi:10.1080/07370008.1985.9649008.

Duncker, K. (1945) "On problem-solving," *Psychological Monographs*, 58(5), pp. i–113. doi:10.1037/h0093599.

Gick, M.L. and Holyoak, K.J. (1983) "Schema induction and analogical transfer," *Cognitive Psychology*, 15(1), pp. 1–38. doi:10.1016/0010-0285(83)90002-6.

Hattie, J. (2008) *Visible learning: A synthesis of over 800 meta-analyses relating to achievement*. 1st edn. Routledge.

Kapur, M. (2010) "A further study of productive failure in mathematical problem solving: Unpacking the design components," *Instructional Science*, 39(4), pp. 561–579. doi:10.1007/s11251-010-9144-3.

Kapur, M. (2014) "Productive failure in learning math," *Cognitive Science*, 38(5), pp. 1008–1022. doi:10.1111/cogs.12107.

Loibl, K. and Leuders, T. (2019) "How to make failure productive: Fostering learning from errors through elaboration prompts," *Learning and Instruction*, 62, pp. 1–10. doi:10.1016/j.learninstruc.2019.03.002.

Petanjek, Z. *et al.* (2011) "Extraordinary neoteny of synaptic spines in the human prefrontal cortex," *Proceedings of the National Academy of Sciences*, 108(32), pp. 13281–13286. doi:10.1073/pnas.1105108108.

Peter R., H. (1979) "Synaptic density in human frontal cortex: Developmental changes and effects of aging," *Brain Research*, 163(2), pp. 195–205. doi:10.1016/0006-8993(79)90349-4.

Chapter 7

Berlyne, D.E. (1954) "A theory of human curiosity," *British Journal of Psychology. General Section*, 45(3), pp. 180–191. doi:10.1111/j.2044-8295.1954.tb01243.x.

Berlyne, D.E. (1960) *Conflict, Arousal, and Curiosity*. New York: McGraw-Hill.

Burnette, J.L. *et al.* (2023) "A systematic review and meta-analysis of Growth Mindset Interventions: For whom, how, and why might such interventions work?," *Psychological Bulletin*, 149(3–4), pp. 174–205. doi:10.1037/bul0000368.

Dweck, C.S. (2006) *Mindset: The New Psychology of Success*. Random House Publishing Group.

Edmondson, A.C. (2018) *The Fearless Organization: Creating Psychological Safety in the Workplace for Learning, Innovation, and Growth*. New Jersey: John Wiley & Sons Inc.

Kapur, M. and Bielaczyc, K. (2012) "Designing for productive failure," *Journal of the Learning Sciences*, 21(1), pp. 45–83. doi:10.1080/10508406.2011.591717.

Mazziotti, C. *et al.* (2019) "Probing boundary conditions of productive failure and analyzing the role of young students' collaboration," *npj Science of Learning*, 4(1). doi:10.1038/s41539-019-0041-5.

Sinha, T. and Kapur, M. (2021) "When problem solving followed by instruction works: Evidence for productive failure," *Review of Educational Research*, 91(5), pp. 761–798. doi:10.3102/00346543211019105.

Tipton, E. *et al.* (2023) "Why meta-analyses of growth mindset and other interventions should follow best practices for examining heterogeneity: Commentary on Macnamara and Burgoyne (2023) and Burnette *et al.* (2023)," *Psychological Bulletin*, 149(3–4), pp. 229–241. doi:10.1037/bul0000384.

Yeager, D.S. *et al.* (2019) "A national experiment reveals where a growth mindset improves achievement," *Nature*, 573(7774), pp. 364–369. doi:10.1038/s41586-019-1466-y.

Chapter 8

Atomic Habits: An Easy and Proven Way to Build Good Habits and Break Bad Ones (2023) James Clear.

Conclusion

Csikszentmihalyi, M. (1975) *Beyond Boredom and Anxiety: Experiencing Flow in Work and Play*. San Francisco, CA: Jossey-Bass.

Acknowledgments

This book is a culmination of almost two decades of work. There are too many people to thank and acknowledge, and I know as I write this, that I will definitely miss someone. I will fail. But for a book on Productive Failure, I hope I will be forgiven.

I could not have written this book without the unconditional support of my family: my partner, Minni Lakotieva, and our four-year-old son, Arvi. They were first and foremost my foundation that I took for granted, neglected at times on work evenings and weekends to be able to write this book on top of my regular work commitments. Thank you for suffering through and supporting me. I will always be grateful.

Special thanks go to two people who read my work end to end as I wrote it, and gave me endless feedback on what was working and what needed improvement. First, my elder, twenty-one-year-old son, Dev Kapur, whose intellect, wit, maturity, and emotional strength continue to inspire and amaze me, and I am immensely grateful to life for blessing me with him. Second, my closest colleague, friend, and mentor, Pierre Dillenbourg, who held me scientifically in check and made giving feedback as one of his top priorities on top of being in the senior leadership of a university. For that, I am immensely grateful.

Then there are people who gave me feedback on specific parts of the book, be it the proposal or particular chapters: Carol Soon, Ido Roll, and Eram Schlegel, thank you for your constructive comments and suggestions, and even more so for always being there to give feedback on a short turnaround.

Esmond Harmsworth, my literary agent, someone who saw my first TED talk on Productive Failure and thought it should be a book. Thank you for believing in my work, pushing me, and working with me tirelessly over more than a year on producing the book proposal that got an offer from the publishers.

My publishing editor, Amy Fandrei, and her team at Jossey Bass/Wiley, for taking me through the world of publishing, providing me with guidance and support, development editing, and for believing that a book on Productive Failure would not be a failure. Thank you, and I hope you are right. Fingers crossed, time will tell. Big thanks also to my development editor, Danielle Noble, for encouraging me to do more of what I was doing right, and nudging me to improve the structure and readability of the book. The book has benefited tremendously from your feedback.

This book is also built on the back of several close colleagues and mentors who have supported and believed in me at different stages of my academic career: Charles Kinzer, John Voiklis, the late Florence Sullivan, Kate Bielaczyc, Nikol Rummel, and David Hung. I am most thankful.

Then there's a group of people who are the delight of my academic life: my students, research assistants, doctoral and postdoctoral scientists. Too numerous to name everyone here, but I have thoroughly enjoyed living in the world of ideas with you, designing and testing them, failing, refining, adapting and trying again, in other words, living Productive Failure with you. Thank you.

Finally, I am grateful for my birth lottery: My late father, Sudhir Kapur, whom we lost to cancer in 2017, my mother, Rita Kapur, for being a pillar of strength, and my unusually devoted younger brother, Tanuj Kapur. Without their backing, I probably would not have been able to take the risk to quit my job and move halfway across the world to New York to pursue my doctoral studies. I thank you.

And as it must be obvious by now, I am indeed lucky.

About the Author

Manu Kapur is currently the Director of the Singapore-ETH Center and Professor for Learning Sciences and Higher Education at ETH Zurich, Switzerland, where he also led The Future Learning Initiative. Before that Manu held professorial and leadership positions at universities in Hong Kong and Singapore. A mechanical-engineer-turned-math-teacher-turned-academic, Manu holds a doctorate in the learning sciences from Teachers College, Columbia University. He also holds double Masters: a Master of Science in Applied Statistics from Teachers College, Columbia University, and a Master of Education from the National Institute of Education in Singapore. Manu conceptualized the ground-breaking theory of Productive Failure, profoundly impacting the learning sciences as well as STEM education. In addition to substantial funding and media attention worldwide, Manu is a sought-after keynote speaker, having delivered two TEDx talks, and has held prestigious visiting professorships and advisory roles globally. His contributions extend across high-profile journals and conferences, influencing educational policies and practices internationally. Visit www.manukapur.com for more information.

Index